Englishness

Until the Brexit referendum, there was widespread doubt as to whether English nationalism existed at all, at least beyond a small fringe. Since then, it has come to be regarded an obvious explanation for the vote to Leave the European Union. Subsequent opinion polls have raised doubts about the extent of continuing English commitment to the Union of the United Kingdom itself. Yet even as Englishness is apparently reshaping Britain's place in world and perhaps, ultimately, the state itself, it remains poorly understood.

In this book Ailsa Henderson and Richard Wyn Jones draw on data from the Future of England Survey, a specially commissioned public attitudes survey programme exploring the political implications of English identity, to make new and original arguments about the nature of English nationalism.

They demonstrate that English nationalism is emphatically not a rejection of Britain and Britishness. Rather, English nationalism combines a sense of grievance about England's place within the United Kingdom with a fierce commitment to a particular vision of Britain's past, present, and future. Understanding its Janus-faced nature—both England and Britain—is key not only to understanding English nationalism, but also to understanding the ways in which it is transforming British politics.

Ailsa Henderson is Professor of Political Science at the University of Edinburgh and the co-author of *The National Question and Electoral Politics in Quebec and Scotland* (with É Bélanger, R Nadeau, E Hepburn, McGill-Queen's University Press, 2018).

Richard Wyn Jones is Professor and Director of the Wales Governance Centre at Cardiff University. He is co-author of *The Welsh Criminal Justice System: On the jagged edge* (with R Jones, University of Wales Press, 2022).

Englishness

The Political Force Transforming Britain

AILSA HENDERSON AND
RICHARD WYN JONES

OXFORD
UNIVERSITY PRESS

Great Clarendon Street, Oxford, OX2 6DP,
United Kingdom

Oxford University Press is a department of the University of Oxford.
It furthers the University's objective of excellence in research, scholarship,
and education by publishing worldwide. Oxford is a registered trade mark of
Oxford University Press in the UK and in certain other countries

First published 2021
First published in paperback 2022

Published in the United States of America by Oxford University Press
198 Madison Avenue, New York, NY 10016, United States of America

British Library Cataloguing in Publication Data
Data available

Library of Congress Cataloging in Publication Data
Data available

ISBN 978-0-19-887078-4 (Hbk.)
ISBN 978-0-19-286759-9 (Pbk.)

DOI: 10.1093/oso/9780198870784.001.0001

Acknowledgements

We have incurred many debts during the course of this project. The most significant is to Charlie Jeffery and Dan Wincott, friends and colleagues with whom we have cooperated for many years on the Future of England Survey and associated publications. We are hugely grateful to them for so many insightful conversations, as well as general support and unrivalled camaraderie.

The Future of England Survey has lived a hand-to-mouth existence, with only one iteration—the 2014 Survey—receiving financial support from a conventional funding agency. So, while warmly acknowledging the support of Michael Keating and the Economic and Social Research Council for the 2014 survey, we would also like to offer our particular thanks to Cardiff and Edinburgh universities for their support in the other years. Daniel Wincott and Claire Sanders at Cardiff were instrumental in conjuring up support when all other avenues appeared closed.

We are also deeply conscious of and grateful for all the support we have received from our colleagues at YouGov—a level of support that has gone well beyond the call of duty. Not only have they been consummate professionals in conducting the surveys; they have also been patient and flexible during the planning stages. All the YouGov staff with whom we have worked have been hugely helpful in their different ways, but we are sure that they will not object if we make special mention of Adam McDonnell, as well as their now former colleague Laurence Janta-Lipinski, on whom we relied so much for support and sage advice.

The book has also benefited significantly from the fact that analysis of data from our three initial surveys was published in report form—of the first two by the IPPR and the third by the ESRC's 'Future of UK and Scotland' programme. All three reports sparked considerable interest and debate in the media and among policymakers, as well as among our fellow academics. These debates helped us both hone our existing arguments and develop our analysis in new directions. We are grateful to the IPPR (supported in this case by the Joseph Rowntree Charitable Trust) and the Future of UK and Scotland programme for publishing these papers and, of course, to our co-authors on these works and other articles.

Debate surrounding the publication of these papers also led to a series of invitations to present our arguments in all kinds of other fora, ranging from literary festivals to party conferences, as well as to academic conferences across the UK and further afield. We have also been invited to conduct seminars with senior civil servants and to present our findings to various committees and meetings of politicians and their advisers in London, Edinburgh, and Cardiff. We will not try to list all of these various events; suffice it to say that we are extremely grateful to all of the organizers and to all those present who have engaged with our ideas. This book is much the richer for their interest and contribution.

During the preparation of this book a Fellowship at the Institute for Advanced Studies in the Humanities at the University of Edinburgh allowed Richard Wyn Jones to spend a term in Edinburgh. We are grateful to the institute for its generosity, as well as to Cardiff University for supporting a period of study leave.

In addition, we are especially grateful to all those who contributed by reading part or all of the typescript, or by otherwise providing support and encouragement. They are Nick Bibby, Adam Evans, Rob Ford, Lucy Hammond, Jerry Hunter, Guto Ifan, Charlie Jeffery, Rob Johns, Jac Larner, Alex Massie, James Mitchell, Jesús Rodríquez Moreno, Ed Gareth Poole, Cian Siôn, Eli Stamnes, Lisa Turnbull, and Dan Wincott. Finally, we would also like to extend our grateful thanks to Dominic Byatt at Oxford University Press, as well as the typescript reviewers for their helpful comments and suggestions.

All errors remain our responsibility.

Contents

List of Figures   ix
List of Tables   xi

Introduction: Englishness and the New British Politics   1

1. England Speaks: The 2015 UK General Election and
   the 2016 EU Referendum   8

2. On Englishness and Britishness   35

3. The English on England and the United Kingdom   57

4. The English on Britain in the World   80

5. The English World View   103

6. England, Scotland, and Wales Compared   135

7. Accommodating England   167

8. Analysing England   195

Bibliography   217
Index   231

List of Figures

2.1. 'Forced-choice' national identity, England, 1992–2016   39

2.2. Pride in Englishness/Britishness, 2016   53

2.3. Relative sources of pride by national identity   54

5.1. What makes you especially proud to be English?   113

5.2. What makes you especially proud to be British?   115

5.3. Devo-anxiety, Euroscepticism, and national identity in England   118

6.1. Relative identity strength in Scotland, Wales, and England   145

List of Tables

2.1. Trends in 'Moreno' national identity, England, 1997–2016   41

2.2. Trends in 'Moreno' national identity, England, 2011–16   42

2.3. Identity strength by 'Moreno' national identity, 2016   43

2.4. National identity (Moreno) by social group, 2016   47

2.5. Predictors of Britishness and Englishness in England   50

2.6. Pride across primes and national identity   55

3.1. Attitudes in England towards public spending in England and Scotland, 2011–15   61

3.2. Attitudes in England towards public spending across the UK, 2016   61

3.3. Scottish MPs should not vote on English laws, 2011–16   62

3.4. Attitudes in England towards English culture, 2014–16   63

3.5. Scottish MPs should not vote on English laws, 2000–15   64

3.6. English attitudes towards Scotland's share of public spending, 2000–15   64

3.7. Constitutional preferences for England, 2011–16   65

3.8. Attitudes towards England and its place in the union, by national identity, 2016   67

3.9. Attitudes in England to how Scotland should be governed, 1997–2015   69

3.10. Views in England on the desired status of the other constituent parts of the UK, by national identity, 2011   71

3.11. Views in England if Scotland votes Yes, 2014   73

3.12. Views in England if Scotland votes Yes, by national identity   75

3.13. Views in England if Scotland votes No, 2014   76

3.14. Views in England if Scotland votes No, by national identity, 2014   77

4.1. Attitudes towards the EU by Moreno national identity, 2016   83

4.2. Comparative attitudes towards the relative influence of the EU   84

4.3. Perceptions of the costs and benefits of EU membership, 2016   85

4.4. Attitudes to immigration by Moreno national identity, 2016   90

4.5. Hostility to migrants by national identity (mean scores), 2015–16   92

4.6. Attitudes towards Britain's place in the world, 2016   95

5.1. Attitudes towards England's two unions   117

5.2. Modelling devo-anxiety and Euroscepticism   122

5.3. The dimensions of an English world view   126

5.4. Who holds the English world view?   130

6.1. National identity (Moreno) in Scotland, Wales, and England   136

6.2. Predictors of Britishness and sub-state identity in Scotland,
      Wales, and England   142

6.3. Relative territorial identities in Scotland, Wales, and England   146

6.4. Attitudes to Britain's two unions?   147

6.5. National identity and political attitudes   149

6.6. National identity and attitudes to Europe   156

6.7. Euroscepticism by vote intention (F=ANOVA by Euro vote intention)   160

6.8. Territorial grievance in Scotland, Wales, and England   162

7.1. The governance of England in party manifestos, 1997–2019   175

7.2. Regional-level governance in England since 1997—Timeline   184

Introduction

Englishness and the New British Politics

There is a forgotten, nay almost forbidden word, which means more to me than any other. That word is England. Once we flaunted it in the face of the whole world like a banner. It was a word of power. It humbled the pride of the tyrant, and brought hope and succour to the oppressed. To the lover of freedom it was the one sure rock amid shifting sand. But today we are scarcely allowed to mention the name of our country.

Winston Churchill (1974)

This is a blessed nation. The British are special. The world knows it. In our innermost thoughts we know it. This is the greatest nation on earth.

Tony Blair (2007)

In the aftermath of the referendum vote to Leave the European Union on 23 June 2016, the United Kingdom of Great Britain and Northern Ireland was plunged into political crisis. During the protracted period of disruption that followed, any talk of those traits that were once thought to characterize British politics—stability, continuity, moderation—came to appear hubristic at best. Rather, parliamentary gridlock and an almost unprecedented breakdown of party discipline intersected with an ever-more voracious media cycle to generate a succession of 'decisive' moments, none of which seemed to change much if anything at all. Multiple ministerial resignations, open dissent within the cabinet, and a parliament seeking to seize control of the legislative programme and timetable from the executive—any of which before the referendum would have been regarded as shocking—seemed to pass with little more than a shrug of the collective shoulders. It was a political system that combined febrile, feverish activity with almost complete paralysis—a negative dialectic that, all sides seem to agree, served to diminish the country's much vaunted global reputation.

But this may have been one of the few things that did unite across a bitterly divided political landscape. For, in the wake of the referendum, a chasm opened up between two blocs, each regarding the other with mutual incomprehension leavened with no little distain. Members of these opposing blocs seemed to understand the world around them in fundamentally different ways. In such a context, 'losers' consent' proved to be as rare and elusive as 'Bregret'. Rather, questioning the patriotism (certainly) and even the sanity of the opposite side not only become commonplace but even socially acceptable. 'Remoaners' versus 'Gammon'; 'Saboteurs' versus 'Little Englanders': it is perhaps not surprising that psychologists reported an uptick in Brexit-related referrals (Lockett 2016; Watts 2016; Kinder 2019; cf. Degerman 2019). Meanwhile, at the geopolitical level, the referendum result raised (and continues to raise) real questions about the very future of the state as a union of four constituent parts. A border poll in Northern Ireland and a second independence referendum in Scotland have come to be increasingly regarded as among the inevitable, if unintended, aftershocks of the seismic constitutional change brought about by Brexit.

Having largely failed to foresee the result of the Brexit referendum, commentators in both the media and the academy struggled to understand its aftermath, despite no lack of effort on their part. Quite the opposite, in fact. Old and new media outlets competed to provide microscopically detailed accounts of the latest developments across multiple different platforms. This was accompanied by an ever-burgeoning literature on the underlying causes of the referendum result itself, with multiple factors being identified as playing a key role, including: a rejection of austerity; the frustration of those 'left behind' by globalization; inherent racism and xenophobia; a sepia-tinted longing for Empire; diffuse nostalgia for the past among an older generation; opposition to mutual interdependence and concern for parliamentary sovereignty; and objections to the EU as a protectionist cabal. Yet, because 2016 and its aftermath seem to offer such a fundamental challenge to the established paradigms for understanding British politics, there remained a great deal of bafflement—and in many cases, anger—at what had occurred. Understanding remained incomplete and inchoate.

In this book, we offer a new perspective on the current remaking of British politics by focusing on what we regard as the motor force behind it—namely, Englishness. This perspective remains every bit as relevant in the aftermath of the UK general election of December 2019 as it was before it, not least because the Conservative Party's decisive victory served to highlight the political divisions that exist *across* the four territories of the union. Even as they inflicted a humiliating defeat on Labour in England, the Tories lost more than half of their own seats in Scotland, while Labour remained by some distance the largest party in Wales. In addition, the contrast between the Conservatives startling advance in the so-called red-wall seats in England *profonde* and Labour's continuing strong performance in London, in particular, serves to underline the differences *within* England that we explore in the following pages. Furthermore, although the Conservative Party's election slogan 'get Brexit done' served to secure a comfortable majority and hence end the parliamentary impasse, most if not all of the major questions around Britain's future place in the world remain unanswered. As such, the fundamental differences in identities and related values and world views that drove the referendum result retain their defining importance.

Even if we have been pointing to the relationship between Englishness and Eurosceptic sentiment for longer than most, we are certainly not alone in making this link. Indeed, since 2016, the argument that English nationalism is somehow at the heart of the decision to leave the European Union has been heard relatively frequently. Yet the relationship remains contested and poorly understood, in part owing to the multiple ways in which the whole notion of English nationalism challenges prevailing assumptions.

Commentators on British politics have long assumed that there were no politically salient differences related to national identity within the English core of the United Kingdom. In England, choosing to describe oneself as British or English was generally regarded as being a matter of taste or, in particular, of context, rather than a matter of political consequence. So, while there has certainly been recognition that England is divided on the basis of class—indeed it was for many decades a staple of academic studies of electoral behaviour—little thought has been given to the possibility that there might be or might have developed national-identity-related differences too. To the extent that nationalism was considered at all, it was as a feature of political life in the state's periphery—that is, in Scotland, Wales, and Northern Ireland. England and the English were different.

Not only that, but even when there has been a willingness to concede that English nationalism might exist, the specific nature and character of English nationalism has been poorly understood. This, arguably, is because for most observers it is precisely the nationalisms of Ireland, Wales, and Scotland that provide the natural point of reference and comparison. But, in their contemporary manifestations, at least, Irish, Scottish, and Welsh nationalists tend to reject Britain and Britishness. This is emphatically *not* the case for English nationalism. As will become clear in the remainder of this book, English nationalism combines both concern about England's place within the United Kingdom as well as fierce commitments to a particular vision of Britain's past, present, and future. So, returning to the quotations at head of this Introduction, it combines a sense that England has been 'forgotten' and unfairly submerged, with the belief that Britain, self-evidently, is or should be 'the greatest nation on earth'. Understanding its Janus-faced nature—both Churchill and Blair, as it were—is key not only to understanding English nationalism, but also to understanding the way that English nationalism is transforming British politics.

Until relatively recently, another barrier to understanding English nationalism has been the lack of available data with which to explore and elucidate the nature of English nationalist sentiment. For scholars such as ourselves, whose work makes extensive use of data from social attitudes surveys, this problem is especially acute. Such surveys are expensive undertakings and almost always reliant on external funding, funding that is, understandably enough, directed towards questions or issues that are deemed by funding organizations (and their academic advisers) to be of particular relevance or salience. Given that national identity was not considered a salient political cleavage within England, apart from a brief period around the advent of political devolution when some work sought to detect an 'English backlash' to constitutional change in the rest of the UK, there have been relatively few survey datasets available that might allow scholars to bring English nationalism into sharper focus.

This book draws on data from a survey vehicle established to facilitate an exploration of patterns of national identity in England and any relationship that might exist between those patterns and political and, in particular, constitutional attitudes. Working alongside our main collaborators, Charlie Jeffery and Dan Wincott, we fielded the first Future of England Survey (FoES) in 2011 and have repeated the exercise eight times since. The first three outings led to reports that were widely cited in the press and by political parties: *The Dog that Finally Barked: England as an Emerging Political Community* (Wyn Jones et al. 2012); *England and its Two Unions: The Anatomy of a Nation and its Discontents* (Wyn Jones et al. 2013); *Taking England Seriously: The New English Politics* (Jeffery et al. 2014). Since then, we have explored how Englishness helps us to understand developments in domestic politics as well as attitudes to Brexit (Henderson et al. 2016, 2017, 2020; Jeffery et al. 2016). Our goal here is larger. Using data from successive rounds of the FoES, we outline what we know about England and Englishness (and Britishness) and how it is reshaping politics in Britain. Where relevant, we supplement our data with those from other surveys—for example, to show trends over time or to show how we depart from other survey vehicles.

The book's argument is organized into eight chapters. Chapter 1 focuses on the campaigns that preceded the 2015 UK General Election and the 2016 EU Referendum. In part this is because these two electoral events were clearly linked: it was the Conservatives' unexpected victory in the former that paved the way for the latter. But both campaigns also highlight different aspects of the English nationalism that is discussed in the remainder of the book. In 2015, the Conservative campaign successfully mobilized English suspicion at the prospect of the influence of the Scottish National Party (SNP) over a minority Labour government—a suspicion rooted in a deep sense of English grievance about Scotland's alleged unfairly privileged position within the union. Only a year later, England was hardly mentioned by the Leave campaign. Yet, as we shall see, in England, its vision of and for Britain appealed overwhelmingly to those with a strong sense of English identity but not, perhaps ironically, to those who feel exclusively or predominantly British.

In Chapter 2 we ask who are the English and where might they be found? Using different survey measures, we show that, even if English identity has strengthened since the early 1990s, those who view themselves as strongly English remain deeply attached to Britishness. We also demonstrate that, with the partial exception of London, there is very little regional variation in terms of patterns of national identity. There are, however, socio-economic and demographic differences. Older people, Anglicans, those in social class DE, and those born in England are all more likely to feel strongly or exclusively English. By contrast, younger voters, 'non-white British', and those born outside England are more likely to identify themselves as British.

Chapter 3 explores English attitudes to England and its place within the United Kingdom, attitudes that are strikingly different from those held by that proportion of England's population that views itself in primarily or exclusively British terms. English identity is strongly linked to what we term devo-anxiety—namely, a belief that England is not treated fairly in the union as currently constructed, as well as support for the recognition of England as a unit within the UK state. In Chapter 4 we turn our attention to the other side of the English nationalist coin—namely, English views of Britain and its place in the world. We show how Euroscepticism and negative attitudes towards immigration are both prevalent among those who feel exclusively or predominantly English, as well as a strong sense of kinship with (some) of the nations of the so-called Anglosphere.

Linking together the analysis in the previous three chapters, Chapter 5 delineates what we term the 'English world view'. Our argument is that English attitudes towards England's place in the union and Britain's place in the world are underpinned by a distinctive understanding of what constitutes legitimate government and that devolution and European integration offend, in part at least, because they offend against it. There is a clear sense among English identifiers that they no longer live in a state that is interested in them or acts on their behalves. We go on to demarcate more clearly those parts of England's population that hold this world view.

The subsequent chapter, Chapter 6, shifts our focus beyond England and compares the attitudes found in England to the attitudes of other identity groups across Britain. We show that many of the attitudes that attach to Englishness in England attach to Britishness in Scotland and Wales. This serves to underline the key point that Britishness means different things in different parts of Britain. The views of the predominantly or exclusively British in England do not align with those of the predominantly or exclusively British in Scotland and Wales. At least on some of the issues explored in this book, they are in fact closer to the views of those in both countries who feel predominantly or exclusively Scottish and Welsh.

Following from these primarily data-driven chapters, Chapter 7 assesses the political challenges that arise in the context of the rise of English nationalism. In particular, we discuss the ways in which three constraints—the pattern of public attitudes in England, the institutional fusion of English and all-UK institutions, as well as the overwhelming size of England relative to the other constituent territories of the union—all serve to shape, limit, or undermine attempts to accommodate England within the post-devolution UK.

Finally, Chapter 8 focuses on the analytical challenges posed by English nationalism. We explore how the academic literature on nationalism helps us better to understand the politicized English identity that has been the subject of the previous chapters, including the relationship between English and British nationalism. We also outline methodological and, for want of a better term, infrastructural implications of our findings for the future study of 'British politics' if we are, indeed, to take England and Englishness seriously.

It has become commonplace—a cliché, even—for discussions of England and the political implications of Englishness to repeat the opening stanza of G. K. Chesterton's 'The Secret People' (1907):

> Smile at us, pay us, pass us; but do not quite forget;
> For we are the people of England, that never have spoken yet.

Doing so again here serves to underline from the outset how our discussion is different from previous treatments of the subject. For Chesterton and most of those who cite these lines, Englishness is conceived of as a potential but not (yet) actual force in political life. The starting point for this book, by contrast, is the contention that England *is* speaking. Indeed, such is the power of this voice that British politics is currently being transformed as a result of its intervention. As such, it is not Chesterton's words but rather those of another, altogether more significant poet that now appear most relevant. In his *Little Gidding*, T. S. Eliot ([1942] 1971) says,

> History is now and England.

1

England Speaks

The 2015 UK General Election and the 2016 EU Referendum

The moment at which England and, in particular, distinctively English attitudes towards the government and governance of their country were launched onto the mainstream British political agenda can be traced with unusual precision. At 7.00 a.m. on the morning of 19 September 2014, Prime Minister David Cameron emerged from the front door of 10 Downing Street to greet the result of Scotland's independence referendum. After informing the world's media that the future of Scotland's relationship had been resolved, he went on to say this:

> I have long believed that a crucial part missing from this national discussion is England. We have heard the voice of Scotland—and now the millions of voices of England must also be heard. The question of English votes for English laws [EVEL]—the so-called West Lothian question—requires a decisive answer. (Cameron 2016)

Scotland had had its moment in limelight; now it was to be England's turn.

Cameron's decision to respond to the ostensible resolution of Scotland's constitutional relationship with the United Kingdom by raising the issue of England's governance was greeted with fury by Scottish unionists. Alistair Darling's immediate reaction on being told by Cameron of his plans to use his post-referendum remarks to argue that moves to give Scotland more powers needed to be 'balanced' with a move to EVEL was to turn to his wife and proclaim: 'He's going to fuck it up' (cited Pike 2015: 159). Gordon Brown's assessment of 'this most ill-judged of interventions' and 'political manoeuvring' was less colourfully phrased but just as damning: 'the Prime Minister's statement was not a proposal for greater English rights, but for fewer Scottish rights . . . he lit a fuse that to this day still threatens the integrity of the United Kingdom' (Brown 2015: 328). Scottish unionists' sense of resentment and even betrayal has continued to reverberate. During the 2016 EU referendum campaign, Brown refused to participate in a joint appearance of all living former UK prime ministers to champion a Remain vote because he was still so 'bitter' at Cameron's decision to press the case for EVEL in the immediate aftermath of the Scottish referendum (Shipman 2016: 359).

Scottish unionists had many reasons to resent Cameron's decision to greet the independence referendum result by raising the spectre of England. Timing was clearly one of them. The anomaly that lies at the heart of the West Lothian question had been identified as long ago as the debates over Irish home rule in the nineteenth century and had been endured in practice since the introduction of devolution in 1999. In this context, the prime minister's decision to focus on it at the very moment of Scottish unionism's referendum triumph appeared gratuitous. The substance of his position served only to add insult to injury. Following a campaign that had proven to be much more challenging and closely fought than most had expected, the Scottish politicians that had led the 'Better Together' anti-independence campaign were now confronted with the sight of a UK prime minister vocally championing a policy that they regarded as diminishing their own status at Westminster (Brown 2015: 329). The limitations of the argument dear to some No campaigners, that the rest of the UK would be so grateful if Scotland chose to remain in the union that it would be allowed to 'dictate [the] terms' of its future relationship, could hardly have been more immediately or brutally exposed (Rowling 2014).

But it is also hard not to detect a sense that Cameron was, in effect, highlighting a problem that did not really exist and doing so for the basest of motives. Many unionist politicians in Scotland and, indeed, Wales—especially those on the centre left—have been loath to accept that the English might wish to see a distinctive, all-England approach to territorial governance within the UK. They have been even more resistant to the idea that this might be a reasonable or legitimate political position. Rather they have viewed proposals for EVEL—the pronunciation of the acronym is evocative—as a crude attempt to bolster the position of the Conservative Party in the House of Commons. From this perspective, Cameron's post-referendum statement on England was not only poorly timed, but entirely unnecessary and nakedly partisan (see Pike 2015: 158–66).

From the perspective of David Cameron and his advisers, however, it all appeared very different. During the fraught final weeks of the campaign, unionists had sought to counter apparent pro-Yes momentum by making ever more lavish rhetorical promises to the Scottish electorate about what an alternative to independence within the UK might look like. Scotland, claimed Gordon Brown, would be left in a position 'as near to federalism as is possible' (cited in Macwhirter 2014: 124). This rhetoric was buttressed by the Brown-inspired 'Vow' printed on the front page of the tabloid *Daily Record*, which, *inter alia*, appeared to guarantee to Scotland in perpetuity relatively high levels of public spending compared to England, in particular. Notwithstanding their questionable impact in Scotland, this language and accompanying commitments generated substantial disquiet south of the border, particularly though far from exclusively among Conservative backbenchers. In their view, these promises had not been shared with let alone sanctioned by the English electorate, and they, as their parliamentary representatives, certainly did not agree with them.[1]

Given that speaking out at such a sensitive juncture would have been such an obvious gift to independence campaigners, self-discipline could be relied upon to ensure that this disquiet would be relatively muted during the referendum campaign itself. Downing Street was well aware, however, that it was set to spill out into the public realm once the union had been secured. In particular, Conservative backbenchers and their right-wing media allies were likely to use the apparent capitulation to 'Better Together'—in many respects, the Brown government *redux*—as yet another stick with which to beat the prime minister. Indeed, such was the level of backbench disquiet that Cameron was threatened with 'a rebellion to dwarf the past Commons revolts...over Europe' (see Ross 2015: 142; also Laws 2017: 447; Cameron 2019: 555). It is important to note, in this regard, that the war inside the Conservative Party over Europe had not abated during the referendum campaign, and this despite the existential threat to England's other union.

Barely three weeks before referendum day, the Conservative MP for Clacton, Douglas Carswell, had defected to UKIP and triggered a by-election.[2] Rumours abounded that other defections were imminent (in the event, Mark Reckless would follow Carswell's lead nine days after referendum day). Given that his more Eurosceptic backbenchers also tended to be among those most exercised at the way that England was (in their view) being ignored and even disadvantaged by the flurry of hurried concessions to Scotland, a failure by the prime minister to stand up for English interests was almost certain to be portrayed as yet another betrayal. But, by making it clear, immediately and in

---

[1] Cf. Gordon Brown's complaints (2015: 329) that Cameron's proposals for EVEL had not been shared with the Scottish electorate before the independence referendum vote.

[2] Carswell describes his politics as being 'rooted in the tradition of English radicalism', but his defection was apparently unrelated to what we term 'devo-anxiety' (Goodwin and Milazzo 2017: 126).

the highest profile of circumstances, that more powers for Scotland had to be balanced with the recognition of English aspirations—'balance' was the key word in his post-referendum remarks—Cameron would have hoped to close down one line of attack. At the same time he could also hope (perhaps optimistically) to contain any damage to the union that might result from less-measured attempts from his party colleagues to articulate English grievance.

There were other potential benefits to be gleaned from (metaphorically) waving the St George's cross. Downing Street was already conscious of the link between English national identification and UKIP support.[3] Demonstrating that the Conservatives, too, 'got' English disquiet might help shore up one flank at a time in which there was a real danger (from a Conservative perspective) of UKIP developing further momentum after gaining most votes in England in the European elections earlier in the year. On the other flank, speaking out in the name of English sentiment was also a way of differentiating the Tories from their Liberal Democrat coalition partners. It was, after all, the Liberal Democrats—more precisely, the vehement opposition of Scottish Liberal Democrat MPs—that had blocked the McKay Commission's 2013 proposals for a form of EVEL.[4] Labour was also vulnerable, given that party's tortuously convoluted attitude towards England and Englishness. By claiming to amplify the 'millions of voices of England', Cameron (2016) could reasonably hope to reinforce his party's position as the dominant electoral force in the union's largest constituent nation.

Controversy about the motivations for and the appropriateness of the then prime minister's decision to respond to the Scottish referendum result by linking the promise of more powers to Scotland with the recognition of English aspirations will, doubtless, continue to rage—north of the border, at least.[5] But what is surely beyond doubt is that, by making this link, David

[3] Not least because some of the prime minister's advisers had been taking a close interest in data from the Future of England Survey (FoES), with members of the research team invited to provide briefings on our findings on several occasions in the run-up to the 2014 referendum.

[4] The Liberal Democrat Parliamentary Party's meeting to discuss the McKay recommendations has been described as the 'most difficult' of its time in coalition, with Scottish Liberal Democrat MPs attending *en masse* to express their very strong opposition to any form of EVEL. (Interview with Joanne Foster, Deputy Chief of Staff to the Deputy Prime Minister, 2011–14.)

[5] In his excupatory account of his time as prime minister, David Cameron (2019: 555) expresses qualified regret at his decision to raise the prospect of EVEL on the morning after the referendum: 'The idea that I could have ignored the issue altogether is nonsense, but I now wish I'd left it until the party conference.' But, given that the party conference to which he refers started only nine days later, it is far from clear that any such delay would have done much to placate the hostility of Scottish Unionists, some of whom—as we have seen—regard the very principle of EVEL as abhorrent.

Cameron was signalling his belief that a distinctive English sense of grievance about how England is governed was not only politically salient, but also (potentially) mobilizable. This assessment was essentially correct, as was to be amply demonstrated during the course of the general election campaign that would commence almost as soon as the votes of the Scottish independence referendum had been counted.

England and the 2015 UK General Election

When the serious academic study of voting behaviour in UK elections commenced around the 1964 general election, in political terms at least the United Kingdom could be viewed as forming 'one nation'—one nation with two dominant political parties, each deeply entrenched on either side of a class divide and enjoying the loyal support of most members of 'their' respective classes (Butler and Stokes 1971). While a token smattering of Liberal holdouts representing peripheral, rural constituencies leavened the mix in the House of Commons, those seeking an understanding of electoral behaviour could largely ignore their supporters.[6] Rather, in this world of 'two-party politics' and 'uniform national swings', studies could focus on class voting and its obverse, 'class deviance' (*sic*), confident that this captured by far the most important dimensions of electoral competition.

Territorial differences across the UK hardly featured at all. Even where they existed—and note, for example, that relative Conservative weakness in Scotland (compared to England) emerges at this time and in Wales long predates 1964—they had little impact on the overall 'national result' elections and could again be largely ignored (Wyn Jones et al. 2002; Wyn Jones and Scully 2015). Northern Ireland provided the only real exception, and indeed voters there were not asked to participate in the pioneering 1964 election study 'mainly because [Northern Ireland] lies outside the mainstream of British party competition' (Butler and Stokes 1971: 537). But, for those of a less rigorous bent than these early academic psephologists, even Northern Ireland could be viewed as part of the two-party system to an extent that is now barely imaginable. After all, the Ulster Unionist Party (UUP)— which won all twelve northern Irish constituencies in the 1964 general

---

[6] The Liberals returned nine MPs at the 1964 general election, eight of whom represented constituencies located either in or off the far north of Scotland (party leader, Jo Grimond, represented Orkney and Shetland), in mid-Wales, or in the south-west of England.

election—was umbilically linked to the Conservatives at Westminster (Walker and Mulvenna 2015). So, even though the UUP's dominance of the six counties of Ulster reflected the influence of a very different social cleavage from that holding sway across (most) of the rest of the union, the territory was nonetheless fully integrated into the UK's party system.

In retrospect, however, it appears that the 1964 general election took place around the high-water mark of this particular period in UK electoral history. Signs of the ebbing were already apparent. The one non-rural seat to return a Liberal MP in 1964, Orpington, located in London's suburbia, had been gained by the party in a remarkable by-election coup two years previously—a moment now widely regarded, in retrospect, as having heralded the start of the Liberal revival and the rise of three-party politics in England. The tide was subsequently to recede with remarkable rapidity. In 1966, Labour secured a scarcely credible 60.7 per cent of the votes cast in Wales in the May general election, returning thirty-two out of thirty-six MPs. Yet only two months later the party went on to lose the Carmarthen by-election to Plaid Cymru, signalling an abrupt change in the electoral fortunes of Welsh and then—after the 1967 Hamilton by-election—Scottish nationalism. By October 1974, the SNP, now securing 30.4 per cent of the popular vote in Scotland, was winning in constituencies where, only a decade before, it could not even muster a candidate. The same election offered graphic evidence of the depth of the rupture between the Conservatives and their erstwhile Ulster Unionist allies when Enoch Powell was elected as the UUP MP for South Down, Powell having previously left the Conservatives and even advocated a vote for Labour because of his former party's (then) pro-Common Market stance—a harbinger, perhaps, of future Conservative agonies over 'Europe'.

To compare the results of the 1964 and 2015 general elections is to underline just how much electoral politics in the UK has changed over the previous half century and in particular how one 'national' electorate had become four national electorates. In 2015, for the first time in the UK's democratic history (but repeated twice since), four different parties topped the polls in the state's four different constituent territories. These results were presaged by campaigns that were not only nationally distinctive to an extent that had also not been seen before, but also based on stressing national divisions.

Territorial differentiation is, of course, part and parcel of general-election campaigning in the UK. The first-past-the-post (or single member plurality) system used to elect members of the House of Commons encourages a 'target-seat' approach, whereby certain constituencies are accorded significantly higher priority by political parties than other, non-target seats. Campaigners will also regularly tailor their messages to the perceived concerns of a particular community, be that by focusing on the prospects for specific, locally relevant industries, or opposing 'threats' to local services, and so on. National territorial differentiation—that is, tailoring specific policies and messages for the component territories of the UK—also has a long history. The two largest British parties have produced UK general-election manifestos for Wales and Scotland at (almost) every election since the late 1950s (Craig 1990: 519–21).[7] What was new and distinctive about the 2015 election is the way in which the Conservatives became the first major party to produce a manifesto specifically and explicitly targeted at voters in the largest of the UK's constituent territories—namely, England.

'Explicitly' is important here. Since the establishment of the Scottish and Welsh devolved legislatures in 1999 and the transfer of significant legislative and executive power over 'bread-and-butter' political issues to Edinburgh and Cardiff, the main general-election manifestos produced by the dominant British parties have all been, to a significant extent, English manifestos by default, for the simple reason that, if a party was invited to form the United Kingdom's government, then the existence of devolution meant that, for example, most of the health and education policies contained in these documents would apply only in England. Despite this, the parties had all (until 2015, at least) tended to be reluctant to drop the pretence that their main manifesto policies would apply across the state as a whole.

Significantly, the introduction to the Conservatives' English manifesto—signed by David Cameron—links the publication directly to his appearance outside Downing Street in the aftermath of the Scottish independence referendum.

> When I spoke on the steps of No. 10 Downing Street on the morning after the Scottish Referendum I reiterated that the Conservative Party is the party of the Union—and we will always do our utmost to keep our family of nations together. As a result of our plans, more powers are now going to Scotland, to Wales and to Northern Ireland—and we have published Manifestos for each one of those nations. At the same time, it is absolutely right that a new and fair settlement applies to all parts of our United Kingdom. So it is in that spirit that we are publishing the first English Manifesto for a General Election.

---

[7] The sole exception is the February 1974 general election, when Labour produced a manifesto for Wales but not for Scotland, reflecting the fact that, at that time, the party was proposing devolution for the former while actually opposing it for the latter.

But the then prime minister also went on to embrace the broader reality that, notwithstanding the transfer of further powers in the aftermath of the Scottish independence referendum, devolution to Scotland, Wales, and Northern Ireland had already created a situation in which the UK government's policy writ often runs only to Welsh and Scottish borders in a state of affairs he described as 'effectively' constituting English devolution.

> Of course, the UK Parliament in Westminster will always retain powers over vital issues such as our national security. But just as Scotland, Wales and Northern Ireland have full responsibility for some policy areas, so does England. Our great National Health Service, our education system, our support to help first time buyers—all these policies are effectively devolved to England, just as they are devolved to Scotland and Wales.
>
> (Conservative Party 2015a: 5)

Even if it was an unintended consequence of the devolution process in the rest of the UK, a distinctive English polity had now emerged and—once again—the Conservatives were determined to act as its champions.

We should perhaps not overplay the significance of the publication of an explicitly English manifesto, not least because its existence was not widely publicized at the time, and it remains exceedingly difficult to locate traces of it online. That said, the fact that it was produced at all serves as another indication of the Conservative Party leadership's awareness of the political potential of 'England' and 'Englishness'. They were to find another way of playing the English card to far greater—even devastating—effect. Ironically enough, the opportunity to do so was generated by the leading role played by their then Labour allies in the Better Together campaign.

The independence referendum broke the Scottish Labour Party. For decades, Scotland's dominant political force, its position at the head of the cross-party Better Together campaign left the party at odds with much of its base in what remains the most important and most vigorously contested democratic vote in Scottish political history. In response, a large proportion of its erstwhile supporters shifted their support to the SNP. The result was the political equivalent of what palaeontologists term an 'extinction event': it would go on to lose forty out of its forty-one Scottish MPs at the 2015 general election.

This was, however, a political death foretold. Even if the announcement of some of the individual results still managed to take the breath away, that the 2015 general election would see Scottish voters flock to the SNP banner to an unprecedented degree had been obvious from the polling that had taken place in the months before May (Johns and Mitchell 2016; Rose and Shepard 2016; Diffley 2017). As the election approached, the only real question was how close to the 'full house' of fifty-nine Scottish constituencies the nationalists might reach. It was the likelihood of sweeping gains for the SNP—and concomitant losses for Labour, especially—that set the scene for what became the central feature of the Conservatives' campaign—namely, 'the Tories' total focus on stoking English fears about the [post-election] influence of the SNP' (Ross 2015: 45). So successful were these efforts that '[t]he effect of the political earthquake in Scotland', in the words of Tim Ross, 'was to send tremors south of the border that were felt in the homes of Liberal Democrat voters in Devon, Somerset and Cornwall, and those tempted to back Nigel Farage in Kent, Essex and Lincolnshire' (Ross 2015: pp. xi–xii).

The Conservatives had been quick to realize the potential electoral significance of an SNP breakthrough in the context of a hung parliament. Lynton Crosby, who masterminded the party's campaign, began to conduct focus groups exploring 'the attitudes of the English to their Scottish neighbours' in the immediate aftermath of the independence referendum:

> His research was startling. Participants in focus groups consistently showed that the one thing English voters who were tempted by UKIP or the Lib Dems hated more than any other was the prospect of a Labour government propped up by the SNP.
>
> (Ross 2015: 72. The timeline is confirmed in Cowley and
> Kavanagh 2016: 246)[8]

By the end of the year, M&C Saatchi, the advertising agency long closely associated with Conservative Party election campaigns, was testing—and getting powerfully negative responses to—adverts that gave central billing to Alex Salmond. According to Jeremy Sinclair, Chairman of Saatchi, this reflected the fact that

> [w]e [sic] hate being ruled or bossed by foreigners. French, Germans, Scots, anyone—and it looked as though we were going to be run by Alex Salmond...it is a most powerful thing when people are threatened by government by outsiders.   (Sinclair and Atkinson 2017: 115–16)

---

[8] This is not, however, the whole story. We are aware from personal experience that some of Cameron's team were already keenly interested in data highlighting English attitudes towards Scotland at least eighteen months before the independence referendum.

Focus groups of swing voters in English seats provided further confirmation of the way that Alex Salmond, in particular, acted as a lightning rod for English suspicion: 'Nicola Sturgeon was seen negatively, the SNP were disliked, but Alex Salmond...was poison' (see Ross 2015: 144).[9] It was thus clear to both Crosby and Sinclair that what the latter termed the 'Scottish dimension' could play a major role in determining the result of the general election that was to follow only 230 days after the independence referendum (Sinclair and Atkinson 2017: 116).

The Conservatives' campaign proceeded to focus relentlessly on the apparently dangerous prospect of a Labour government reliant on SNP support. The Conservative's core message was brutally and brilliantly distilled in a Saatchi-produced poster depicting Labour leader Ed Miliband perched in Alex Salmond's pocket—by some distance the most memorable image of the election (reproduced in Cowley and Kavanagh 2016: 151).[10] This basic message dominated the Conservatives 'air war' and 'ground war' alike; it featured centrally from the very start of the campaign, reaching a fevered crescendo in the final week before polling day.[11]

In addition to featuring on Conservative posters displayed on some of the country's most prominent and expensive billboard sites, the threat of SNP influence also dominated the party's social media campaign. Or, in the words of journalist Iain Watson (2015: 51, 48): 'On the internet and at selected poster sites, the star of their campaign wasn't David Cameron—it was the SNP's Alex Salmond.' The alleged dangers of a Miliband government 'propped up by the SNP' also provided the core theme for the Conservatives (twice

[9] Though, by contrast, Iain Watson (2015: 150) cites 'a senior Conservative strategist' who claimed that Sturgeon's heightened profile south of the border as the campaign progressed meant that she eventually came to be seen 'as even more noxious in the seats that they [the Conservatives] had to win' than her predecessor.

[10] Cameron's autobiography furnishes a rather curious postscript to this episode, with the former prime minister keen to take personal credit for recognizing the potential impact of this 'devastating poster'. It was, apparently, Cameron (and Osborne) who insisted on its widespread use in the face of Crosby's scepticism—the latter having apparently assessed the poster as 'bullshit' (Cameron 2019: 566). It should be noted that Saatchi produced other posters ploughing this particular furrow. Perhaps most striking in the context of the present discussion was an image of Salmond stealing money from the pocket of an English voter, this only a few months after Cameron had signed up to a 'Vow' pledging to maintain Scotland's 'Barnett bonus' apparently in perpetuity (Ross 2015: 148). Predictably, perhaps, the former prime minister's autobiography is silent on this apparent inconsistency.

[11] Some academic commentators as well as political opponents have argued that the Conservatives focus on the 'SNP threat' emerged in an apparently unplanned way during the course of the campaign. Andrew Gamble (2015: 154) argues that it was a response to the failure of more familiar electoral strategies. David Laws (2017: 312) claims to have observed the 'first signs' of the Conservatives focus on the Scottish National Party (SNP) in early March 2015, while UKIP's Paul Nuttall believed that the Tories' focus on the SNP emerged 'by accident not design' after the first televised leaders debate in early April 2015 (cited in Goodwin and Milazzo 2017: 248). The evidence does not support these arguments.

repeated) 'final' Party General Election Broadcast (Conservative Party 2015b). Indeed, Phil Cowley and Denis Kavanagh (2016: 172) estimate that fully 60 per cent of all Conservative press releases during the campaign featured references to the SNP and/or its leading figures. The ostensible dangers of SNP influence featured in the paid 'wrap-arounds' adorning local newspapers in 100 or so seats targeted by Crosby and his colleagues. It provided the punch line to the Conservatives' centrally generated script for canvassers (Cowley and Kavanagh 2016: 259).[12] It was also a core feature in the 'personalized' letters produced by the very extensive Conservative direct-mail operation focused on voters in target constituencies. The ubiquity of the message is underlined by a comment from one Labour strategist who spoke to Cowley and Kavanagh: 'The Tories claimed to segment their messages but I'm not sure I ever saw anything that veered off the lines of warning about the dangers of an "Ed Miliband government propped up by the SNP"' (Cowley and Kavanagh 2016: 267).[13] Indeed perhaps the only significant adjustment to the Conservatives' messaging during the course of the campaign was a switch from an almost exclusive focus on Salmond as the personification of the 'SNP threat' to a dual focus on both Salmond and Sturgeon. Labour's campaign launch event held in Manchester on 13 April was picketed by fifteen Conservative activists and a *Sun* reporter all wearing Sturgeon masks, as well as six lorries mounted with posters featuring both Salmond and Sturgeon with Miliband in their respective pockets, all accompanied by Tory party Chair, Michael Gove.[14] By the end of April, Conservative activists were regularly hounding Miliband's public appearances sporting Sturgeon masks (Watson 2015: 44, 149; Cowley and Kavanagh 2016: 179). This followed from the latter's strong performances in the televised leaders' debates broadcast during the campaign (Emes and Keith 2017). But, even if the cast was adjusted, the core message remained unchanged: it was only by electing a Conservative government that English voters could avoid a weak Labour government dependent upon—and being manipulated by—perfidious and spendthrift Scottish nationalists.

This core message was taken up and echoed by Conservative Party outriders in what was, even by UK standards, a particularly partisan press

---

[12] According to the script, the first question for a potential voter was whether or not s/he thought that it was important to have a strong government delivering a strong economy. The follow-up question was whether s/he approved of a government reliant on the SNP.

[13] Cf. Andrew Cooper's claim (2017: 129) that there were 'literally hundreds of small but important variations' in Conservative direct-mail scripts.

[14] *Scottish Sun*, 13 April 2015, https://www.thescottishsun.co.uk/archives/news/127105/gove-gatecrashes-manifesto-with-gang-of-tory-sturgeons/.

(Deacon et al. 2017: 187–90). The London editions of the *Sun* and the *Daily Mail* (though not their Scottish equivalents) were particularly vocal about the threat of SNP influence, the latter famously branding Sturgeon as 'the most dangerous woman in Britain' in a front page headline.[15] In its declaration of support for the Conservatives, *The Times* decried the 'tyranny' of potential SNP influence, while *Sunday Telegraph* columnist Janet Daley argued that any pact between Labour and the SNP 'would be an outrage to democracy' (cited in Cowley and Kavanagh 2016: 312, 327). In parallel with these lurid pseudo-constitutional proclamations, and with a certain grim predictability, parts of the press responded to Nicola Sturgeon's newfound prominence south of the border with unpleasant personal attacks (Cowley and Kavanagh 2016: 328). The unprecedented number of opinion polls published during the campaign served to ensure that the broadcast media were also consumed by speculation about potential post-election deals involving Labour and the SNP.

Those on the receiving end of the Conservatives' campaign have attested to its effectiveness. During the campaign, the feedback reaching the Liberal Democrats' headquarters focused on the 'growing impact' of Conservative warnings about the SNP—an impact that was 'very palpable on the doorsteps' and 'incredibly powerful' (Cowley and Kavanagh 2016: 269). According to Nick Clegg (2016: 157), 'fear of Scottish Nationalists holding the rest of the country to ransom became an abiding concern for many English voters...masterfully exploited by the Conservatives'. He describes the way in which

> Conservative central office was posting letters from David Cameron to tens of thousands of Lib Dem voters in the South-West of England that essentially said, 'I know you're a Lib Dem, that's okay, we've worked with them very well for five years, but if you really don't want Ed Miliband in charge, with Alex Salmond pulling the strings, then on this occasion please lend us your vote.' It was a devastatingly effective tactic.   (Clegg 2016: 123)[16]

---

[15] *Daily Mail*, 4 April 2015, http://www.dailymail.co.uk/news/article-3024983/SNP-s-Nicola-Sturgeon-tells-Ed-Miliband-ll-call-shots-now.html.

[16] The party's post-election review made the point in the following, rather plaintive terms: 'Despite our failings, we might not have done so badly except for the strength of the late Tory message about the weakness of Ed Miliband and English voters' fear of the SNP in control in Westminster. No party had a response to this...And where this overarching message was combined with hundreds of thousands of pounds of central and local money spent in Conservative target seats, Liberal Democrat chances were simply swept away' (Liberal Democrats 2015).

Even Clegg's pledge—two weeks before polling day—that under no circumstances would his party participate in any kind of post-election arrangement involving the SNP was not enough to save the Liberal Democrats from utter humiliation (Laws 2017: 54–541). In her retrospective account of an election campaign in which she played a key behind-the-scenes role, Liberal Democrat peer Olly Grender (2017: 151) describes the way in which 'the chill SNP wind from the North was used ruthlessly [by the Conservatives] to create a climate of fear. For the Liberal Democrats... it was a battle against a wind which made a tsunami look tame.' The Liberal Democrats' Commons contingent would be reduced to 1964 levels.

From his very different vantage point, Nigel Farage is equally clear about the electoral damage inflicted on his own party by the way in which the Conservatives managed to peel off potential UKIP voters by focusing on the potential influence of the SNP on a minority Labour government. In doing so, the Conservatives were capitalizing on the existence of what he describes as 'some quite vehement anti-Scottish sentiment out there'—a sense that 'the Scottish tail has wagged the English dog in the most remarkable way' with the Scots 'getting our money' while 'being horrible about us' (cited in Ross 2015: 173). Farage's framing here is revealing: notice in particular the focus on finance as well as the characterization of Scotland as an appendage to the main body of the state, which is formed by the English, both themes to which we will return.[17] Suffice it to say on this point that Farage displayed an astute understanding of the attitude towards Scotland among a very significant segment of the English electorate.

This was an attitude on which he himself had initially hoped to capitalize, confident that the surge in support for SNP would 'fuel feelings of nationalism among English voters', in particular among erstwhile Labour supporters put off by the way that Ed Miliband, in the UKIP leader's words, 'denies Englishness at any given opportunity' (cited in Goodwin and Milazzo 2017: 131, 216). Goodwin and Milazzo (2017: 237) describe one appearance by Farage in the South Thanet constituency where he was a candidate:

'Our modern political class', he said with a St George's flag draped behind him, 'think it's shameful to be English'. The UKIP leader, who talked often about his belief in the power of Englishness to propel his party forward... then outlined his party's plan to make St George's day a public holiday.

---

[17]   On the latter point, it is striking the extent to which Farage provides a mirror image for Gordon Brown's claims (2014: 332) in the run-up to the 2014 independence referendum that Scotland should be 'leading Britain—not leaving it'.

During the subsequent televised leaders' debates, he sought to highlight the Barnett formula and what he regarded as the unfairly generous treatment of Scotland that results from it.[18] A little over a week before polling day, he used a series of high-profile media interviews to suggest that the surge in support for the 'openly racist' SNP was a manifestation of 'anti-English hatred' in Scotland (see Bennett 2015: 281–2).

UKIP's problem, however, was that—unlike the Conservatives—it could not offer those English voters concerned about the 'threat' of SNP influence a credible governmental alternative. Or, as Farage himself put it while reflecting on his own failure to win in South Thanet, 'I talked to lots of [voters]...and they just said: "Look Nigel, we love you but we can't have Nicola Sturgeon running the country"' (Bennett 2015: 331).[19] It should be pointed out that this was a sentiment that the Conservatives—victorious in South Thanet—worked very hard to cultivate. Voters there had been 'bombarded...with literature and phone calls, warning them again and again about the likelihood of a Labour–SNP coalition' (Goodwin and Milazzo 2017: 263). UKIP was, in effect, hoisted by its own petard in the face of a Tory campaign that the UKIP's Chief Press Officer, Gawain Towler (2017: 165), was to describe (with no apparent irony) as 'astonishingly nationally divisive'. All of which underlines the success of the Conservatives' strategy of appealing to those who 'were planning to vote UKIP but hated the idea of Labour doing a deal with the SNP more than they disliked the prospect of voting Conservative' (Ross 2015: 174–5). In the words of one UKIP organizer: 'the SNP narrative killed us' (cited in Goodwin and Milazzo 2017: 280).

The main targets of the Conservative campaign were potential Liberal Democrat and UKIP voters who, in the words of David Cameron, were asked to 'lend their vote' in order to stop the formation of an Labour–SNP government (Cowley and Kavanagh 2016: 2015). But there is nonetheless ample evidence that it was a message that resonated even among potential Labour supporters. So, for example, Labour's (unsuccessful) candidate in Rochester and Strood, Naushabah Khan (2016: 66), reports that, 'even in Medway, five hundred miles from Scotland, I was asked time and time again if the rumours were true, "would Ed Miliband form a coalition with the Nationalists"'—five hundred miles is, in fact, a considerable but possibly

---

[18] Available at https://www.youtube.com/watch?v=vc6YH4-IHME.
[19] This was not simply an act of post hoc rationalization on Farage's part, as he had publicly acknowledged the effectiveness of the Conservative message in the weeks before polling day—for example, in an interview with BBC News on 28 April (cited in Bennett 2015: 277).

telling overestimate. Policy was part of the issue. Labour canvassers in Harlow, for example, encountered the

> belief that the SNP would offer a set of policies that were alien to a core group of voters (some of whom were previous Labour supporters). These concerns centred around perceptions of an SNP-influenced Labour government as economically extravagant, and dove-ish on defence and foreign policy.   (Stride and Quagliozzi 2016: 58)

But, at an even more fundamental level, national identity mattered too. Tristram Hunt (2016a: 2), Labour's (successful) candidate for Stoke-on-Trent, recalls 'fears of "betraying" England to the Scottish Nationalist Party [*sic*] via a post-election coalition deal' as the dominant theme of the campaign 'both in the mass media and on doorsteps'. The fear that Labour was about to collude in a process that would leave English voters worse off than their Scottish counterparts is also palpable in a comment by one shadow cabinet member quoted by Cowley and Kavanagh (2016: 377): 'It was just the idea that Scotland might be getting a better deal out of the government than they would in Bolton.'

Labour's response was uncertain and vacillating. In part this may be attributed to the fact that the growing pressure being applied by the Conservatives through their relentless focus on the 'threat' of SNP influence placed the party in a genuinely invidious position. Given that the polls were suggesting that a hung parliament was the almost inevitable outcome of the election, it appeared that Labour's only realistic route to power was through some form of accommodation with the SNP. For Labour definitively to rule out any such arrangement was, therefore, gravely to weaken its expected post-election position and perhaps to rule itself out from even attempting to form a government. Moreover, even if the party was to declare that there were no circumstances in which it would deal with the Scottish nationalists, it was far from certain that this would be enough to draw the poison. After all, the SNP could—and did—make it clear not only that it was determined to 'lock out' the Conservatives from power, but that it would be willing to support a minority Labour government's legislative programme on a case-by-case basis without seeking a confidence and supply-type arrangement, let alone a formal coalition.[20] Those nervous about SNP influence could have good cause to

---

[20] The phrase was used by Nicola Sturgeon during the televised seven-way leaders' debate broadcast on 2 April 2015.

remain concerned, whatever Labour said. In addition, there was strong pressure from the party's beleaguered but still influential Scottish leadership not definitively to rule out some form of deal with the SNP, lest the electorate north of the border interpret that as anti-Scottish.[21] Eventually, just a week before the polling day—in part having had to accept that his party's position in Scotland was hopeless—Miliband went as far as he possibly could in ruling out any form of understanding with the SNP: even if doing so 'meant we weren't going to be in government…then so be it' (Watson 2015: 169). But by this point the damage had been done.

Steven Fielding (2015: 67) quotes 'a prominent Labour insider' who conceded that the party just 'didn't have a narrative strand to challenge' the Conservatives' focus on a potential SNP influence. It is arguable, however, that the problem was more fundamental than that. To read the accounts by various Labour politicians and activists of the election campaign in England is to be struck by the existence of a cultural chasm between the leadership group, on the one hand, and much of the English population, on the other. This chasm is symbolized above all, perhaps, by a now famous incident that took place, not during the general-election campaign itself, but rather during the by-election held in late November 2014 in Rochester and Strood following Mark Reckless's defection to UKIP. Canvassing in the constituency, Shadow Minister and MP for Islington South Emily Thornberry came across a modern terraced house adorned with three St George's cross flags and with a white van in the drive, of which she promptly tweeted a photo accompanied by the caption 'Image from #Rochester' (Donald 2014; Khan 2016: 62–7). This apparently innocuous act was widely interpreted as an expression of metropolitan disdain towards patriotic, working-class voters—even towards the very idea of England—and denounced as such in the most forthright terms, not least by her own party colleagues. By the end of the day she had resigned her shadow cabinet position.

Setting the peculiarities of the Thornberry episode to one side, the sense that the Labour leadership did not understand contemporary English society—in particular the growth of support for UKIP and the response south of the border to the prospect of SNP influence—is a recurring theme (see the various contributions to Hunt 2016). Cowley and Kavanagh (2016: 86) cite the blunt assessment of one member of Labour's NEC that '[i]f you're Scottish

---

[21] This was the view of Scottish Labour leader Jim Murphy although he was strongly opposed by the party's (UK) general election coordinator, and (then) fellow Scottish MP, Douglas Alexander (Watson 2015: 48-9).

or from London, you just don't get that demographic...'. John Spellar, a veteran Labour MP who had long been warning his party of the UKIP threat, is reported to have accused Labour campaign co-ordinator Douglas Alexander of not understanding UKIP because he sat for a seat in Scotland; in turn, Alexander accused Spellar of being 'racist' (Cowley and Kavanagh 2016: 86). Polarization along national lines was clearly featuring in intra- as well as inter-party disputes.

Unsurprisingly, some unionists were deeply discomforted by the tone of the Conservative campaign. Gordon Brown accused the Tories of fuelling a 'dangerous and insidious' English nationalism, while former Tory Minister Lord (Michael) Forsyth warned his own party that it was pursuing a 'short-term and dangerous view which threatens the integrity of our country' (cited in Ross 2015: 300, 301). Their warnings were echoed in Northern Ireland by the DUP's Nigel Dodds (Cowley and Kavanagh 2016: 328). The implication, of course, is that the Conservatives' anti-SNP line was shading into—and fanning—a more general anti-Scottishness. It is a suggestion indignantly rejected by Lynton Crosby, who claims that the focus was the SNP not Scotland as such, and was a means to an end—the end being to expose Ed Miliband as a weak leader (see Ross 2015: 157, 293–4).

But this is hardly the whole story. As Tim Ross argues, it is 'debatable' whether voters' undoubted dislike of the idea of a Labour–SNP tie-up was rooted in any 'rational assessment of the SNP's public spending priorities'. Rather, the Conservatives appear to have been able to make political capital from 'a visceral antipathy' towards Scots among English voters (Ross 2015: 294). 'Visceral antipathy' represents a very strong claim, of course. Nonetheless, it certainly tallies with Sinclair's view from the centre of the Conservative campaign that 'we'—presumably the English—view Scots as threatening 'foreigners' and 'outsiders'. Even if we were to resist such a stark conclusion, it nonetheless cannot be gainsaid that there is ample evidence for the existence of, at the very least, a strong sense of grievance among the English at what is regarded as Scotland's unfairly privileged treatment within the United Kingdom. The Conservatives were aware of this and were knowingly capitalizing upon it. In other words, 'anti-Scottish' or not, theirs was a strategy that deliberately aimed to make political capital from a national territorial cleavage within the UK, and, in doing so, served to deepen that cleavage. It would be disingenuous to pretend otherwise.

Commenting on the Conservatives' success in staving off the UKIP threat, Ross (2015: 179) suggests that, having unsuccessfully tried various approaches to the problem,

[f]inally, they turned to the root motive for many of UKIP's supporters in marginal English seats: a deeply held sense of national identity and a fear that it was under threat from a powerful foreigner from the north. Crosby and Cameron beat Farage by turning UKIP's most potent weapon on itself.

But it was not only Farage who was (for the moment) defeated by this strategy. As we have seen, it was Clegg and Miliband too. A year later, however, having apparently misunderstood both the nature and power of this 'national identity', Cameron himself was to be consumed by the flames he had helped fan as the United Kingdom voted to quit the European Union.

Britain and the 2016 Referendum

The Conservative Party's success in mobilizing English concerns about the SNP and, more generally, Scotland's apparently privileged position within the union helped secure an unexpected election victory that made a referendum on the UK's continuing membership of the EU inevitable.[22] Yet it is striking that in the run-up to that referendum, held only 413 days after the general election, 'England' featured hardly at all. Rather, the relentless rhetorical focus of both the Leave and the Remain campaigns alike was on 'Britain'. Not only that, but both sides portrayed Britain in remarkably similar ways, even while drawing different conclusions as to the implications of this portrayal for continuing EU membership. But what is also beyond doubt is that, even if England was hardly ever mentioned directly by the Leave campaign, its arguments about Britain's future nonetheless resonated in particular with those voters with a strong sense of English national identity (Henderson et al. 2016, 2017, 2020).

That both campaigns tended to portray Britain in similar ways is a fundamental if often overlooked aspect of the referendum campaign (for an exception, see Barnett 2017). Britain 'the island nation'; Britain with its truly glorious, buccaneering past; Britain the land of cherished democratic institutions; Britain the global power managing to punch well above its still considerable weight; Britain the natural, international leader: these were the tropes that formed the common currency of the referendum campaign.

---

[22] The party's 2015 election manifesto included a pledge to 'legislate in the first session of the next Parliament for an in–out referendum to be held on Britain's membership of the EU before the end of 2017' (Conservative Party 2015c: 73).

One striking illustration of this can be found in the two draft articles—one pro-Remain and the other pro-Leave—penned on the same day in early 2016 by Boris Johnson as he pondered which side to support in the referendum (reproduced in Shipman 2016: 609–18). The endorsement of this high-profile politician was a highly sought-after prize for both campaigns, and the fact that Johnson could apparently have so easily fallen either way is regarded by his critics as yet another sign of his perfidity. But, for present purposes, more interesting is the significant overlap between the arguments in both his Leave and Remain missives in terms of the way they conceive of Britain. Writing in his Leave guise, Johnson claimed:

> We have become so used to Nanny in Brussels that we have become infantilised, incapable of imagining an independent future. We used to run the biggest empire the world has ever seen, and with a much smaller domestic population and a relatively tiny civil service. Are we really incapable of cutting trade deals?

But, donning his Remain persona, Johnson could argue with apparent conviction: 'Britain is a great nation, a global force for good. It is surely a boon for the world and for Europe that she should be intimately engaged.' Whatever side of the argument he was on, there was clearly no doubting Britain's illustrious past, its moral integrity, let alone its rightful, global role. British exceptionalism was beyond question.

In this, at least, Johnson was entirely representative. The core tenets of British exceptionalism appear and reappear innumerable times on both sides of the referendum divide.[23] Take, for example, David Cameron's own rhetoric. In his Bloomberg speech in January 2013, when he announced his party's commitment to renegotiate the UK's relationship with Europe and a subsequent in–out referendum on EU membership, the then prime minister claimed that 'our geography has shaped our psychology. We have the character of an island nation—independent, forthright, passionate in defence of our sovereignty. We can no more change this British sensibility than we can drain the English Channel' (Cameron 2013). In his November 2015 speech ahead of that renegotiation, he was eager to point out that 'I am not saying for one moment that Britain couldn't survive outside the European Union. Of course

---

[23] For reasons of space we will not deal with the arguments of those small left-wing groups who championed Brexit from a left-of-centre perspective: so-called Lexit. Suffice it to say that these arguments are also premised on their own version of British exceptionalism.

we could. We are a great country. The fifth largest economy in the world... Our capital city a global icon. The world, literally, speaks our language' (Cameron 2015). Speaking to a journalist in the midst of the subsequent referendum campaign, Cameron eagerly pointed out that he was 'teaching his children that Britain is "special"' and that he believed that Britain could be a 'swashbuckling, trading, successful, buccaneer nation of the 21st century' (McTague 2016).

All of this sounds remarkably similar to the rhetoric deployed by the person whom he had replaced as prime minister in 2010. Writing in a special issue of the *New Statesman* ahead of the referendum, Gordon Brown (2016a) waxed lyrical about 'our great island nation' 'whose history, values and general temperament impel us to lead when others fail to do so' (see also Edgerton 2018: 518). The former prime minster had recently published a book arguing that Britain should be 'leading, not leaving' Europe (Brown 2016b).[24] Even if bad blood following Cameron's support for EVEL meant that they would not share a stage during the campaign, they nonetheless remained in fundamental agreement about the core features of Britain and Britishness and their exceptional character.

As were their opponents at the head of the Leave campaign. Take, for example, Daniel Hannan, widely lauded as one of the leading intellectual lights of the Eurosceptic movement (for his key pre-referendum contribution, see Hannan 2016a). According to Hannan (2016b), because the British 'don't sit on great natural resources in this green, damp, exquisite island home of ours, we have to make our way in the world by what we buy and sell'. This has meant, as spelled out in the title of one of his most popular and influential books, that the British became the 'inventors' of freedom worldwide (Hannan 2015). On his reading, even historic defeats serve only to underline the country's leading role: the leaders of American struggle for independence 'were arguing not for the rejection but for the assertion of what they took to be their birthright as Englishmen [*sic*]'. The subsequent 'spread of "Western" values was, in truth', the result of 'a series of military victories' by the English-speaking states that represent the British Empire's legacy to the world (Hannan 2013). What Boris Johnson (2018) termed Britain's 'historical national genius' meant it was always destined to be more than, in the words of Nigel Farage (2015: 122), 'just one star on their EU flag'.

---

[24] As has already been noted, he was in fact recycling a phrase he has used in the run-up to the 2014 referendum, when he had argued that Scotland should be 'leading Britain—not leaving it' (Brown 2014: 332)—a phrase not repeated in the post-referendum version of the book (Brown 2015).

In short, both sides of the referendum debate conceived of Britain in remarkably similar, exceptionalist terms. Not only that, but—in stark contrast to the 2015 general-election campaign—there was relatively little national territorial differentiation in terms of either campaign strategy or messaging. Rather, with relatively minor exceptions, the official Remain campaign and the various rival Leave campaigns alike all tended to treat the UK as an undifferentiated whole, foregrounding messages that focused almost exclusively on Britain, Britishness, and their associated rhetorical tropes and symbolic trappings.

Paradoxically this was partly a result of the very Anglo-centrism of David Cameron, who ignored an unprecedented joint request by the First Ministers of Scotland and Wales and the First and Deputy Ministers of Northern Ireland not to hold the referendum only weeks after the elections to the devolved legislatures in early May.[25] In doing so, the prime minister ensured that—as predicted by the devolved leaders—there would be little by the way of a ground campaign in any of these territories, where, for political campaigners across the parties, the referendum became, quite literally, an afterthought.[26] Had Cameron heeded advice on timing, then it is is likely that, on the Remain side, at least, the organizations established by the official 'Britain Stronger in Europe' campaign for the devolved territories—'Scotland Stronger in Europe', 'Wales Stronger in Europe', and 'NI Stronger in Europe'—would have developed into powerful national campaigns of their own right with their own distinctive country-specific messaging. But that was not to be (Davies 2018: 55–84).

Yet, even if the prime minister had made doubly sure that England would be the key battleground, the Remain campaign, in particular, ignored the lessons of the 2015 general election. Indeed, it was as if campaign strategists were determined to pretend that the the period between 19 September 2014 and 7 May 2015 had never happened. It was, in fact, the Better Together campaign of 2014 that provided them with their model. Given that, despite overwhelming media support as well as deeper pockets than their rivals, Better Together had managed to fritter away a large proportion of its opinion-poll lead in the final six months before the referendum, this may

---

[25] See 'David Cameron Urged to Delay EU Referendum by First Ministers', BBC news website, 3 February 2016, https://www.bbc.com/news/uk-politics-35483522.
[26] Indicative of the Cameron camp's fundamental lack of understanding of the changes to the political infrastructure of the UK brought about by devolution is the fact that his closest advisers were apparently surprised at the relatively low turnout in Scotland on (2016) referendum day (Shipman 2016: 402).

strike many readers as counter-intuitive. Nonetheless, accounts of the Remain campaign are replete with examples of the ways in which it sought to follow the 'Better Together playbook' (Oliver 2016: 81, 225, 274; Shipman 2016: 242–3, 362). With the Scots and the Londoners in charge, figuratively if not necessarily literally, 'Britain Stronger in Europe' ignored the lessons of Conservative success in 'borrowing the votes' of potential Liberal Democrat, Labour, and UKIP supporters.

There was to be no 'England Stronger in Europe' campaign or even branding. Not only that, but Remain campaigned as if the UK was a comfortably multinational as well as multi-ethnic polity and society rather than a country characterized by territorial grievance. This was evidenced, most obviously, in the choice of participants for the set-piece TV debates that provided the main focal points of the campaign, and in particular the (demographically wholly disproportionate) prominence accorded to Scottish devolved politicians. Both Nicola Sturgeon and Ruth Davidson were chosen to make the case for staying in the EU: two out of a total of six Remain participants in the debates.[27]

Notwithstanding Nicola Sturgeon's undoubted prowess as a debater, given that the Downing Street representatives at the head of the campaign would have been well aware of the evidence from Conservative focus groups about her deep unpopularity among a large segment of English voters—indeed, they even had confirmation of this from the Remain campaign's own focus groups—it is genuinely difficult to discern what strategy the leaders of the campaign thought they were pursuing in handing her such a prominent role.[28] While those leading the Remain campaign had persuaded themselves that, because Davidson does not have 'a cut-glass, received-pronunciation

---

[27] The other four were Angela Eagle, Sadiq Khan, Frances O'Grady, and Amber Rudd. The list therefore included two of the most prominent politicians in Scotland as well as the newly elected mayor of London, who was also the state's most prominent ethnic-minority politician: in retrospect, the Remain campaign's choice of debate participants appears to have been drawn from segments of the electorate already likely to support Remain. Leave used the same three representatives for both set-piece TV debates. Andrea Leadsom and Boris Johnson were accompanied by German-born, Birmingham-domiciled Labour MP Gisela Stuart, whose presence was clearly designed to appeal to potential Labour Leave voters but also to reassure any other potential supporters who had been given pause by the Leave campaign's increasingly strident anti-immigration rhetoric. While Leave was intent on both shoring up and attempting to appeal beyond its base, Remain seemed to have little idea how to appeal to those tempted to vote for its opponents.

[28] Craig Oliver (2016:287) claims that '[w]e wouldn't have chosen Nicola to be on the platform, as she goes down badly with English voters, but ITV insisted'. One can only imagine how a Lynton Crosby or Paul Sinclair might have responded to such a demand. Reporting back on a post-debate Remain focus group in Durham, Ryan Coetzee told his colleagues that '"a few" English voters 'responded very badly to Sturgeon, as was the finding in Worcester last week [sic]. I hope her presence in that debate helped drive up SNP support levels because despite her good performance, I don't think she really did us much good' (Shipman 2016: 334).

accent…she speaks in an accent that's less foreign to Labour voters in the north of England', the high profile accorded to the Scottish Conservative leader was also of doubtful utility, given the imperative need to appeal to what Tony Blair once dubbed 'middle England' (Shipman 2016: 393–5). One can only conclude that the Remain campaign did not take seriously the realities of territorial politics in the United Kingdom, and of English grievance in particular, despite the sharp lesson dealt by the very recent general election. Indeed, the fact that prominent Remainers, including Cameron himself, could so regularly use 'little England' and 'little Englanders' as a casual insult with which to belabour their opponents suggests an almost wilful blindness (Oliver 2016: 296).

None of the rival Leave campaigns was to make an *explicit* effort to mobilize specifically English opinion (for accounts, see Banks 2016; Bennett 2016). Yet despite this, and despite the fact that many of the tropes used to characterize Britain and Britishness were also utilized by the Remain campaign, it is clear that Leave in its various manifestations was far better attuned to the views and sensitivities of what we might term 'middle-English' voters. Leave's Britain was not the equal partnership of nations ostensibly championed by the unionist parties in the run-up to the 2014 Scottish independence referendum. Neither was it the vibrant and confident multi-ethnic, multinational-yet-still-one-nation Britain their opponents in the Remain campaign were seeking to project and valorize. Theirs was rather Anglo-Britain or, less diplomatically, Britain-as-Greater England (Wyn Jones 2017; Henderson 2018). Which is one reason why, even if England was hardly mentioned directly by Leave, Nigel Farage nonetheless had a point when he described the rise of UKIP and, by extension, the wider Eurosceptic movement as 'our very English rebellion' (cited by Goodwin and Milazzo 2017: 8).

To illustrate how the Leave campaign appealed to characteristically English views of Britain and briefly to anticipate arguments we will illustrate in much greater detail in the following chapters, let us focus on two of the most memorable 'sound bites' associated with it. First, arguably the single most well-known newspaper headline to feature in what was an overwhelmingly Eurosceptic press appeared early in the campaign (on 3 February 2016). Published amid concern among Leave supporters that members of the UK cabinet, as well as other leading Conservative luminaries, would be unwilling to risk the possible consequences of affiliating openly with the Leave campaign, the *Daily Mail* used its front page to ask: 'Who will speak for England?' The headline was accompanied by a highly unusual front-page editorial urging them to do just that. In the event, of course, amid bitter recriminations and fractured personal relationships, the *Mail* leader writer's hopes would be realized, as several cabinet members joined with Boris Johnson in leading the official Leave campaign.

The headline offered one of the few examples of England being mentioned directly during the campaign, and, even though the newspaper was quick to point out that 'of course, by "England"…we mean the whole of the United Kingdom', it is telling that neither the headline nor the accompanying editorial was repeated in that day's Scottish edition of the newspaper. But, even as it called England in aid, the headline very deliberately evoked a key event in British history by repeating Leo Amery's famous anti-appeasement cry across the House of Commons chamber—'Speak for England'—as Neville Chamberlain's policy of placating Hitler finally began to unravel in the face of continuing Nazi aggression. It was Winston Churchill who would ultimately (and figuratively speaking) answer Amery's call, and one need hardly be an expert in semiotics to work out what the *Mail* was attempting to signal to the author of a recent bestselling book on Churchill (Johnson 2014). But framing the referendum battle-to-come in the context of the Second World War was about far more than appealing to the conscience and/or vanity of one man. Rather, the newspaper that has regarded itself (not without reason) as the authentic voice of 'middle England' was calling in aid a period in history that has particular—even overwhelming—national-cultural significance for Anglo-Britons. The subtext was not really a subtext at all: supporting the Leave cause was, once again, to cast aside appeasement and resist continental authoritarianism.

If 'Who will speak for England?' was probably the best-known Leave supporting headline, then the highest-profile and best-known Leave campaign slogan was, without a shadow of a doubt, 'Take back control'. Apparently devised by Dominic Cummings, the campaign director of the officially designated Vote Leave campaign, 'Take back control' was pitch perfect. It managed to span the two key themes of the Leave campaign—namely, sovereignty and immigration—doing so in a way that evoked a sense of national history that resonates particularly strongly with those who identify as English. Restoring the 'sovereignty of parliament' and restoring the state's borders in order to stop 'uncontrolled' immigration: these are both tropes whose undoubted power resides in a quintessentially English nostalgia for a glorious past in which the monarch in parliament was sovereign and in which the United Kingdom was more ethnically homogenous. But this is not only some sepia-tinted hankering for a lost age. It also manifests in a very contemporary, normative understanding of what appropriate government should (and should not) look like: a sovereign parliament wielding unfettered control over its own territory and walking tall in the world. Past, present, and (potential) future are all perfectly encapsulated in three little words.

It is here that the crux of the difference between the Leave and Remain campaigns comes into focus. Yes, both sides embraced the familiar tropes of British exceptionalism, yet, in doing so, they also came to very different conclusions about what EU membership meant for Britain and Britishness. For both David Cameron and Gordon Brown alike, EU membership provided a stage from which Britain—naturally, playing the leading role—could continue to project its positive influence worldwide. Cameron was explicitly clear that he did not regard Europe as an end in itself but, in a phrase repeated in both the 2013 and 2015 speeches from which we have already quoted, 'a means to an end'. That end was to maintain and to amplify the already undeniable Greatness of Britain (Barnett 2017). Pooling sovereignty with continental Europeans might be irritating, occasionally infuriating, and certainly something to be kept to a minimum, but it was nonetheless a price paid to allow Britain to be Britain in a contemporary context.

But, for Leavers, the message and moral of these core beliefs about Britain and Britishness were simpler and more direct—and for many, it would seem, more emotionally satisfying. To be true to its glorious past, to allow Britain's unique parliamentary democracy to flourish, to unlock the innate, exceptional talents and spirit that would make Britain great again, the country had to cast off the tethers that had tied it to—indeed, made it subservient to—continental Europe.[29] Here, Britain's best future had its roots in the country's glorious past. Only in this way could the nation achieve—to adopt American parlance—its manifest, global destiny. In other words, core beliefs about the past that made Britain exceptional served as a blueprint for renewal and a Greatness fully restored.

Conclusion

In a retrospective reflection on the EU membership referendum result, Remain-campaigner Peter Mandelson claimed:

> We lost because of the mountain of anti-EU sentiment in *the country*, driven by Rupert Murdoch and Paul Dacre and the rest of the Brexit press over

---

[29] Further to underline the extent to which British exceptionalism is common ground between Remain and Leavers, it is worth recalling the subtitle of Nick Clegg's post-Brexit referendum book: *How to Stop Brexit (and Make Britain Great Again)* (2017).

many years, the hopelessness of the Labour leadership, and our own campaign's lack of dexterity and reading of public opinion. Having said that, given the underlying drivers working against us, including the prevailing anti-politics, anti-establishment feelings in the West, the achievement of 48 per cent of the vote begins to look like a small miracle.

(Shipman 2016: 595; our emphasis)

The third leg of New Labour's leading triumvirate and, by any reckoning, one of the canniest operatives in UK politics over the past few decades, Mandelson deserves to be taken seriously. Indeed, notwithstanding the distinct air of bathos surrounding the final sentence, there can be little doubt that many disappointed Remainers share Mandelson's broad analysis. But it is repeated here, not in order to debate the merits of these exculpatory remarks, but rather to highlight the way in which he clearly regards the referent object of his comments—'the country'—as entirely unproblematic. He simply assumes that it is self-evident to which definite-article country he is referring.

For the avoidance of doubt, Mandelson is hardly alone in making such an assumption. For most analysts and participants in the political process, the identity of 'the country' remains a matter of simple common sense. But, as our review of political and constitutional developments between September 2014 and June 2016 in this chapter should have made clear, this is an assumption that increasingly appears to be at odds with reality. In September 2014, not only did 45 per cent of the Scottish electorate vote to end what its supporters like to claim is the most successful political union in history, but we also saw emerging into clear focus a powerful sense of English grievance about their country's place within that same union. Eight months or so later, that sense of grievance was to play a pivotal role in a general election in which English suspicion not only of the SNP but of Scotland more generally was mobilized to great effect by the Conservative campaign. That campaign's success was in turn a necessary condition for the European membership referendum in June 2016, a referendum whose results also served to call into further question any straightforward invocation of 'the country'.

Taken in combination, the 2015 general election and the 2016 referendum suggest that, even in the context of a single state, to suggest the existence of a singular, let alone united country is—at best—to gloss over deep national divisions. Yet, neither is it obvious how we should understand the political terrain exposed by these linked electoral events. In England, in particular, it is clearly not some simple story of fracture and (potential) break-up. Even if the result of the 2015 election hinged on the success of an electoral strategy based on mobilizing English grievance about the apparently unfair treatment of England within the United Kingdom, the 2016 vote demonstrated that the English, in particular, remain deeply attached to a particular version of Britishness and vision for Britain. Unlike Irish, Scottish, and Welsh nationalisms, which by the twenty-first century, and with only relatively minor caveats, can all be plausibly interpreted as a rejection of Britishness, English nationalism continues to hold Britain dear. But, precisely because politicized Englishness is different, its nature and implications remain very poorly understood. Before we move to expand upon and evidence our own understanding of contemporary English nationalism, it is first necessary to address the question of who in England feels English. This is the subject of Chapter 2.

2

On Englishness and Britishness

It was not meant to be like this. Unlike the overly emotional Celts or those of their ilk, the English were thought to be indifferent about or even antipathetic towards nationalism.[1] As a former imperial power that had imposed modes of governance as well as values, first, on immediate neighbours and, subsequently, worldwide, England was above such narrow 'tribal' identity politics. Back in the self-styled 'mother country', even the American veneration of flag seemed rather gauche. For the English it was class identity rather than national identity that mattered both politically and culturally (Schopflin 2000—for classic treatments of the relationship between class and nation in England, see Thompson 1965; Nairn 1981a; Anderson 1992). In a world dominated by nations and nationalisms, England, it seemed, was *sui generis*.

It is highly doubtful whether this was ever in fact the case. Comparative study would suggest that dominant nationalities are often characterized by nationalisms that derive much of their rhetorical power from the claim that, unlike the nationalisms of their challengers, they alone are rational and natural: our patriotism to their tribalism; our established order to their disruptive tendencies; our 'thousand years of history' to their 'invented tradition' (Hobsbawm and Ranger 1983; Billig 1995). But, notwithstanding the past, recent years have demonstrated very clearly that England and the English are far from immune to nationality politics. As discussed in Chapter 1, English grievance, against Scotland in particular, was a central theme in the 2015 general election campaign and, according to participants on all sides, a key determinant of the result.[2] The EU referendum that resulted from the Conservative election triumph subsequently saw the Leave campaign make a series of arguments based on Britain's past, present, and potential future that

---

[1] The tendency to juxtapose emotional, mercurial Celts with the stoic, 'teutonic' English has a very long-standing pedigree, but is particularly associated with Arnold (1867).

[2] So far, at least, surprisingly little academic analysis of the result of the 2015 general election has been published, perhaps because it was followed so closely by the Brexit referendum and two subsequent general elections, which has inevitably led to the prioritization of data collection over analysis.

resonated particularly strongly with English-identifying voters (as shown in Henderson et al. 2017, 2020).

It should be noted that the emergence of English national identity as a potent political force will not have come as a surprise to anyone familiar with the literature on Englishness. From the late 1990s onwards, much of that literature took on a conditional even expectant tone. The apparent docility of the English could no longer be taken for granted. Rather, it was widely conjectured that the establishment of new legislatures in Edinburgh and Cardiff, accompanied by the return of devolution to Northern Ireland, would loosen the bonds across the union, particularly in the light of the continued under-representation of English MPs at Westminster and the fact that per capita public expenditure is higher outside England. Pressure for integration within Europe, the 'uncontrollability of international business', and end of empire were also cited as reasons to anticipate a change in English mood (see for example Paxman 1999: viii).

At the time, researchers awaited an English backlash that would make itself felt in two ways, both focused on the domestic union of which England is a part (departing from the European Union would have appeared a fanciful prospect in this period). The first element was an anticipated 'what about us?' response that would see a demand for some sort of institutional accommodation for England and, relatedly, a greater attachment to Englishness. The second was an expectation that the English would eventually demand an end to the perceived privileges granted to Scotland, Wales, and Northern Ireland. Writing in 2000, John Curtice and Anthony Heath claimed that English national identity was on the rise, but that there was as yet no call for institutional accommodation for England, nor did English national identity appear to structure voting preferences. Notwithstanding the presence of 'little Englanders',

> [t]he English seem to be comfortable with the existence of separate institutions in Scotland and Wales without wishing to set up similar arrangements in England, whether at the national or regional level. This is probably why the somewhat muted attempts by the Conservative Party to identify itself as the party of English interests have met with an even more muted response.   (Curtice and Heath 2001: 172)

In retrospect, however, it appears to have been a backlash deferred rather than a backlash avoided.

The subsequent literature on Englishness is multidimensional. Some authors continue to focus on the role of sport, and football in particular, as an outlet for expressions of Englishness (King 2000; Abell et al. 2007; Gibbons 2011, 2014, 2017; building on previous work by Bale 1986; Houlihan 1997; Carrington 1998). Unsurprisingly, perhaps, the relationship between Englishness and Britishness also remains an area of interest, not least in the context of race (Madood et al. 1997; Gilroy 2002), as do, relatedly, the changes in the use of different national labels over time, and the changing national myths or narratives associated with both Englishness and Britishness (Curtice and Heath 2001; Bryant 2003; Kumar 2003; Condor et al. 2006; Curtice 2009; Skey 2011). Noteworthy, too, are discussions of the way that notions of race, religion, and ideology combine in different ways to underpin distinct and perhaps competing visions of English national identity and Englishness (Condor 2010). But, following on from earlier prognostications and warnings, increasing attention has also been paid to the more directly political dimensions of English national identity, including the relationship between English nationalism and attitudes to Europe (Wellings 2012, 2019), options for English governance (Kenny 2014), and support for political parties (Mycock and Hayton 2014).

We will return to many of these contributions throughout the following chapters, but first this chapter sets itself the task of exploring the patterns of national identity found in contemporary England. It proceeds in the following steps. First, we deploy different measures of national identity to explore how English and/or British the electorate of England feels. As will become clear, each measure serves to highlight different dimensions of national feeling. Secondly, we illustrate and explore the different demographic and socio-economic characteristics associated with particular national identities. This helps us to determine if there is a particular type of person more likely to describe her or himself as English or British. Third, we explore the different institutions, traits, and characteristics that our survey respondents associate with Englishness and Britishness. All of this serves to prepare the ground for the following chapters, in which we focus in more detail on the attitudes—and in particular the constitutional preferences—held by those with different national identities in England.

Englishness and Britishness in England

Social surveys offer a number of routes through which to investigate the national identities to which individuals adhere. Given the complex and multifaceted nature of national identity, especially in a context such as England's in which individuals often have more than one national identity, it is arguably the case that none of these routes suffices on its own. In combination, however, they allow us to build up a rich and relatively sophisticated understanding of social reality. In this section we present data drawn from three different measures of national identity. The first enables respondents to select particular national labels to describe themselves. A second measure focuses on the relative strength of two nested identities. In a multinational state like the United Kingdom, but also in Spain or in Canada, this typically includes the national identity associated with the state—in our case Britishness—and the identity associated with the sub-state nation—in this case Englishness. In some states multiple identities are prevalent, while in others they sit in zero-sum opposition. By reflecting on the relative relationship of national identities, we can detect not only whether individuals feel closer to one pole or another but also whether single or dual identities predominate. Our third measure focuses on the intensity with which these identities are held, allowing us—*inter alia*—to draw out empirically what will already have become apparent in Chapter 1—namely, the intensity of the *English* relationship to England and Britain, Englishness and Britishness.[3]

The simplest and perhaps crudest measure of national identity is known to researchers as the 'forced-choice' question. This is a two-stage question: respondents are first asked to choose which national identities (from a list of options) they would apply to themselves, with respondents allowed to pick as many or as few as they deem relevant; then they are asked to select one option that 'best describes the way you think about yourself'. Figure 2.1 combines data from two sources—namely the British Social Attitudes Survey (BSAS) (from 1992 to 2016) and our Future of England Survey (FoES) (from 2011 to 2016). We use these two data sources to show that FoES data are consistent with other data sources on national identity in the UK.

In 1992, people in England described themselves as British rather than English by a ratio of 2 to 1. That is no longer the case. By 2011, data from both the FoES and the BSAS show that those in England are more likely to describe themselves as English, albeit by differing margins (by two points for the BSAS, by seven for the FoES). Since then the two data sources have shown slightly different trends, with the FoES showing Englishness ahead by zero to six points and the BSAS showing Britishness ahead by one to eight points. This in itself is striking, but the rates of change are worth exploring. The rate at which

---

[3] These different questions were asked throughout the first half of each questionnaire, with various multi-item question batteries in between to weaken priming effects of previous responses. In 2016, for example, this included Q3 on national-identity strength (0 to 10), Q8 on Moreno (English not British), and Q18 and Q19 on 'any' and 'best' national identities.

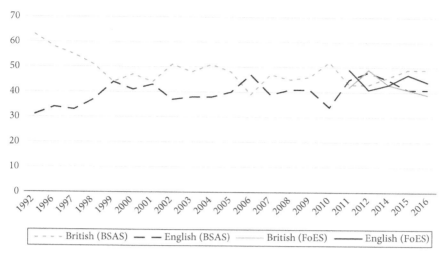

Figure 2.1 'Forced-choice' national identity, England, 1992–2016 (%)
Sources: BSAS 1992–2016, FoES 2011–2016.

people have stopped thinking of themselves as British is far greater than the rate at which people have started to think of themselves as English. The story is, therefore, less about the rise of Englishness and more about the precipitous fall in the salience of Britishness as an identity label in England. Even the more conservative estimates of the BSAS show a fourteen-point drop in Britishness and a ten-point rise in Englishness. Interestingly, much of this change seems to have taken place before the establishment of the devolved legislatures in Edinburgh and Cardiff in 1999, although subsequent chapters will go on to explore how and why identities have changed since.

As has already been noted, however, in multinational states like the United Kingdom, many people have multiple overlapping or nested national identities. In such a context the forced-choice approach to measuring national identity may be regarded as artificial, as imposing a false choice rather than simply a forced choice. To investigate nested identities further, we can examine data from the first part of the forced-choice question in which respondents are asked to pick any and all national identities that apply to them. Data from both the BSAS and the FoES show that majorities of respondents identify as both English and British.

To understand the relative strength of these identities, we employ what has become a standard measure of dual identities, the so-called Moreno question, adapted by Luis Moreno for a Scottish context from work conducted by Juan Linz on multilevel identities in Spain (for a retrospect, see Moreno 2006). The Moreno question asks respondents to locate themselves on a spectrum of options from exclusively English to exclusively British (English not British, more English than British, equally English and British, more British than English, British not English). One of the perceived benefits of the question is that it allows us to examine the relative importance of different identities but also to explore whether people choose to hold a single identity exclusively. The Moreno question has been employed by the BSAS since 1999. It was typically assumed to work better in a Scottish and Welsh context, where sub-state national identities were more obviously demarcated from a British identity. In England, however, there was a belief that the question made less sense, with individuals less likely to be able to disentangle Englishness and Britishness as distinct identities (Cohen 1995). There is some evidence that this is the case. When the British Election Study (BES) first adopted the Moreno question in 1997, almost half of respondents felt equally English and British, with relatively few (indeed always fewer than one in ten) at either the exclusively English or exclusively British pole. By 1999, however, when the BSAS adopted the question, the proportion of those describing themselves as English not British had jumped ten points and those prioritizing Englishness formed almost one-third of the sample. The jump is noteworthy, but we cannot know whether to attribute it to different survey teams using slightly different sampling methods, or to the new devolved legislatures that opened their doors in 1999 (Table 2.1). The trend has remained relatively stable since then, although the proportion of those describing themselves as Equally English and British bounces around from the low thirties to mid-forties in percentage terms.

Since we began conducting the FoES in 2011, we have found consistently higher levels of support for English identity on the Moreno question (Table 2.2). When compared to the BSAS results, our data show slightly smaller proportions of English residents describing themselves as English not British, but we show consistently larger proportions of those who prioritize their sense of Englishness as a whole, and these results are relatively stable over time (from a high point in 2011). It is worth noting that we do not find that identity is particularly responsive to individual events. Even our 2012 survey, conducted shortly after the London Olympics, shows no bounce in Britishness, which might well have been expected. We find also that the 2016 data, conducted in the aftermath of the Brexit referendum, show no bounce in either identity, although the 2015 data, gathered half a year after the Scottish independence referendum, show a slight increase in the proportion of respondents describing themselves as English. Across the various sources of data, two findings are obvious. First, we find far higher proportions of people in England prioritizing their Englishness over their Britishness than

Table 2.1 Trends in 'Moreno' national identity, England, 1997–2016 (%)

	BES	BSAS											
	1997	1999	2000	2001	2003	2007	2008	2009	2011	2013	2014	2015	2016
English not British	7	18	19	18	17	19	19	18	24	16	19	18	15
More English than British	17	14	14	13	20	14	16	16	13	12	14	10	11
Equally English and British	45	37	34	41	31	31	46	34	44	43	47	42	43
More British than English	14	11	14	9	13	14	9	10	7	8	9	8	8
British not English	9	14	12	11	10	12	7	12	9	12	9	12	12
Other/none	6	7	8	8	9	10	3	7	2	8	2	9	11
Don't know (DK)	0	0	0	0	0	0	0	0	0	0	0	0	0
n	2,492	2,718	1,928	2,761	4,432	859	2,558	1,940	2,448	2,799	2,087	3,778	2,525

Sources: BES 1997, BSAS 1999–2016 Results are column percentages.

Table 2.2 Trends in 'Moreno' national identity, England, 2011–16 (%)

	2011	2012	2014	2015	2016
English not British	17	15	11	12	12
More English than British	23	20	20	24	21
Equally English and British	34	39	41	37	37
More British than English	9	10	12	14	14
British not English	7	7	6	6	6
Other	6	6	4	4	5
DK	3	3	5	4	5
n	1,507	3,600	3,695	3,451	5,103

Source: FoES 2011–2016. Results are column percentages.

was the case in 1997, a fact that is consistent with a general increase in the use of English as a label of choice and a stark fall in the use of British as an identity label. Second, these are enduring trends, stable within the BSAS and FoES data collection and not subject to significant swings. Englishness is here and here to stay.

That said, two important caveats need to be entered. First, while the balance of the identity profile is more towards the English rather than the British end of the Moreno spectrum, those who describe themselves as equally English and British always form the largest group. Secondly, it would be wrong to assume that those people in England who prioritize their English identity are necessarily indifferent towards Britishness. This becomes clear when we turn to our third and final way of measuring of identity.

Thus far the measures we have used have offered a fairly crude way to capture identity. The 'best' measure helpfully identifies labels that apply to individuals, and the Moreno question forces individuals to reflect on the relative importance of the two dominant state and sub-state national identities. But neither measure tells us anything about the intensity of national senti-ment, nor do they recognize that individuals can be nested in more than two national communities. So, for example, one individual who does not feel her national identity particularly strongly, could describe herself as Equally English than British, while another, who feels fiercely attached to both England and Britain, might also use the same identity label to describe himself. To provide additional depth to our understanding of English identity, and to show how these two territorial identities—one sub-state, the other at the level of the state—might relate to still further identities, we look at how strongly different identities are held and, critically, compare these to what we

Table 2.3 Identity strength by 'Moreno' National Identity, 2016

	English	British	European
English not British	9.3 (1.6)	5.8 (3.1)	1.7 (2.6)
Very strongly (10) (%)	76	14	2
Not at all (0) (%)	1	12	56
More English than British	9.2 (1.4)	7.7 (1.9)	3.1 (2.8)
Very strongly (10) (%)	64	22	2
Not at all (0) (%)	0	1	30
Equally English and British	8.9 (1.7)	8.9 (1.7)	4.4 (3.4)
Very strongly (10) (%)	57	55	9
Not at all (0) (%)	0	0	24
More British than English	6.8 (2.2)	8.6 (1.7)	4.8 (3.1)
Very strongly (10) (%)	14	46	9
Not at all (0) (%)	2	1	17
British not English	3.4 (3.5)	8.5 (1.9)	4.6 (3.6)
Very strongly (10) (%)	78	45	11
Not at all (0) (%)	40	1	27
Other	2.3 (3.1)	4.2 (3.8)	5.5 (3.8)
Very strongly (10) (%)	4	14	27
Not at all (0) (%)	56	36	22
DK	5.6 (3.5)	5.6 (3.3)	4.6 (3.4)
Very strongly (10) (%)	22	15	12
Not at all (0) (%)	20	18	24

Source: FoES 2016. Results in each identity row are mean scores with standard deviations in parentheses. Results in other rows indicate percentage choosing either 10/10 very strongly or 0/10 not at all.

know already about our respondents' identities. We asked respondents to reflect on how strongly English, British, and European they felt on a scale that runs from 0 (not at all) to 10 (very strongly).

Table 2.3 shows the responses to this question by Moreno identity categories. Each cell contains four pieces of information. It tells us the mean score (and standard deviation) for each identity row. In the case of people who describe themselves as English not British captured in the first row of data, the average score on the 0 to 10 English identity question is 9.3 (although typically responses could be 1.6 points lower or higher than that). In addition, each cell indicates the proportion of people who put themselves at the maximum and the minimum points on our 0 to 10 scale. So, for those describing themselves as English not British, over three-quarters said they were not only English, but 10/10 English. Less than 1 per cent said they were not at all English (which is reassuring, given the Moreno category they have selected!).

There are three things worth highlighting about the findings in this table. First and as already suggested, feeling '*x* not *y*' does not mean that on a 0 to 10 scale people feel absolutely no attachment to the identity they profess *not* to hold. In fact, the average strength of British identity among those who profess to be 'English *not* British' is almost 6 out of 10. At the other end of the spectrum, those who regard themselves as 'British not English' have an average English identity score of just over 3, even while almost 8 per cent say they feel very strongly English. The Moreno question has many advantages. It offers a useful shorthand for the relative strength of identities, and, in terms of understanding how those identities relate to other attitudes or values, it provides a useful way of disaggregating individuals. For all that, though, it appears to underestimate the extent to which identities can be mutually held and in particular underestimates the extent to which those at the poles of the spectrum may well have a meaningful attachment to an identity label they, by other measures, appear to have rejected.

Second, and importantly, the identity patterns are asymmetrical. At the centre of the spectrum, those who identify as 'equally English and British' appear to have a very similar relationship to both identities, with an average score of just under 9 for both. But at the poles we can see clear differences between those who are 'English not British' versus those who are 'British not English'. The exclusively English identifiers ('English not British') still retain a strong British identity, with an average score—as we have seen—of just under 6 and with 14 per cent saying that they felt very strongly British. The 'British not English' identifiers, however, feel less English. There is a larger gap between the two mean scores for 'British and English', a smaller proportion feel strongly about the identity they profess not to hold, and the proportion saying they are not at all English is larger. In short, the 'English not British' are much more British than the 'British not English' are English. In addition, those who prioritize their English identity have stronger identities—or rather hold both identities with greater strength—than those who prioritize their British identity.

Finally, we also asked people to assess the strength of their European identity, and we see interesting patterns both across the English and British identity groups and for 'Other' identifiers. In general, those who prioritize their Englishness have weaker European identities. In addition, if we look at all those who said that they had an identity other than English or British, or who said they did not know how to answer the Moreno question, we see stronger European identities. However useful the shorthand grasp of dual identity provided by the Moreno question, it nonetheless both masks differences in the strength with which multiple identities are held and underestimates the complexity and nuance of their interrelationships.

As we see from the preceding discussion, different measures draw attention to different aspects of the complex pattern of national identity found in contemporary England. Overall, English identity has clearly strengthened since the early 1990s, with the English dimension of dual Anglo-British also more prominent. That said, most of those who prioritize their English identity remain strongly attached to Britishness—a sentiment that is not reciprocated among those who prioritize their British identity. Finally, European identity is particularly weak among those who prioritize their English identity.

Who Are the English?

Having demonstrated that English identity is on the rise in absolute terms and relative to Britishness, and that English identity is held strongly, we now move to examine how this maps onto the English electorate as a whole. There is not, presumably, a uniform pattern within England, and we can expect that certain demographic or socio-economic groups are more likely to describe themselves as English than others. To assist in unpacking this, we turn, briefly, to previous work on Englishness and Britishness and, critically, how they relate to each other (a literature to which we will return at various points in this book).

Two themes are worth noting at this point. First is the tendency to view England as having been rather late to the party, so to speak (although cf. Greenfeld 1993); and for fairly unsurprising reasons. As England was the dominant partner in a larger state, its national identity was always more likely to be conflated within Britishness. Thus, more so than in Scotland or in Wales, English national identity was perceived to express itself through pride in Britain and British accomplishments. Rather than viewing Britain and Britishness as a supplementary identity or even 'the other', England and Englishness were and are the beating heart. This coincides with an alleged English antipathy to nationalism as something unseemly or vulgar (Walden 2004; see also Aughey 2012)—an excessively emotional political project best reserved for the Celtic fringes. These two features combine to create a national identity informed by the belief that nationalism is both literally and meta-phorically beyond the pale and takes pride in Britain's former imperial role exporting values, modes of governance, and a sense of global horizons designed explicitly to overcome petty tribal loyalties.

Second is the identification of multiple fault lines running between Englishness and Britishness. For some, the distinction is between an ethnic and a civic identity, with Englishness portrayed as the identity of a white English population and Britishness as its multicultural, multi-ethnic inclusive (if imperfect—see Modood et al. 1997) foil. Related to this is a view that Britishness is outward looking, the identity of choice for those interested in the UK on a world stage, compared to an insular, self-interested Englishness—hence 'little Englander'. Still others take a very different, even inverse view, distinguishing between a peaceful and gentle Englishness and a colonizing and violent Britishness.

These different understandings are interesting in themselves, and we return to them below (in particular in Chapter 8). At this juncture they are helpful because they help us to identify who would be more likely to describe themselves as English or British (or both). In particular, if membership of a political community is perceived to rest on blood rather than a belonging that is freely chosen, it is perceived to be ethnic rather than civic, and we would look to ethnic rather than civic markers or characteristics when identifying those who hold those identities strongly. In the specific context of England and Britain, there are several obvious starting points.

There is a considerable body of work on national identity and race that has demonstrated that visible minorities and immigrants are more likely to describe themselves as British and less likely to describe themselves as English. With respect to immigrants, this is consistent with evidence from other states of a tendency to adopt a national identity that matches the state rather than a sub-state community (Bilodeau et al. 2010, 2015; White et al. 2015). We also anticipate a positive relationship between age and Britishness, reflecting the salience of formative events to British identity, not least the Second World War experience (in both memory and myth), as well as between right-wing political views and Englishness, in part because of the framing around Englishness by parties on the right (UKIP, Conservatives) in contrast to the deep reluctance of most on the left and centre left even to use the term (see Chapter 7). We anticipate that London will contain a smaller proportion of English identifiers, in part because of compositional effects: London contains more of those individuals that, by race, migration, and age, are less likely to describe themselves as English.

Table 2.4 shows the relationship between different socio-economic and demographic characteristics (including place of birth, ethnicity, age, social class, religious denomination, etc.) and the different Moreno identity categories. As is immediately clear, the balance of most groups is towards the

Table 2.4 National identity (Moreno) by social group, 2016 (%)

	English not British	English > British	Equal	British > English	British not English	Other	n
All	12	21	37	14	6	5	5,103
Place of birth							
England	13	23	40	14	4	2	4,529
Other UK	2	4	11	10	41	26	227
Outside UK	4	6	22	12	14	26	347
Citizenship							
UK	12	21	38	14	6	3	4,955
Other	3	7	7	5	5	48	148
Ethnicity							
White British	13	23	39	14	6	3	4554
Non-white	3	4	28	24	16	9	549
Age							
18–24	7	17	34	28	7	4	607
25–39	9	16	36	15	7	6	1,031
40–59	11	21	38	14	7	5	1,722
60+	16	25	39	10	6	4	1,743
Gender							
Male	13	22	35	15	7	4	2,286
Female	11	20	40	13	6	5	2,817
Social class							
AB	9	19	39	17	10	5	1,527
C1	10	21	38	14	7	5	1,582
C2	13	23	37	12	5	4	889
DE	18	22	34	10	6	4	1,105
Religious denomination							
None	9	22	44	15	4	3	69
C of E	15	25	41	11	4	2	1,113
RC	10	16	34	16	8	11	317
Other Christian	12	18	35	15	12	5	179
Muslim	3	2	42	20	13	2	60
Region							
North-East	8	21	45	11	6	4	288
North-West	11	22	39	13	6	4	601
Yorkshire & Humber	14	20	40	13	6	4	550
East Midlands	12	23	39	14	5	4	547
West Midlands	16	21	37	13	6	2	434
East	14	24	33	14	7	5	538
London	9	15	30	17	9	10	710
South-East	13	22	37	15	5	5	830
South-West	11	22	41	13	6	4	607

Source: FoES 2016. Results are row percentages for unweighted data. Individual religious denominations reported only if more than 50 adherents.

more exclusively or strongly English end of the Moreno spectrum, with this tendency particularly apparent among older people, among Anglicans, those in social class DE, and among those born in England. The exceptions are those born outside England but in the rest of the UK, 'non-white Britons', Muslims, and younger people, where the balance tends to prioritize a more British sense of identity.

As we can also observe, there is only modest regional variation in national-identity patterns. In all of the regions bar one, the balance is towards the English end of the English–British Moreno spectrum. Reflecting the demographic mix of the English/UK capital, London stands out as the exception, not only because it has the smallest proportion of residents who describe themselves as exclusively or primarily English but also because it has more than double the proportion of residents who describe their national identity as neither English nor British.[4] By contrast, the area with the greatest proportion of residents describing themselves as English only or predominantly English is the East, with almost two in five choosing these labels. In general, though, what we have is a contrast between London and everywhere else rather than significant variations in patterns of national identity across the regions of England.

It is one thing, however, to examine patterns of national identity against single demographic variables or even across individual regions. In reality, each of us combines various social and other characteristics. We can, therefore, build up a more sophisticated and potentially useful picture by integrating these various variables into a simple model of identity. This can allow us to identify the impact of, for example, social class, once we control for other variables such as religious denomination and age. To do this we focus not on the particular identity labels chosen, which as we outlined before can hide some of the nuances in dual and single identities, but rather employ our 0 to 10 identity strength variable for Englishness as well as Britishness and a constructed relative measure (relative territorial identity, in this case Englishness minus Britishness). Our 'predictor' variables include those already introduced. To our regions, we add a measure indicating whether someone lives in a town or a rural area. We also add variables tapping the extent to which

---

[4] The notably high proportion of respondents in the North-East describing themselves as 'Equally English and British' is out of line with what we know from the 2011 census, which included for the first time a question on identity along the lines of the 'forced-choice question'. In general, however, census data serve to confirm the picture that emerges from FoES data—namely, that there is little regional variation outside London, with English identity more widely used than British identity (Office of National Statistics 2012).

someone might be embedded within life in England or Britain. These include the previously mentioned place of birth, the length of time in England, citizenship, as well as two indices that have been devised to measure embeddedness. The first of these is a measure of religiosity, which reflects frequency of religious observance. The second is a measure of social capital based on participation in a range of social groups or clubs, including trade unions, the National Trust, campaigning organizations or wildlife charities, local community organizations, and/or whether respondents are engaged in charitable work or active in non-profit or religious organizations or sports clubs. This allow us to determine whether there is something about the embeddedness of individuals in different communities that relates to their sense of national identity.

The results in Table 2.5 help us to identify the type of person more likely to express a strong English or British identity. Four findings are relevant. First, many of the same predictors help to explain a strong English and British identity. Residents in London are significantly less likely to hold a strong identity, regardless of whether it is English or British, and the same is true of age, where there is a positive relationship for both; older respondents are more likely to feel English *and* more likely to feel British. Second, there are differences in the strength of some predictors across identities. Embeddedness matters for Englishness more, but citizenship is the sole measure of embeddedness that has a stronger significant effect for Britishness than for Englishness. Those who do not take out citizenship are not as attached to the national identity of the polity, although we should obviously query the direction of the causal arrow here. It is likely that this category could include those who are ineligible to apply for British citizenship. Third, some predictors influence one identity but not the other. Trust matters for British identity, and being right wing makes one more likely to hold a strong English identity. Efficacy is the only predictor that works in opposite directions for the two identities. Those with lower levels of efficacy—in other words, those who believe they cannot influence politics—are more likely to have a stronger English identity and a weaker British identity.

Fourth, we modelled not just strength of English and British identity but the relative strength between the two. Someone who feels strongly English can also feel strongly British. To isolate those who hold a strong English identity and a weaker British one, we create a composite measure that tracks the difference between the two variables. This serves to clarify those factors that explain Englishness but not Britishness. Individually, the strength of English or British identity is more affected by demographic or socio-economic

Table 2.5 Predictors of Britishness and Englishness in England

	Strength of English identity		Strength of British identity		English relative to British identity	
	Model 1	Model 2	Model 1	Model 2	Model 1	Model 2
Age	0.17 (0.04) ***	0.15 (0.05) ***	0.13 (0.05) ***	0.09 (0.05) **	0.04 (0.06)	0.06 (0.06)
Gender	-0.01 (0.01)	0.00 (0.01)	0.01 (0.02)	0.02 (0.02)	-0.02 (0.02)	-0.03 (0.02)
Education	-0.05 (0.02) ***	-0.04 (0.02) **	-0.01 (0.02)	-0.01 (0.02)	-0.05 (0.02) **	-0.03 (0.02)
Income	-0.05 (0.03)	-0.05 (0.03)	-0.02 (0.03)	-0.03 (0.03)	-0.04 (0.04)	-0.02 (0.04)
Non-white	0.04 (0.04)	0.09 (0.04) **	0.08 (0.04) *	0.11 (04) ***	-0.03 (0.05)	-0.03 (0.05)
Non-Christian	-0.10 (0.04) ***	-0.11 (0.04) ***	-0.02 (0.04)	-0.02 (0.04)	-0.08 (0.05) *	-0.08 (0.05) *
Non-citizen	-0.24 (0.07) ***	-0.24 (0.07) ***	-0.44 (0.07) ***	-0.43 (0.07) ***	0.20 (0.09) **	0.19 (0.09) **
Born UK	-0.36 (0.02) ***	-0.36 (0.02) ***	0.02 (0.02)	0.01 (0.02)	-0.38 (0.02) ***	-0.37 (0.02) ***
Born outside UK	-0.20 (0.04) ***	-0.20 (0.04) ***	-0.07 (0.04) *	-0.08 (0.04) **	-0.13 (0.05) ***	-0.1 (0.05) ***
England <5 yrs	-0.07 (0.10)	-0.05 (0.10)	0.04 (0.11)	0.05 (0.11)	-0.10 (0.13)	-0.10 (0.13)
London	-0.10 (0.03) ***	-0.01 (0.03) ***	-0.10 (0.03) ***	-0.10 (0.03) ***	-0.01 (0.04)	0.01 (0.04)
South-East	-0.06 (0.03) **	-0.05 (0.03) *	-0.03 (0.11)	-0.03 (0.03)	-0.03 (0.04)	-0.02 (0.03)
Midlands & East	-0.01 (0.02)	0.00 (0.02)	-0.06 (0.03) **	-0.05 (0.03) **	0.05 (0.03)	0.05 (0.03) *
North, Y & Humber	-0.03 (0.03)	-0.02 (0.02)	-0.01 (0.03)	-0.01 (0.03)	-0.01 (0.03)	-0.01 (0.03)
Town & fringe	0.03 (0.02)	0.02 (0.02)	0.04 (0.02) *	0.03 (0.02)	-0.02 (0.03)	-0.01 (0.03)
Rural	0.01 (0.02)	0.00 (0.02)	-0.01 (0.02)	-0.03 (0.02)	0.02 (0.02)	0.03 (0.03)
Religiosity		-0.11 (0.03) ***		-0.08 (0.03) ***		-0.02 (0.03)
Social capital		0.05 (0.06)		0.07 (0.06)		-0.01 (0.07)
Political interest		0.04 (0.03)		0.05 (0.03) *		-0.01 (0.04)
Trust		0.05 (0.04)		0.17 (0.04) ***		-0.13 (0.05) **
Right wing		0.17 (0.04) ***		0.05 (0.04)		0.12 (0.05) **
Low efficacy		0.06 (0.04) *		-0.10 (0.04) ***		0.16 (0.05) ***
Constant	0.88 (0.04) ***	0.69 (0.06) ***	0.82 (0.04) ***	0.74 (0.06) ***	0.06 (0.05)	-0.04 (0.08)
Adj R²	0.45	0.47	0.12	0.17	0.29	0.31

Source: FoES 2016. Results are unstandardized coefficients from OLS regression with standard errors in parentheses. *=p<.1, **=p<.05, ***=p<.01.

characteristics, but the gap between them is explained by attitudinal features, the results of which are sharper than for either identity category on its own. Here we see that attitudes to the community and the democratic system offer particular insights. Individuals who prioritize their sense of Englishness over a British identity have lower levels of trust, have lower levels of efficacy, and are more right wing. In addition, those born outside the UK or in the rest of the UK have lower levels of relative English identity. Non-citizens, however, who are less likely to feel English and to feel British, are particularly unlikely to feel a strong sense of British identity. This could be related to the fact that Britishness is perceived to be tied to the wider state in which they do not hold citizenship.

We know that the proportion of those describing themselves as English has been increasing and we know a bit about the type of people likely to describe themselves as strongly English (and strongly English relative to British identity). Specifically, we know that this is related to certain immutable factors about a person (place of birth, ethnicity), but how one navigates the wider social and political environment around them also matters. This raises an important question: what is it that people think of when they think of England (and Britain) and how relevant is that to politics?

What does it Mean to be English and/or British?

If we want to know what people think of Englishness and Britishness, we can ask, first, whether England and Britain conjure similar images or feelings. Within England, for example, this would mean exploring whether or not Englishness is perceived to have the same contours and dimensions as Britishness. Next, we might ask whether understandings of national identity vary within the population. For Anthony Cohen (1996), for example, Britishness in Scotland is different from Britishness in England (just as Scottishness in Glasgow is different from Scottishness in Shetland or the Gàidhealtachd). We would likewise expect variation within England, if not regionally then certainly across those who think of themselves as English or British. As such, we want to know not only what people think of when they think of England or Britain, but whether those who hold particular national identities see different things. Put another way, do those who prioritize an English identity describe Englishness differently from those who prioritize a British identity?

Many of those writing on national identity have sought to distinguish between the political and cultural content of identities. In their study of national culture in England and Scotland, Frank Bechhofer and David McCrone (2013) anticipated that the symbols people associated with Englishness would be more cultural than political, in part owing to the absence of distinctively English political institutions. Their survey data suggested that respondents in England associated Britishness with political markers or symbols of the state such as British democracy, the monarchy, flag, and national anthem, as well as more cultural values or markers—specifically, a sense of fair play—and sport. For Englishness, by contrast, respondents tended to prioritize primarily cultural features, makers, and values, such as language, fair play, and the before countryside. They also found that the national-identity labels peoples used to describe themselves mattered. British identifiers were more likely to focus on the political elements of Britishness, while English identifiers were more likely to associate Britishness with the royal family and the Union Jack. There were no meaningful differences across identity categories in terms of how people conceived of Englishness, with the exception that English identifiers were more likely to identify the St George's cross with England than were British identifiers.

Our FoES data also allow us to explore what makes individuals proud to be English or British. Our goal here was to distinguish further the symbols that attach to English and British identity and to establish how the different identity groups view their relative importance, In order to conduct our analysis, we divided our sample into four. Half of the respondents were asked about England and Englishness and the other half were asked about Britain and Britishness. Within each of these two groups, half of our respondents were asked simply to note whatever came to their minds, while the other half were asked to select up to three responses from a series of (closed-ended) options. This is a method of investigation that not only allows us to determine whether those thinking of England or Britain provide different answers, but also what people think of when they are not constrained by our response options. The (closed-ended) options are listed below. While they are listed here in alphabetical order, in the survey itself they were presented in a random order to each respondent.

Question: People think of different things when they think of Britain/ England. What about you? What makes you especially proud to be British/ English? (Please rank the top 3, where 1 is the most important.)
- Britain's/England's willingness to work with European partners to overcome the legacy of past conflicts
- British/English countryside

- British/English openness to different cultures and faiths
- British/English pop music
- British/English sense of fair play
- British/English sense of humour
- British/English sporting achievements
- British/English tradition of democracy
- English language and literature
- NHS
- Parliament
- The Queen
- Union Jack/St George's cross flag

The response options allow us to move beyond a cultural/political dichotomy to cover a range of institutions (NHS, monarchy, parliament), culture (music, sport, language, and literature), values (sense of fair play, openness, humour), history (democracy, working to overcome past conflicts), as well as various visual symbols (flag, countryside).

The responses to the closed-ended options (Figure 2.2) suggest that, in general, individuals are less likely to cite cultural or symbolic manifestations of either England or Britain (flags, pop music, sport) and more likely to cite institutions (NHS, Queen), items that relate to a proud past (the tradition of democracy, sacrifice in world wars) and values (a sense of fair play, openness, humour).

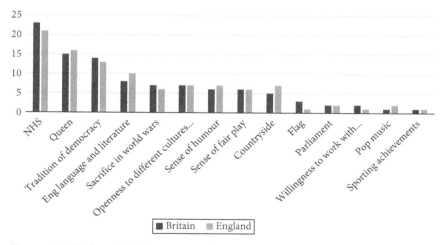

Figure 2.2 Pride in Englishness/Britishness, 2016

Source: FoES 2016. Results are proportion in each identity group claiming items make them proud.

Priming for Britain rather than England makes very little difference. The three most popular response options (the NHS, the Queen, and the tradition of democracy) are the same for both Englishness and Britishness, suggesting that respondents find it difficult to distinguish clearly between them (a key point to which we return in later chapters). That said, in two of these cases those asked about Britain were prouder of these things than were those asked about England, which might lead us to suggest – at least hesitantly – that the Health Service and democratic tradition are most readily seen in British garb. Beyond these, there are some variations at the margins. More significant, perhaps, is that whilst the tradition of democracy is prized, the most obvious institutional manifestation of democracy, Parliament, is not.

We were also interested to know, in addition, whether those who prioritized their British or English identity offered different answers to these questions. The differences are, in most cases, small. When asked about Britain, English identifiers are less likely to cite institutions of social solidarity such as the

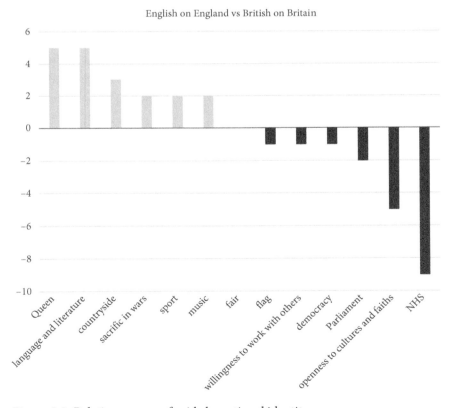

Figure 2.3 Relative sources of pride by national identity
Source: FoES 2016.

NHS and more likely to cite the Queen and sacrifices in world wars as a source of pride. If asked about England, English identifiers show greater pride in the Queen (and less in the NHS) but it is more accurate to say that the differences are marginal.

Another way to look at this is to examine what English identifiers think of England and British identifiers think of Britain. To visualise this, we can calculate the proportion of English identifiers declaring, for example, that they are proud of an English sense of fair play and subtract from this the proportion of British identifiers saying the same of British fair play. The resulting graph (Figure 2.3) shows the relative importance of various items. Above 0, English identifiers associate it more with English identity than British identifiers do. Below 0, British identifiers associate it more than English identifiers with British identity. The results show that English identifiers are more likely to cite the Queen, literature, sacrifices in world wars, and countryside, whereas British identifiers are more likely to be proud of openness to other cultures and faiths, as well as shared institutions such as the NHS.

Table 2.6 Pride across primes and national identity

	British identifiers	English identifiers
… about Britain	NHS 25	Queen 18
	Queen 14	British tradition of democracy 16
	British tradition of democracy 15	NHS 19
	British openness to different cultures and faiths 9	Britain's sacrifices in world wars 10
		English language and lit 8
	English language and lit 7	British sense of fair play 7
	British sense of fair play 6	British sense of humour 6
	British sense of humour 6	British countryside 5
	Britain's sacrifices in world wars 4	British openness to different faiths and cultures 5
	British countryside 4	
… about England	NHS 24	Queen 19
	English tradition of democracy 15	NHS 16
	Queen 15	English tradition of democracy 14
	English language and lit 9	English language and lit 12
	English openness to different cultures and faiths 8	English sense of humour 7
		English countryside 7
	English sense of humour 6	England's sacrifices in world wars 6
	England's sacrifices in the world wars 6	English sense of fair play 6
	English sense of fair play 6	English openness to different cultures and faiths 4
	English countryside 6	

Source: FoES 2016. Results list the proportion of those who ranked it first as a source of pride among all possible first rankings

Conclusion

This chapter has explored patterns of national identities in England, including consideration of the use of and relationship between different measures of national identity, as well as trends over time. In addition, we have identified the correlates of Englishness and Britishness as well as investigated what it is that individuals think of when they think of England and Britain. The overwhelming message that has emerged from this discussion is that Englishness and Britishness are thoroughly intertwined. Thus, while on some measures there has been a growth in English and a steeper fall in British identity, other measures underline that Englishness and Britishness should not be regarded as occupying opposite ends of some kind of national-identity seesaw, where one end rises as the other crashes down to earth. Neither the forced-choice nor even the Moreno question fully captures the complexity of the interplay between English and British identity in England. In particular, they fail to capture the striking asymmetry that means that the primarily or exclusively English feel more British than the primarily or exclusively British feel English. We have also seen how those who prioritized their English identity also tend to have a stronger sense of national identity (English or British) than those who prioritize their Britishness.

Englishness and Britishness are also intertwined in the sense that the symbols, values, and institutions evoked in the context of both identities are largely the same. One way of potraying this is to say that English national identity is populated primarily by British content. An alternative reading, however, is that the history of the establishment of the British state—whereby an English core expanded through either conquest or treaty—means that institutions, symbols, and values that in the rest of the state are regarded as quintessentially British are viewed by those who ascribe to a sense of English identity as theirs—English in all but name. The latter point becomes especially germane when we recall that the key attitudinal distinction we have uncovered between those who feel English and those who feel British relates to efficacy. English identifiers are more likely to say that they are unable to make a difference and that the state is uninterested in hearing their voice. As we shall see in Chapter 3, this is accompanied by a strong sense among them that England is unfairly disadvantaged—and insufficiently recognized—within the UK.

3

The English on England and the United Kingdom

It was long taken as axiomatic that the British electorate was more concerned about 'bread-and-butter' issues such as health, education, and the state of the economy than they were about constitutional questions—the latter tending to be regarded as the preserve of the chattering classes and/or the terminally crankish.[1] Such was the prevailing wisdom among political scientists, among political commentators, and even—if regretfully—among proponents of constitutional reform themselves. Now, however, everything would seem to have been turned on its head. Since 2014 significant popular mobilization around two referendums focusing on constitutional questions, first in Scotland and then across the UK as a whole, have had an utterly transformative (and, for traditional politics, disruptive) effect on almost every aspect of the state's political life. So, does this mean that it is time to reverse the traditional dictum, accepting that constitutional questions now play a more important role in British politics than 'bread-and-butter' issues?

In our view, no. Chapter 1 should already have begun to lay bare the limitations inherent in any tendency to regard 'bread-and-butter' politics as existing in some kind of binary relationship with the politics of constitutional change. What is so striking about the 2014 and 2016 referendum experiences is that, whatever their other manifold differences, both were defined by the way in which members of the electorate linked ostensibly 'bread-and-butter' issues with the fundamentals of the constitution. Thus, in September 2014, many Yes voters seem to have supported independence on the basis that it would allow the creation of a more socially equal Scotland (Henderson 2019). In June 2016, many Leave voters seem to have believed that departure from the European Union would reduce pressure on public services in Britain by dramatically cutting levels of immigration, while simultaneously releasing

---

[1] A point to which we return in Chapter 5. Northern Ireland was regarded as different from the UK 'norm' in part precisely because its main political fault line was constitutional/sectarian rather than socio-economic.

billions of pounds of additional funding for the health service. Given this, to seek to separate out constitutional questions from the politics of the everyday is to impose an analytical distinction that is (at certain times, at least) actively unhelpful if we are seeking to understand popular opinion. It is precisely the link between them that is (potentially) relevant.

This would not surprise students of nationalism. The key argument at the heart of Miroslav Hroch's *Social Preconditions of National Revival in Europe*—one of the foundational texts of contemporary nationalism studies—is that nationalist arguments develop mass appeal when they become viewed as a means for securing desired material outcomes (Hroch 1985). The success or otherwise of nationalists in persuading their target audience of the material relevance of their cause is, therefore, central to understanding the fate of particular nationalist movements. This insight appears relevant as we seek to understand not only the outcomes of the 2014 and 2016 referendums, but also the success of the Conservative Party's campaign in England in the 2015 UK general election. Indeed, the key lesson from nationalism studies for those seeking to understand these pivotal electoral events is that we need to be attentive to the ways in which politicians and campaigners seek to present apparently abstract constitutional concerns as solutions to material concerns/grievances.

What follows from this is the realization that not all constitutional questions are created equal. Even if, say, House of Lords reform or the future of local government have historically tended to receive far more attention in terms of mainstream political debate, their *potential* to act as a basis for transformative/disruptive political mobilization is less significant than the question of the position of England as a whole within the United Kingdom, precisely because the latter has the potential to form the basis for popular, nationalist mobilization. Note that the caveating is important here. There is nothing preordained about the success of any particular attempt at nationalist mobilization. But, if the nature of the 2015 election campaign was not enough confirmation in itself, data from the Future of England Survey (FoES) suggest that people in England, and in particular those with a strong sense of English national identity, are indeed concerned about England's place within the UK and that this is tied to a sense of material grievance about the division of resources across the state as well as broader concerns about equity of treatment.

The following chapter explores these data, proceeding in two steps. First, we explore the dimensions of English grievance: the sense that England is unfairly treated both financially and politically within the union, a sentiment that we have termed *devo-anxiety*, and the accompanying sense that more needs to be done to recognize England as a distinctive unit of government and administration within the UK. Given the dire warning from unionists in the rest of the state about the possible consequences of recognizing England, the strong support that exists in England for such a move raises in turn the question of English commitment to the union. Just how strong is unionist sentiment at the 'heart' of the union? This we explore in the second substantive section of the chapter. As we shall see, even if those who feel English also tend to be strongly committed to Britain and Britishness, their support for the territorial integrity of the state in its current form is strikingly low.

Devo-Anxiety and English Recognition

In the months before and the years immediately following the Scottish and Welsh devolution referendums of 1997, more or less dire warnings were sounded about the likely impact of the establishment of institutions of devolved government in both countries on opinion in England (see, e.g., Heffer 1999; Marr 2000). The people of England, it was claimed, would become increasingly resentful of the anomalies that would inevitably arise in the context of asymmetric devolution—that is, a position in which some parts of the UK had devolved institutions and others did not. The most striking of these anomalies is crystallized by the famous and obviously rhetorical West Lothian question: how can it be right that an MP representing West Lothian (or indeed Carmarthen West or West Belfast) can have a voice in determining, say, education policy in England when, as a result of devolution, English MPs cannot similarly influence education policy in Scotland, Wales, and Northern Ireland (see Crampton 2014)?[2] It was also suggested that devolution would lead to a situation in which English taxpayers became increasingly aware and resentful of the fact that levels of public spending are higher in the devolved territories than in England itself.

In truth, however, academic work in the early years of devolution suggested that these fears had been overstated: the available evidence was interpreted as

---

[2] The West Lothian question is now associated with Tam Dayell, who was Labour MP for West Lothian and a passionate opponent of his own party's plans for Scottish and Welsh devolution in the late 1970s. The term itself, however, was coined by Enoch Powell—by then, as has already been noted, the Ulster Unionist Party (UUP) MP for South Down—during a Commons debate on 14 November 1977. See https://hansard.parliament.uk/Commons/1977-11-14/debates/5b5223e8-2a89-4bbd-a64e-ee2ba1a8493/ScotlandBill#contribution-6e2d7e1a-400c-4482-8522-44ff7e74618c.

suggesting that the English remained blithely indifferent to it all (Curtice and Heath 2001; Curtice 2009). While generally supportive of developments in Scotland and Wales, voters in England remained firmly attached to the Westminster system of government (as Labour was to discover during its abortive attempts to create elected regional assemblies in England.) As for differences in levels of public expenditure, the English electorate may well have been peeved, but they certainly did not seem unduly perturbed. Moreover, even if badges of English identity such as the St George's cross had undoubtedly become more prevalent—with the 1996 UEFA European Football Championship having already acted as something of a watershed moment—there was little sign that a strengthening English self-awareness demanded or required expression through distinct English political institutions.[3] If, as Jeremy Paxman once claimed, 'the English have not spent a great deal of time defining themselves because they haven't needed to', then initially at least, it appeared as if devolution had done little to encourage such introspection (Paxman 1999: 23). This despite the fact that one of the unintended consequences of the establishment of devolved institutions for Scotland, Wales, and Northern Ireland was to ensure that, if only by default, England would also emerge as an increasingly distinct policy space.

By the time the FoES was established, however, it appears that the situation had changed. Tables 3.1 and 3.2 set out data from the period between 2011 and 2016 highlighting attitudes in England towards the relative levels of public spending across the UK. While there is some fluctuation year on year, the overall pattern is clear enough. As Table 3.1 demonstrates, people in England believed that their country was being treated less than fairly while Scotland was getting more than its fair share. That this sense of unfair treatment focuses on the relative position of Scotland in particular appears to be confirmed by findings from the 2016 survey, which probed the views of our respondents in England about the relative positions of the four constituent territories of the UK. As Table 3.2 makes clear, while a higher proportion of our England-based respondents claimed that both Wales and Northern Ireland receive more, rather than less, than their fair share, the gap is relatively narrow (Wales at three percentage points and Northern Ireland at six percentage points), certainly compared to Scotland (at thirty-four percentage points).

---

[3] It has become customary in this regard to contrast the Union Jack-bedecked crowds at Wembley during England's triumph at the 1966 football World Cup final with the overwhelming predominance of the St George's cross among English supporters at the same stadium thirty years later.

Table 3.1 Attitudes in England towards public spending in England and Scotland, 2011–15 (%)

	2011	2012	2014	2015
England's share of public spending				
More than their fair share	7	8	8	8
Pretty much their fair share	26	27	25	26
Less than their fair share	40	40	31	37
Don't know (DK)	27	24	36	29
Scotland's share of public spending				
More than their fair	45	52	38	52
Pretty much their fair share	21	18	20	15
Less than their fair share	4	4	4	3
DK	31	35	38	30
n	*2,836*	*3,600*	*3,705*	*3,451*

Source: FoES 2011–15. Results are column percentages.

Table 3.2 Attitudes in England towards public spending across the UK, 2016 (%)

	England gets	Scotland gets	Wales gets	Northern Ireland gets
More than their fair share	8	38	16	15
Their fair share	22	15	23	23
Less than their fair share	29	4	13	9
DK	41	43	48	54

Source: FoES 2016. Results are column percentages.

Public finance forms only one dimension of a broader sense of unfair treatment. The FoES also provides clear evidence that people in England had become resentful—even deeply resentful—of the possibility that Scottish MPs could play a role in passing laws that applied only in England. Indeed, respondents agreed rather than disagreed with the proposition that 'Scottish MPs should not vote on English laws' by a ratio of at least 6 to 1 (Table 3.3). In this case, all our data focus on attitudes to Scottish MPs only rather than MPs from Northern Ireland and Wales, in part because of the tendency of the (English) media to focus on the Scottish dimension, but also because the tortuous evolution of the Welsh devolution dispensation and regular suspensions of the Northern Irish devolution meant that, in the past at least, the role of Welsh and Northern Irish MPs has tended to raise fewer constitutional issues. It is also important to point out that a focus on 'English laws' tends to oversimplify a much more complicated reality, not least because of the way

Table 3.3 Scottish MPs should not vote on English laws, 2011–16 (%)

	2011	2012	2014	2015	2016
Strongly agree	53	55	35	43	37
Agree	26	26	27	25	27
Total agree	79	81	62	68	64
Neither/nor	—[a]	8	15	12	13
Disagree	8	4	9	7	7
Strongly disagree	2	2	3	4	3
Total disagree	10	6	12	11	10
DK	11	5	10	9	10
n	2,836	3,600	3,705	3,451	5,103

Source: FoES 2011–2016. Results are column percentages. (a) The 2011 FoES did not provide a middle 'neither/nor' option.

that the Barnett Formula (which determines the level of funding to the devolved administrations from UK central government) links changes in levels of public spending in Scotland, Wales, and Northern Ireland to funding decisions for England. Caveating aside, however, what is important to note is the existence in England of a strong perception of a country being unfairly treated within the union, and at the expense of Scotland in particular.

In addition to a sense of unfair treatment, there is also a palpable sense that England is being overlooked and is deserving of more recognition and even celebration. In Table 3.4 we find a strong plurality of respondents agreeing that, '[r]ecently, people in England have become more aware of English national identity' as well as overwhelming majority support for a bank holiday on St George's Day. While it is perhaps unwise to read any great political significance into a desire for an additional public holiday, this finding appears more consequential when we recognize that there exists even stronger agreement with the statement that 'English culture is not valued as highly in England as other cultures are'. It is not just that England is perceived as failing to receive its due within the UK, compared to Scotland, in particular; it is that English culture is regarded as being undervalued within England itself. There is more (limited) support, however, for the contention that '[i]n England our values make us different from the rest of the UK'. Given what we know about the relationship between Englishness and Britishness as identities, this latter finding is perhaps unsurprising. Even so, we are left with a clear sense that people in England—and, as we will discover shortly, in particular those who feel English—have become more aware of their national identity, believe that their English culture is not valued, and desire some positive recognition of Englishness.

Table 3.4 Attitudes in England towards English culture, 2014–16 (% agree)

	2014	2015	2016
Recently, people in England have become more aware of English national identity	45	47	—
St George's Day should be a public holiday	66	69	65
English culture is not valued as highly in England as other non-English national cultures are	75	71	69
In England our values make us different from the rest of the UK	—	27	26
n	*3705*	*3451*	*5103*

Source: FoES 2014–16. Results are column percentages.

All of this raises the question: when and why did apparent English acquiescence and/or indifference give way to a sense of unfair treatment? Tables 3.5 and 3.6 reproduce some of our longest time series of evidence on English attitudes to the territorial constitution of the UK—namely, data from the British Social Attitudes Survey (BSAS) on attitudes towards relative levels of public spending in Scotland and the continuing role of Scottish MPs in the passage of 'English laws'. With regards to the potential role of Scottish MPs in determining English laws, it would appear that opinion in England was always hostile, with hostility perhaps masked by the fact that—until the run-up to the 2015 general election, at least—there seemed little prospect of a UK government being formed that did not also enjoy a clear majority among English MPs.

Attitudes to relative levels of public spending provide yet more evidence of change over time, with the 2007 data apparently marking a watershed. But, while it might be tempting to attribute this development to, say, the elevation of Scot Gordon Brown to the UK premiership or the establishment of a minority Scottish National Party (SNP) administration in Edinburgh, in truth our ability to provide a definitive accounting for the hardening of opinion in England is limited, not only because we need to recall the old adage that correlation does not imply causality, but also because our data are imperfect. Even if the BSAS provides the most complete time series of relevant data, we nonetheless have no data on this particular issue between 2003 and 2007. If such data did exist, we might find that the gradual, post-devolution divergence in the package of public services on offer on both sides on the Scotland–England border—and the perception to its south that the Scots were getting a better deal—served (perhaps gradually) to heighten English perceptions of unfair treatment.

Table 3.5 Scottish MPs should not vote on English laws, 2000–15

	2000	2001	2003	2007	2009	2012	2015
Strongly agree	18	19	22	25	31	30	30
Agree	45	38	38	36	35	38	33
Total agree	63	57	60	61	66	68	63
Neither/nor	19	18	18	17	17	14	19
Disagree	8	12	10	9	6	6	9
Strongly disagree	1	2	1	1	1	1	2
Total disagree	9	14	11	10	7	7	11
DK	9	11	11	12	10	10	6
n	*1,695*	*2,341*	*1,530*	*739*	*773*	*802*	*1576*

Source: BSAS 2000–15.

Table 3.6 English attitudes towards Scotland's share of public spending, 2000–15

	2000	2001	2002	2003	2007	2008	2009	2010	2011	2012	2013	2015
More than fair	21	24	24	22	32	41	40	38	45	44	36	39
Pretty much fair	42	44	44	45	38	33	30	29	29	30	37	31
Less than fair	11	9	9	9	6	3	4	4	3	4	5	8
DK	25	23	22	25	22	23	25	28	23	22	22	22
n	*1,695*	*2,761*	*2,897*	*1,917*	*859*	*982*	*980*	*913*	*967*	*939*	*925*	*940*

Source: BSAS 2000–15. Results are column percentages.

This is, of course, speculation. What seems beyond doubt, however, is that, no matter when or exactly how they got there, by the second decade of the new millennium a significant part of the population of England felt a sense of what we have termed 'devo-anxiety'—a sense that England was being unfairly disadvantaged by changes to the territorial constitution of the UK, and in particular with respect to the operation of devolved government in Scotland. This was accompanied by a sense that some (constitutional) redress was required, a point that becomes apparent from the data presented in Table 3.7

We have noted already that, in the immediate aftermath of the introduction of devolution, English opinion appeared generally supportive of or ambivalent

Table 3.7 Constitutional preferences for England, 2011–16

	2011	2012	2014	2015	2016
Status quo	24	21	18	18	16
EVEL	34	36	40	41	40
Regional assemblies	9	8	9	9	9
English Parliament	20	20	16	12	16
Other	n.a.	n.a.	n.a.	n.a.	1
DK	14	16	17	19	18
n	*1507*	*1774*	*1204*	*1113*	*1739*

Source: FoES 2011–16. Results are column percentages.

to developments elsewhere across the state while remaining firmly attached to the status quo as far as England itself was concerned. Table 3.7 shows just how much had changed by the time the FoES entered the field. It presents responses to a group of options for the future governance of England, each of which has been more or less authoritatively suggested as a way of 'balancing' the post-devolution territorial constitution of the UK. They range from doing nothing to establishing an English parliament. At least three points are worth highlighting here. The first is the strikingly low level of support for the status quo, falling by the end of the period 2011–16 to fewer than 1 in 5 of the electorate. The second is the consistently very low support for the establishment of regional assemblies within England. Even if regularly touted by the parties of the centre left as the appropriate English response to devolution or as a possible route to federalism in the UK (see Chapter 7), this is the only constitutional option that consistently received significantly lower levels of support than the increasingly unpopular status quo. The final point to note is that English votes for English laws (EVEL) consistently enjoys the highest level of support, with margins in favour increasing over time. Indeed, even if its eventual introduction has proven to be something of a damp squib (again, see Chapter 7), in our various explorations of constitutional preferences in successive iterations of the FoES, EVEL has consistently garnered more support than the many other options that have been trailed (for more on the findings of successive FoES surveys, see Wyn Jones et al 2012; 2013 Jeffery et al 2014).

Across the population of England as a whole, therefore, there is a clear sense of devo-anxiety—a perception that England is unfairly treated within the territorial settlement that now exists in the UK. Indeed, support for the status quo is remarkably low. Rather, the population supports the recognition of England both culturally (through an annual bank holiday to mark the national day) and also in political–institutional terms (through the introduction of EVEL). Given our discussion at the start of this chapter of the potential for *national* mobilization, what is truly striking is the extent to which it is those who feel predominantly or exclusively English (in Moreno scale terms) who feel most aggrieved at the way England is currently treated and who most strongly desire English recognition. Table 3.8 breaks down the responses from our 2016 survey to the various questions that have featured so far in this chapter by national identity as measured by the Moreno question.

If we review the table, it becomes immediately apparent that there is a strong and significant relationship between the national identity of respondents and their attitudes towards how England both is and should be governed and recognized within the UK. The predominantly or exclusively English are much more likely than the predominantly or exclusively British to feel that England is unfairly treated relative to other parts of the state, and especially Scotland. Similarly, even if a majority of all voters in England want Scottish MPs to be barred from voting on laws that apply only in England, support for such a move is overwhelmingly strong among the predominantly or exclusively English. The same group also feels—again in overwhelming numbers—that English culture is not valued in England and that St George's Day should be marked by a bank holiday. The predominantly or exclusively English are also very significantly more likely than their British equivalents to believe that 'English values make us different from the rest of the UK'. Turning to the way England is and should be governed, we find that support for the status quo stands at remarkably low levels among the predominantly or exclusively English—a segment of the population that also tends to be significantly more supportive of both the all-England approaches to the governance of the country (namely, an English parliament) and, in particular, EVEL. For this group it is clear that there is not only a strong sense of (English) national grievance but also strong support for (English) national solutions: for treating England as a single, discrete unit within the state.

Confirming this general picture, the table also presents data that show very clearly that those who feel predominantly or exclusively English prioritize England's position within the UK above all other constitutional issues except the relationship between the UK and the European Union—an issue over which the English also tend to have particularly strong views. Relatedly, however, the same group is significantly less likely to trust the UK government 'to work in the best long-term interests of England' than those who

Table 3.8 Attitudes towards England and its place in the union, by national identity, 2016 (%)

	English x British	English > British	English = British	British > English	British x English	Other
National grievance						
Scots more than fair share ***	48	51	37	34	33	19
Wales more than fair share ***	24	20	15	12	9	8
Northern Ireland more than fair share						
England less than fair share ***	42	40	28	23	20	14
Scottish MPs should be prevented from voting on laws that apply only to England ***	79	78	64	57	51	51
Recognition—Cultural						
St George's Day should be a public holiday ***	80	76	66	56	46	40
English culture is not valued as highly in England as other cultures are ***	86	82	69	60	52	43
In England our values make us different from the rest of the UK ***	47	36	22	17	18	14
How England should be governed ***						
Status quo	8	10	19	25	27	18
Regional assemblies	8	7	8	12	14	18
English Parliament	24	20	14	11	13	15
EVEL	46	51	41	36	30	21
Constitutional Priorities ***						
Question: Which three, if any, of the following areas do you think require urgent action or change at this time?						
UK's relationship with the EU	67	74	65	61	58	57
How England is governed	44	44	30	26	28	18
A more proportional system for electing MPs	33	37	40	46	46	49
Reforming the House of Lords	31	25	28	33	36	34
Strengthening local government	19	22	28	30	30	27
Scotland's future relationship with the UK	11	11	12	14	17	13
The future of Northern Ireland	4	3	3	6	5	7
Trust to work for England						
How much do you trust the UK government at Westminster to work in the best long-term interests of England ***	18	26	29	32	31	25

Source: FoES 2016. Results are column percentages within categories, indicating % agreeing unless otherwise stated. Asterisks refer to significant chi square scores * = p < .1, ** = p < .05, *** = p < .01.

feel predominantly or exclusively British. While the English clearly desire national recognition and renewal, they do not seem to trust the UK government to deliver it.

Unionism at the Heart of the Union

If this is how the people of England—and English identifiers, in particular—feel about their own place within the union, the obvious question that arises is how committed they are to its continuation? Given the extensive common history and, for the most part, common culture that binds together a state of which—by any objective criteria—England is overwhelmingly the dominant part, it might have been presumed that English attitudes towards the union would be wholly supportive. But it is already clear from our preceding discussion that this is not necessarily the case. In this final section of this chapter, therefore, we review the survey evidence. Let us begin with what might be regarded as the most fundamental issue of all—namely, the degree of support in England for the territorial integrity of the state. In most states, territorial integrity is regarded as nigh-on sacrosanct, yet, as we shall see, in the core territory of the UK, this does not seem to be the case.

Utilizing data from the longest available time series, Table 3.9 shows attitudes in England towards the future of Scotland in the United Kingdom. The pattern that emerges is rather stable. Notwithstanding some apparently trendless fluctuation, it would seem that little has changed since the establishment of the Scottish Parliament in 1999. The intensifying debate in Scotland itself on independence during this period had little discernible impact on attitudes in England. Thus, from 1999 to 2015, a consistent 1 in 5 to 1 in 4 of the English electorate support Scottish independence. At the opposite pole, support for Scotland remaining part of the UK without an elected parliament—that is, the *status quo ante*—fluctuated only a little below the same general level. Support was highest for the constitutional status quo—namely, for a Scottish parliament with taxation powers—the clear plurality choice, even receiving majority support in 2001. There was also some support (at around 1 in 10 of the population) for a weaker form of devolution, although, given what we know about the general lack of political knowledge among the English electorate, it is almost certainly wrong to assume that there exists detailed knowledge of the Scottish devolution settlement in England.

The significance of the fact that support in England for Scottish independence does not seem to be tied to the state of the debate in Scotland becomes

Table 3.9 Attitudes in England to how Scotland should be governed, 1997–2015 (%)

	1997	1999	2000	2001	2002	2003	2007	2011	2012	2013	2015
…become independent, separate from UK and EU, **or** separate from the UK but part of the EU[a]	14	24	19	19	19	17	19	25	24	20	23
…remain part of the UK, with its own elected parliament, which has some taxation powers	38	44	44	53	41	50	36	33	31	38	39
…remain part of the UK, with its own elected parliament, which has no taxation powers	17	11	8	7	11	8	12	11	11	11	10
…remain part of the UK, without an elected parliament	23	13	17	11	15	13	18	19	23	18	20
DK	8	9	11	10	14	11	15	12	11	13	8
n	2,536	2,718	1,928	2,761	1,924	1,917	859	967	939	925	1,865

Sources: BES 1997; BSAS 1999–2015. Results are column percentages. (a) As we are specifically interested in attitudes in England towards the territorial integrity of the UK, we have combined responses to the two independence options.

clearer when we look at how different identity groups within England view the territorial integrity of the state. The 2011 FoES probed attitudes towards the potential future constitutional status of the three other constituent units of the UK. The responses of the different Moreno national-identity groups are presented in Table 3.10. These data make clear not only that the electorate in England differentiates between the various constituent parts of the state, but that there are very clear differences in attitude towards the union within England itself, reflecting different senses of national identity. Even if those with a strong sense of English identity often feel strongly British (discussed in Chapter 2), nonetheless a strikingly large proportion of those who feel exclusively or predominantly English would also appear to support a reduction of the territorial extent of the state. Or, in other words, their commitment to the union does not appear to stretch much beyond its English core.

It certainly does not extend to Northern Ireland, which is—to say the least—deeply ironic, given that territory's centrality to the post-Brexit referendum debate about the relationship between the UK and EU. Indeed, a plurality of the English electorate as a whole would actually like to see that territory depart the UK, with exclusively English identifiers most likely to support one of the three answer options that would bring about such an eventuality. Indeed, excluding don't knows, fully two-thirds of those who describe themselves as English not British support Northern Ireland leaving the union, with the prospect of an independent Northern Ireland eliciting particularly strong support. Views among the More English than British and the British not English are very evenly divided between those who want Northern Ireland to remain part of the union and those who support Northern Ireland's departure. Only among the More British than English is there a decisive margin in favour of Northern Ireland remaining part of the UK, with a smaller margin in favour amongst the Equally English and British.

Attitudes towards Scotland and Wales are different, with a clear majority of people in England wanting both territories to remain part of the UK. It might, therefore, be better to say that a majority of people in England support the territorial integrity of Great Britain but not the territorial integrity of the United Kingdom of Great Britain and Northern Ireland. Yet even here there are some striking differences in attitudes within England across the different national-identity groups. Turning first to Scotland, we find that a clear plurality of the English not British support Scottish independence. Indeed, at 43 per cent, support for independence is higher than for the combination of the other three options, which would see Scotland remain part of the union. As was also the case with Northern Ireland, it is those who identify as More

Table 3.10 Views in England on the desired status of the other constituent parts of the UK, by national identity, 2011 (%)

	All	English not British	More English than British	Equally English and British	More British than English	British not English
How Northern Ireland should be governed						
Become independent, separate from UK and EU, **or** separate from the UK but part of the EU[a]	23	41	19	18	19	14
Become part of Republic of Ireland with own elected Assembly	14	12	17	13	11	20
Become part of Republic of Ireland without an elected Assembly	5	4	5	5	5	7
[TOTAL NI out of UK]	42	57	41	36	35	41
Remain part of UK with own elected Assembly	26	16	29	28	36	33
Remain part of UK without an elected Assembly	12	13	13	13	12	9
[TOTAL NI stay in UK]	38	29	42	41	48	42
DK	20	15	17	23	17	16
How Scotland should be governed						
Become independent, separate from UK and EU, **or** separate from the UK but part of the EU	23	43	23	16	11	16
Remain part of UK with own elected Parliament with some tax powers	22	16	24	22	31	23
Remain part of UK with elected Parliament but no tax powers	19	11	20	21	25	27
Remain part of the UK without an elected Parliament	22	18	24	24	20	20
DK	15	12	10	16	14	14
How Wales should be governed						
Become independent, separate from UK and EU, **or** separate from the UK but part of the EU	17	37	14	11	13	11
Remain part of UK with own elected parliament with some tax powers	22	17	24	21	29	24
Remain part of UK with elected parliament without tax powers	22	13	23	24	24	27
Remain part of the UK without an elected Parliament	24	19	29	27	21	23
DK	16	14	10	17	13	15
N	1506	261	347	511	143	111

Source: FoES 2011. Results are column percentages. (a) As we are specifically interested in attitudes in England towards the territorial integrity of the UK, we have combined responses to the two independence options here and in the rest of this table.

British than English who are most supportive of the constitutional status quo. Yet support in England for the status quo in Scotland should not be exaggerated. Among all groups claiming some form of British identity, the FoES found that support for the weaker or no devolution options is stronger than support for the status quo itself.

Attitudes in England towards the constitutional future of Wales are broadly the same as for those towards Scotland—again suggesting that English attitudes are largely unrelated to the state of the constitutional debate in the territory in question. Even if support for the no devolution option is the plurality choice, the margin over the two devolution options is small. Indeed, support is divided fairly evenly across the four answer options. Differences between the various identity groups are, however, more pronounced. The English not British are, again, the most likely to support Welsh independence (although, at 37 per cent, support for Welsh independence among this group is some six points lower than support for Scottish independence, and is therefore lower than the combined non-independence options.) Among the More English than British and the Equally English and English we find plurality support for no devolution, while a plurality of the More British than English support a Welsh parliament (*sic*) with taxation powers. Only among the British not English do we find plurality support for what was the constitutional position in Wales in 2011—namely, an elected legislature with no taxation powers. Although, again, given that it seems fair to assume that most of the English electorate will not have enjoyed detailed knowledge of what has been a rapidly evolving Welsh devolution dispensation, it is almost certainly unwise to make too much of this apparent endorsement.

In summary, therefore, support in England for the territorial integrity of the UK as a whole is weak; indeed, quite remarkably so. When presented with five possible futures for Northern Ireland, three outside the UK and two within it, a plurality of the English electorate supports the departure of Northern Ireland from the union. Support for a continuation of the union with Scotland and Wales is, by contrast, stronger. Yet, even here, that proportion of the population with an exclusively English sense of national identity is markedly less supportive. Support for this most basic tenet of unionism can clearly not be taken for granted, even within that union's majority.

A possible criticism of these findings is that they derive from a period in which the future of the union was not a live political issue. Even if it was the SNP victory in the 2011 devolved election that would eventually lead to the 2014 independence referendum, when the 2011 FoES was put into the field it is unlikely that many of our respondents could have guessed that Scottish independence would soon become so salient a prospect. It would require the Brexit referendum result to catapult the future constitutional status of Northern Ireland back onto the political agenda, while Wales's constitutional status has never been a burning issue in the rest of the state—or at least not since the Disestablishment controversy of the early twentieth century. The 2014 Scottish independence referendum provided a further opportunity to explore English attitudes towards the union, this time in a period in which its future was genuinely in doubt. Accordingly, in the 2014 FoES (conducted before the referendum) we probed respondents' views towards two different scenarios—one in which the Scottish electorate voted Yes to independence and the other in which they voted in favour of remaining part of the UK. The results offer important insights into views in England of the union, including—again—the marked difference in attitudes across different national-identity groups.

It will be recalled that the Scottish government's prospectus for independence was one that envisaged a strong, continuing, and friendly partnership with the rest of the UK: even if the 'parliamentary union' came to an end, the broader 'social union' binding Scotland to the other nations of the UK would 'flourish and strengthen' (Scottish Government 2013). As is clear from Table 3.11, reporting data from our 2014 survey, this was not on the whole a vision shared by English voters. That survey contained a series of questions designed to determine how supportive—or not—voters in England would be to the Scottish government's reported preferences. On one of the central questions in the independence debate—whether or not an independent Scotland would continue to use sterling by entering a currency union—a clear majority rejected the Scottish government's position. More also disagreed than agreed

Table 3.11 Views in England if Scotland votes Yes, 2014 (%)

	Agree	Disagree	Neither	DK
An independent Scotland should be able to continue to use the pound	23	53	15	9
People should be able to travel between England and Scotland without passport checks	69	13	11	6
The rest of the UK should support Scotland in applying to join international organizations such as the EU and NATO	26	36	26	12
The UK's standing in the world will be diminished	36	29	24	10
Relations between Scotland and England will improve	10	53	26	11

Source: FoES 2014.

that what remained of the UK (rUK becoming the acronym of choice) should be helpful in securing Scottish membership of the EU and NATO. More agreed than disagreed that rUK's standing in the world would be diminished. And a clear majority felt that Anglo-Scottish relations would not improve as a result of independence. Only on passport-free travel—and by a resounding majority—did people in England share the Scottish government's vision of post-independence partnership with the rUK. Overall there is a clear sense that people in England, passport-free travel aside, would have inclined towards a tough line in independence negotiations with Scotland. Part of the union, or else…

Yet, even within this broader context there are some quite pronounced differences in attitude across the different national-identity groups. As Table 3.12 makes clear, when we break down the responses by national identity, it is those who prioritize their English identity, and especially those who regard themselves as English not British, who adopt the most punitive attitude towards an independent Scotland. The same group was also the least likely to agree that the UK's status in the world would be diminished if Scotland were to leave the union. For these voters, it seems that Britain will remain Great even if Britain does not survive in its current form.

But what of attitudes if Scotland were to vote No? Given our preceding discussion, it will be no surprise to learn that, even if majority opinion in England continued strongly to support the continuation of the union with Scotland and Wales (though not Northern Ireland), there was evidence of equally strong support for fundamental reform of the territorial constitution of that union. Such reform would involve not only the explicit recognition of an all-England dimension to (at least) the UK's legislative process, but also—as Table 3.13 makes abundantly clear—a very significant adjustment in Scotland's position within the state.

The first two questions focus on the two issues—tax devolution and welfare devolution—at the heart of the cross-party Smith Commission established after the referendum and the subsequent Scotland Act 2016. It is clear from the responses that opinion in England was supportive of the move to devolve tax and welfare powers to Scotland, plausibly because it establishes clear lines of responsibility in terms of spending funds raised in Scotland. But this was balanced with a very strong sense that additional devolution should be accompanied by EVEL, a proposal supported by a ratio of 5 to 1. Given that the UK government was to introduce a version of EVEL in 2015 (although see the discussion in Chapter 7), here is another example of the UK government introducing reforms that worked with the grain of popular opinion in

Table 3.12 Views in England if Scotland votes Yes, by national identity (% total agree)

	English not British	More English than British	Equally English and British	More British than English	British not English
An independent Scotland should be able to continue to use the pound	17	18	24	27	36
STRONGLY DISAGREE that an independent Scotland should be able to continue to use the pound	48	42	35	31	28
People should be able to travel between England and Scotland without passport checks	62	70	72	75	78
The rest of the UK should support Scotland in applying to join international organizations such as the EU and NATO	19	20	26	35	40
STRONGLY DISAGREE that the rest of the UK should support Scotland in applying to join international organizations such as the EU and NATO	27	24	19	17	19
The UK's standing in the world will be diminished	21	35	39	51	42
Relations between England and Scotland will improve	11	7	8	10	12
n	416	755	1,509	459	206

Source: FoES 2014. Results are column percentages representing total agree unless otherwise stated.

England. This was, however, emphatically not the case with regards to public spending in Scotland. In this case we find a clear majority of respondents in favour of reducing per capita public-spending levels in Scotland to the UK average—a move that, as we have already noted, would imply substantial public-spending cuts north of the border. Yet, just two days before the independence referendum, urged on by Gordon Brown and apparently panicked by prospects of a Yes vote, the (then) three major British party leaders joined forces to sign the 'Vow' printed on the front page of the *Daily Record* pledging to maintain the Barnett Formula—namely the territorial funding regime that has underpinned Scotland's preferential (compared to both England and Wales) financial treatment.

Table 3.13 Views in England if Scotland votes No, 2014 (%)

	Agree	Disagree	Neither	DK
The Scottish Parliament should be given control over the majority of taxes raised in Scotland	42	24	22	12
The Scottish Parliament should be given the power to decide its own policies on welfare benefits	41	26	22	11
Scottish MPs should be prevented from voting on laws that apply only to England	62	13	15	10
Levels of public spending in Scotland should be reduced to the levels in the rest of the UK	56	9	21	13
England and Scotland will continue to drift apart	37	21	29	13

Source: FoES 2014.

When these responses are broken down by national identity (see Table 3.14), we again find some significant differences across the different groups. Even in the context of strong overall support, support for the prospect of reducing Scottish public-spending levels to the UK average and EVEL is overwhelmingly strong among the predominantly or exclusively English, with more than two in three supporting a reduction. The same groups were also the most likely to express pessimism about the future relationship between England and Scotland, expecting both countries to continue to drift apart even in the case of a No vote.

There is, no doubt, an internal coherence to views in England on the future place of Scotland within the UK. Opinion in England is supportive of Scotland having more powers over its own affairs. But, at the same time, the English expect Scotland to become more financially self-reliant and want to see an end to what they clearly regard as unfair financial subventions from taxpayers south of the border. In addition, they strongly support the removal of Scottish influence over the legislative process for England. That said, even if it is clear that a majority of people in England support the continuation of a largely autonomous Scotland within the UK, it remains unclear what territorial–constitutional arrangements for the union-as-a-whole English opinion might be willing to support. At first blush, some kind of federal constitution would appear to be the natural terminus: after all, this is a long-recognized means of accommodating national territorial differences within a single state. It would, however, require a root-and-branch transformation of the UK's current constitutional structures. This would include, *inter alia*, the enacting of a written constitution enshrining shared or even divided sovereignty; the transform-ation of the second chamber in order to ensure territorial representation; a

Table 3.14 Views in England if Scotland votes No, by national identity, 2014 (% total agree)

	English not British	More English than British	Equally English and British	More British than English	British not English
The Scottish Parliament should be given control over the majority of taxes raised in Scotland	45	41	41	53	48
Levels of public spending in Scotland should be reduced to the levels in the rest of the UK	65	67	57	53	49
Scottish MPs should be prevented from voting on laws that apply only to England	77	73	60	61	58
England and Scotland will continue to drift apart	48	44	34	39	30
The Scottish Parliament should be given the power to decide its own policies on welfare benefits	43	40	40	47	45
n	416	755	1,509	459	206

Source: FoES 2014. Results are column percentages.

fundamentally different mechanism for allocating public finance across the territory of the state; the possibility of regional assemblies, which remain, at present, unpopular; and so on. Even if support for the status quo is, as we have seen, strikingly low, there is little evidence that voters in England—even those among them who feel exclusively or predominantly English—are ready for this degree of change, especially when doing so would inevitably mean a fundamental transformation in the ways in which *they* are governed in order to accommodate the constitutional preferences of the other nations that share the/their state.

Conclusion

This chapter has focused on attitudes in England towards its domestic union. It has highlighted the existence of a sense of grievance at England's apparently unfair treatment within the post-devolution state. This is a sense of *national* grievance in two senses. It focuses on England as a national unit within the UK: a unit that has emerged ever more clearly, if only by default, as an inevitable if unintended consequence of devolution to the other three constituent parts of the state. It is also a sense of grievance felt most strongly by those who feel strongly English in terms of their national identity. All of this creates potentially fertile ground for political mobilization, a potential that we have argued was realized in the run-up to the 2015 general election—a potential that might yet be mobilized again.

In focusing on attitudes in England to the union, we have noted what is (in comparative terms) a striking indifference to the territorial integrity of the state as a whole. While there remains strong support for the union with Scotland and Wales, this is simply not the case with regards to Northern Ireland. But here again there are significant differences in attitude within England, reflecting different senses of national identity. Those who feel exclusively or predominantly English are less supportive of the maintenance of the union, including that with Scotland and Wales, than those who feel exclusively or predominantly British. Moreover, it is important not to confuse support for the union (with Scotland and Wales, at least) with support for the status quo as far as the UK's territorial constitution is concerned. Rather, is majority opinion in England were ever to have its way, then the union would continue on a radically revised basis, a basis that would surely cast into doubt its very survival when we recall that reducing per capita levels of public spending in Scotland the UK average would entail swinging cuts in the Scottish government's budget. Yet, were Scotland subsequently to choose independence, attitudes in England towards the newly independent state would be punitive—particularly so among the exclusively and predominantly English.

Turning to the governance arrangements for England itself, if we were to seek to define English nationalism solely in terms of support for the establishment of a distinct national legislature, that is an English parliament, then it is clear from our results that this remains a minority preference, even among English identifiers. Yet, even if England does not follow what we might term standard nationalist practice in this regard, there nonetheless remain striking differences in attitude within England towards that country's governance that are clearly linked to national identity. Support for the (now pre-2015) status quo has fallen to strikingly low levels across the board but in particular among English identifiers. There is also strong support for treating England as a single unit as opposed to 'dividing' the country into regions, the latter option being even less popular than the status quo. Again, this is particularly pronounced among English identifiers. Above all, there is very strong support for EVEL. Thus, while those who prioritize their English identity are most likely to support an English parliament, even among this group, when forced to choose between an English parliament or EVEL, the latter has remained the more popular option. Given, however, that EVEL amounts to nothing more (or less) than a revision to the standing orders of the House of Commons, there must be some doubt as to its ability to assuage English grievance, which extends beyond legislative procedure to encompass perceived financial unfairness and a general denial of recognition. Could it be, in fact, that EVEL was more effective as a political slogan than an actual constitutional palliative for English dissatisfaction?

We shall return to these issues in Chapter 7. In Chapter 4 we turn our focus to the external union—the European Union—where again, as we shall discover, there has been a striking degree of nationally based mobilization around a constitutional issue. In this case, we find those who prioritize their English national identity seeking British self-determination, apparently on England's behalf.

4

The English on Britain in the World

In Chapter 3 we explored attitudes in England towards that country's place within the United Kingdom as well as towards the future of the union itself. As became clear during that discussion, those who feel a predominantly or exclusively English sense of national identity tend to hold rather different— sometimes, very different—attitudes from those who feel predominantly or exclusively British. The former are significantly more likely to feel that England is being unfairly treated within the union, apparently as a result of devolution to its non-English parts; they are also significantly more likely to want to see England explicitly recognized as a distinctive unit of government within the union; at the same time, they are less committed to the territorial integrity of that state. There is, in short, a distinctive English view of England and the state of which it is (overwhelmingly) the dominant part.

But, as the following chapter will make clear, those in England who regard their identity as predominantly or exclusively English also have a distinctively different view of Britain and its place in the wider world as compared to those who view themselves as predominantly or exclusively British. Understanding this is vital if we are to solve the analytical puzzle that emerged from our discussion of the 2015 general election and the 2016 EU referendum campaign in Chapter 1—namely, why is it that campaigns that focused specifically on England and English sensibilities in the former but focused almost exclusively on Britain and Britishness in the latter seem nonetheless to have appealed so strongly in both cases to those who prioritize a sense of English national identity? The answer lies in the distinctive views of both England and Britain held by the English.

This is a key though perhaps unfamiliar point that needs to underlined. While it may be tempting to view the politicization of English national identity as analogous to the development of Welsh, Scottish, or even Irish nationalism, to do so is to erect a false equivalence. In their late twentieth- and early twenty-first-century guises at least, the nationalisms of the three Celtic nations have all entailed a refutation of Britishness as well as an often sharp rejection of Britain's imperial past.[1] But, in stark contrast, the English nationalism that is the focus of this book involves both a focus on England qua England within the UK and the championing of a particular vision of Britain and Britishness in dealing with the rest of the world—a vision of Britain and Britishness, moreover, that, far from rejecting the state's imperial past, embraces it. To complicate matters even further, this means in turn that it is a vision of Britain and Britishness that tends not to be shared by those in England who identify as predominantly or exclusively British.

It is English attitudes towards Britain's place in the world to which we now turn our attention. We shall proceed in three steps. First, we detail English Euroscepticism, showing the close relationship between English national identity and negative attitudes towards European integration. But Euroscepticism is part of a wider understanding of Britain's appropriate place in the world, an understanding that, as we show in the second part of this chapter, is deeply coloured by the legacy of Britain's imperial past—a past that even today continues to have profound implications for collective senses of belonging and—at least as importantly—non-belonging.

Finally, in conclusion, we note the paradox at the heart of English constitutional attitudes, as regards both the territorial constitution of the United Kingdom itself and the relationship between the UK and the European Union. At least by implication, the constitutional views of those who regard themselves as predominantly or exclusively English are very radical indeed. Yet, in our view, it would be a mistake to conclude from this that there exists in England—and among the English, in particular—some kind of penchant for radical constitutional change per se. Rather, the radical implications of English territorial–constitutional preferences are best understood as the corollary of strongly traditionalist views of the state and its history. Constitutional change within the UK itself and, in particular, with regards to the UK's relationship with the European Union, are viewed as necessary in order to preserve or resurrect those constitutional arrangements that English opinion tends to regard as legitimate. Or, in other words, as far as the English are concerned, in the famous words of Lampedusa's *The Leopard* (1961: 29), it appears to be the case that 'if we want things to stay as they are, things will have to change'.

---

[1] This was not the case in the late nineteenth century, when the dominant strands in Irish, Scottish, and Welsh nationalism all tended to stress the compatibility of their national claims with the continuation of links to both Crown and Empire. It was arguably the failure of the state to accommodate the claims of constitutional Irish nationalism that led—eventually in all three countries—to the emergence of nationalisms that sought or seek secession from the British state.

English Euroscepticism

People in England who feel predominantly or exclusively English were significantly more likely to vote to Leave the European Union in the 2016 referendum than those who identified predominantly or exclusively British (see also Henderson et al. 2017, 2020). This correlation between Englishness and Euroscepticism was not some overnight development but had been evident for some time (the available data are discussed in Henderson et al. 2016). In the 2012 iteration of the Future of England Survey (FoES), our respondents were asked how they would vote in any referendum on the UK's continuing membership of the EU. Even then it was apparent that, if a referendum was ever called, overwhelming majorities of the exclusively and predominantly English would probably vote Leave. It was only among the predominantly or exclusively British in England that remaining part of the EU enjoyed plurality support (Wyn Jones et al. 2013: 17–9).

Table 4.1 reports responses to three EU-related questions from the 2016 survey, conducted a week before the referendum. As can be seen, in the context of an overall lead of five points for Leave, the referendum voting intention question shows the same strong correlation between national identity and attitudes towards EU membership, with large Leave majorities among the exclusively and predominantly English and substantial Remain majorities among the exclusively and predominantly British as well as the 'Other' category. Only among the equally English and British identifiers is opinion more or less equally divided on Europe. The same pattern is apparent in responses to a question that asked whether respondents viewed membership of the EU as a good or a bad thing for the UK. The assessment of the predominantly or exclusively English identifiers is negative—among the latter, by a ratio of almost 7 to 1—while the predominantly and exclusively British as well as the Other group are much more positively disposed to EU membership.

The table further shows responses to a question that asks respondents to state which level of government they regard as having most influence over the way 'England is run'. Overall, 35 per cent of our sample claimed that the EU has most influence over the way England is run, but, again, there are some very significant differences between those who identify as predominantly or exclusively English and their predominantly or exclusively British compatriots in terms of their perceptions of the extent of EU influence over domestic policy. Among the English not British, the EU is seen as having more influence

Table 4.1 Attitudes towards the EU by Moreno national identity, 2016 (%)

	All	English not British	More English than British	Equally English and British	More British than English	British not English	Other
How would you vote in referendum on EU membership ***							
Remain	40	14	28	45	58	57	65
Leave	45	73	59	43	31	34	17
Wouldn't vote	4	4	3	3	2	2	14
Don't know (DK)	11	10	10	10	9	8	5
UK's membership of the EU…***							
Good thing	35	10	24	38	53	50	60
Bad thing	42	68	56	39	26	32	17
Neither	13	12	13	13	12	11	18
DK	11	10	7	10	9	8	6
Who has the most influence over the way England is run? ***							
Local councils	3	3	3	2	2	3	3
UK government	47	27	40	50	64	57	61
EU	35	57	47	33	22	26	16
Other	2	2	2	1	3	3	8
DK	13	12	9	13	9	13	13
n	*5103*	*606*	*1068*	*1892*	*707*	*321*	*237*

Source: FoES 2016. Results are column percentages. Asterisks refer to chi square significance tests.
* = p < .1, *** = p < .05, *** = p < .01.

than the UK government over English domestic affairs by a ratio of 2 to 1. So, not only is the EU viewed more negatively, but it also looms much larger in the perceptions of that part of England's population that tends to cleave to an English national identity, which is, of course, entirely consistent with our findings on constitutional priorities set out in Chapter 3.

The significance of these differences in perceptions of the relative influence of the EU along the Moreno identity spectrum becomes even more apparent when we compare our English data with data from other parts of Europe. Table 4.2 compares the proportion of respondents in England stating that they believe that the EU has most influence with the proportion of respondents making the same claim in fourteen other sub-state 'regions' across western Europe (see Henderson et al. 2013 for further details). We see that, on average, English respondents are three times more likely to perceive the EU as having most influence than respondents in next highest-scoring regions (Brittany and Upper Austria). This proportion is substantially higher again among those who identify as predominantly or exclusively English.

Table 4.2 Comparative attitudes towards the relative influence of the EU

	% EU has most influence in 'their' region
England	27
Brittany	9
Upper Austria	9
Galicia	9
Alsace	8
Scotland	8
Castilla La Mancha	8
Vienna	7
Salzburg	7
Wales	7
Catalonia	6
Bavaria	6
Lower Saxony	5
Ile de France	5
Thuringia	4

Sources: For all regions but England: CANS 2009; England: FoES 2011.

At this point, some important methodological caveats need to be entered. First, these data were not all collected simultaneously, with the English data having been collected two years later than data from the other fourteen regions. Secondly and more fundamentally, the fact that all the 'regions' concerned, with the exception of England, have a distinctive, all-region tier of government means that the answer options for respondents were different. In addition to the local, state, and EU levels, respondents in the other fourteen had the option of choosing their regional level of government. Indeed, the main story outside England is the tendency for the proportion saying that the regional level 'should have' most influence to be higher (often, substantially higher) than the proportion saying that it 'has' most influence. Only in England does the (undesirable) extent of EU influence provide the main headline. Notwithstanding these methodological qualms, the fact that the EU seems to loom so much larger for respondents in England—and in particular, but not only, among the English identifiers—must surely give pause. It certainly serves to underline both the very different nature of the debate about the EU in the UK's largest constituent unit as well as the pull of 'take back control' among a large segment of that country's population.

Returning to differences within England, our 2016 survey provides yet further evidence of the way that perceptions of the European Union are closely and significantly linked to senses of national identity. Table 4.3 shows

Table 4.3 Perceptions of the costs and benefits of EU membership, 2016 (%)

	All	English not British	More English than British	Equally English and British	More British than English	British not English	Other
N	5,103	606	1,068	1,892	707	322	237
'European human rights law helps guarantee the basic freedoms of British citizens' ***							
Strongly agree	16	7	9	15	29	27	33
Tend to agree	25	12	25	26	30	24	29
Neither agree nor disagree	20	26	21	22	13	17	15
Tend to disagree	16	23	21	15	11	13	8
Strongly disagree	12	22	16	10	7	9	6
DK	12	11	8	12	9	8	9
'British people benefit greatly from being able to live and work in other EU countries' ***							
Strongly agree	18	5	9	18	28	31	41
Tend to agree	28	14	30	32	33	27	32
Neither agree nor disagree	25	37	30	23	18	22	13
Tend to disagree	13	19	18	12	10	10	6
Strongly disagree	7	16	8	6	3	4	1
DK	10	10	6	9	8	7	7
'The EU helps to promote freedom and democracy across Europe' ***							
Strongly agree	14	6	8	14	22	24	29
Tend to agree	28	14	27	31	35	27	33
Neither agree nor disagree	21	28	24	20	15	17	15
Tend to disagree	15	23	20	13	11	13	8
Strongly disagree	12	20	15	11	8	11	10
DK	11	9	6	11	10	8	6
'The EU produces too many regulations interfering with the lives of ordinary people' ***							
Strongly agree	34	59	47	31	23	24	17
Tend to agree	24	18	29	27	23	22	18

Continued

Table 4.3 *Continued*

	All	English not British	More English than British	Equally English and British	More British than English	British not English	Other
Neither agree/disagree	14	8	10	15	14	14	21
Tend to disagree	12	4	7	13	19	20	18
Strongly disagree	6	3	2	6	11	11	15
DK	10	8	6	9	10	9	10
'The EU has made migration between European countries too easy' ***							
Strongly agree	40	65	52	38	29	29	24
Tend to agree	25	17	28	26	26	27	22
Neither agree nor disagree	13	8	9	15	13	13	14
Tend to disagree	10	3	6	10	18	17	19
Strongly disagree	5	1	1	4	6	9	15
DK	8	6	4	7	8	6	7

Source: FoES 2016. Results are column percentages. Asterisks refer to chi square significance tests. * = p < 0.1, ** = < 0.05, *** = p < 0.01.

responses to five propositions relating to some of the perceived costs and benefits of European membership. As is apparent, none of the apparent benefits associated with the EU are particularly appealing/believable to the predominantly or exclusively English. Be they arguments about economic mobility or rights-based arguments about how the EU buttresses liberty: they all fail to convince. Conversely, the predominantly or exclusively English identifiers are even more negative about the apparent failings of the European project.

One of the areas where the world views of Eurosceptics seem to depart most fundamentally from those of their more Europhile opponents is in relation to rights and freedoms. A standard trope in Eurosceptic rhetoric is that 'our' rights and freedoms are rooted in a wholly indigenous tradition that can be traced back via the Bill of Rights to the Magna Carta and even beyond into the traditions and mores of the Anglo-Saxons.[2] Far from being protected or enhanced by the UK's membership of the EU, these rights and freedoms are perceived to have been systematically undermined by 'Brussels bureaucrats' and their associated courts. Institutions allegedly mired in a collectivist and even quasi-authoritarian continental ethos are viewed in opposition to the tradition of individual freedom that has been Anglo-Britain's most significant legacy to its global offspring in the rest of the Anglosphere.[3] So, while supporters of the UK's external union have tended to celebrate its alleged role in buttressing the rights of UK citizens through European human-rights laws, its opponents have seen the EU's involvement in this area as an unwarranted and unwelcome intrusion.

All of this serves to make the responses of our respondents to the statement that 'European human rights law helps guarantee the basic freedoms of British citizens' particularly interesting. As can be seen, they are heavily polarized along national-identity lines. The predominantly or exclusively English disagree; the predominantly or exclusively British overwhelmingly agree, as do those in the Other category. Indeed, the balance of opinion among the

---

[2] That Scotland has its own legal tradition influenced by both the continental and common-law traditions and an (at least) equally robust commitment to liberty and freedom seems not to trouble proponents of this argument.

[3] While addressing an American audience during one of his most famous post-war speeches (that lamenting the fall of an 'iron curtain' across the European continent), Winston Churchill (1946) attempted to elide the rather significant differences between the Westminster tradition and that of the United States in the following terms: 'We must never cease to proclaim in fearless tones the great principles of freedom and the rights on man which are the joint inheritance of the English-speaking world and which through the Magna Carta, the Bill of Rights, the Habeas Corpus, trial by jury, and the English common law find their most famous expression in the American Declaration of Independence.' For those interested in this trope, see Mead (2007).

exclusively and predominantly English is sceptical, even when faced with a proposition that most observers would surely view as almost entirely uncontroversial. Notwithstanding the role of the EU in the transition from authoritarian rule in southern Europe and the post-Communist transition in central and eastern Europe, they still disagree with the statement that '[t]he EU helps to promote freedom and democracy across Europe'.

Similarly, it is the most predominantly or exclusively English that are most sceptical of another of the oft-cited benefits of EU membership—namely, the fact that it allows UK citizens to live and work in other EU member states. By a margin of almost 2 to 1, more of our English not British respondents disagreed rather than agreed that 'British people benefit greatly from being able to live and work in other EU countries' (though note also the relatively high proportion that neither agree nor disagree with the statement). In this case, however, the more English than British take a different position from the exclusively English, with more of this group agreeing than disagreeing with the proposition. As is clear from the table, agreement becomes even more emphatic and strongly expressed as Britishness becomes a more prominent part of respondents' sense of national identity. Among the Other group, agreement is absolutely overwhelming.

The final two statements crystallize familiar Eurosceptic arguments: 'The EU produces too many regulations interfering with the lives of ordinary people' and '[t]he EU has made migration between European countries too easy'. With the exception of those who do not identify themselves as either British or English, it is striking that there is more agreement than disagreement with these statements across all of our identity categories. That said, there remains a steep gradient from those who identify as English not British to those who chose the British not English category. Both statements were endorsed very strongly indeed towards the most English end of the spectrum—indeed, among the English not British in particular, the proportion disagreeing is vanishingly small. By contrast, towards the more exclusively British end of the spectrum, views are much more evenly divided—and indeed are far closer to those of respondents in the Other category than they are to those of their exclusively English compatriots.

To focus on attitudes towards migration brings us face to face with the sense of grievance that attends England's relationship with its other union (migration has, of course, been a central focus in the subsequent academic literature on the 2016 referendum—e.g. Clarke et al. 2017). Indeed, it is perhaps not difficult to understand why the issue of 'uncontrolled immigration' served as a lightning-rod issue for so many Leave voters: as has already been intimated, it rendered concrete what might appear to be more abstract concerns about 'loss of sovereignty' by linking those issues to concerns about pressure on public services in a period of economic austerity, especially in a context where, as we know, the English electorate not only tends to overestimate the proportion of migrants in their midst (a not uncommon phenomenon) but also overestimate the proportion of EU migrants within the total population of migrants in the UK (see Ipsos-MORI 2016; Eurobarometer 2018).

FoES data confirm a general preference for restricting immigration. On a 0 to 10 scale, where higher figures indicate greater support for restricting immigration, upwards of 40 per cent in 2014, 2015, and 2016 chose 10/10, and the average answer for the sample as a whole was above 7 for each year. Our data also serve to confirm a less remarked-upon feature of attitudes towards immigration—namely, the extent to which they reflect patterns of national identity. Even in the context of an England in which there is a wide-spread sense that EU membership has made immigration too easy and in which a very substantial proportion of the population believe that immigration should be restricted, those who prioritize their English identity were much more likely to express concern about the impact of EU membership on immigration levels as well as expressing strong support for a more restrictive approach on immigration.

In 2016, we presented respondents with a series of paired statements:

- immigration dilutes British culture versus immigration helps to make Britain the vibrant multicultural society that it is today;
- immigration makes an important positive contribution to the UK economy versus immigration is a drain on the UK economy;
- immigration puts too much pressure on education and the NHS versus immigration makes an important positive contribution to education and the NHS.

Each of these paired statements was presented as a seven-point scale, with respondents able to indicate how close to each end their views were. The mean scores (recoded between 0 and 1) show that the more one prioritizes an English identity the more negative one's view of immigration. Another way to explore this is to present the proportion of respondents identifying the very end of the scale (see Table 4.4). More than two-thirds of exclusively English identifiers were not marginally of the view that immigration puts pressure on education and the NHS, but chose the most emphatic option for expressing

Table 4.4 Attitudes to immigration by Moreno national identity, 2016 (%)

	All	English not British	More English than British	Equally English and British	More British than English	British not English	Other
Puts pressure on public service	38	67	46	34	22	26	18
Drains economy	25	46	23	20	12	11	6
Dilutes culture	22	55	29	21	12	13	10

Source: FoES 2016. Results are column percentages of respondents locating themselves in maximum agreement with the statement.

this. As one moves through the identity categories from most English to most British, the proportion who believe this drops. Indeed, it drops quite precipitately—by one-third (for pressure on public services) and a half (for negative impact on economy and culture)—as one moves from those who feel English not British to those who feel more English than British. But, more generally, it is abundantly clear that the sense of grievance about migration and about the EU's apparent role in facilitating 'uncontrolled immigration' is strongest among those who feel predominantly or exclusively English.

England's World: The Imperial Legacy in Contemporary Politics

Given all this, there may be a temptation for some to dismiss English national identity as terminally, irredeemably parochial. Whatever the 'global-Britain' rhetoric of the organic intellectuals of the Brexit movement, are not their supporters simply a bunch of—to use the phrase so often deployed by their opponents—'little Englanders'? While such a conclusion might provide these opponents with the admittedly faint consolation of a sense of moral superiority, it does little to aid our understanding of the views that propelled the Leave side to victory in 2016. To understand English Euroscepticism, we need to recognize, rather, that the views held by the predominantly or exclusively English view of the EU are part of a broader set of assumptions about Britain's place in the world that are not shared by the predominantly or exclusively British. That view, we shall argue, is deeply coloured and contoured by the continuing legacy of Britain's imperial past—a legacy that seems still to determine English identifiers' sense of where (and to whom) they belong. To illustrate, let us first return to attitudes in England towards immigration.

In truth, attitudes to immigration are even more complex than has already been demonstrated. The fundamental point to underline is that not all immigrants are created equal, so to speak: not all engender the same levels of concern and, on occasion, hostility. This can be seen from Table 4.5, which reports responses to a question that asked whether it was 'a good or a bad thing' that people from a given country or region 'come to live here'. We provide the mean response across the sample as a whole as well as by identity group. We have recoded the original 0 to 10 scale so that it varies between 0 and 1, with higher numbers implying these migrants are a 'bad' thing.

As can be seen from the table, we asked the question in different ways in 2015 and 2016. In 2015, using migration to England as the prime, we distinguished between migrants from outside the EU, from places suffering from war and conflict, from within the EU, from Ireland, and from the rest of the UK (rUK). We can see that attitudes are most positive towards the rest of the UK and Ireland, with average responses more welcoming than not. Migrants from outside the EU, from places suffering war and conflict, and from within the EU are viewed as less desirable—indeed, there is perhaps surprisingly little differentiation in overall attitudes to these three categories of migrants. It is also clear that, the more one prioritizes an English identity, the more hostile to migrants one is.

In 2016, we refined the question by priming for Britain and distinguishing between two different countries within the EU (Romania and France) as well as four different places outside—namely, Pakistan, Africa, Australia, and also Syria (the later embroiled at the time in a bloody civil war). Given these options, the rank ordering we identified earlier in the previous year's data breaks down. Top of the list of 'bad' migrants now are those from Romania, while other EU migrants from France are viewed more favourably, as are those from Australia. Indeed, migrants from Australia are viewed more positively than were those from neighbouring Ireland in the previous year.

Apart from Australia and France, overall mean scores rise above 0.5 in all cases, showing greater negativity for immigrants from Africa and Pakistan and most negative attitudes of all towards Romanians and Syrians. With respect to national identity, even if the attitudes among the exclusively and predominantly English are always more negative towards every group than the exclusively or predominantly British, the rank ordering is similar throughout. British identifiers are more positive in their attitudes to migrants

Table 4.5 Hostility to migrants by national identity (mean scores), 2015–16

	All	English not British	More English than British	Equally English and British	More British than English	British not English	Other
2015: Bad for England that people come to live here from							
Outside EU	0.57	0.72	0.61	0.57	0.48	0.49	0.43
Places suffering war and conflict	0.52	0.69	0.55	0.50	0.43	0.44	0.38
Within EU	0.50	0.64	0.54	0.49	0.41	0.43	0.34
Ireland	0.36	0.44	0.39	0.35	0.31	0.33	0.28
Rest of UK	0.25	0.30	0.28	0.24	0.24	0.22	0.20
2016: Bad for Britain that people come to live here from							
Romania	0.66	0.84	0.74	0.64	0.57	0.53	0.48
Syria	0.66	0.83	0.75	0.63	0.55	0.53	0.50
Pakistan	0.61	0.76	0.68	0.59	0.53	0.51	0.50
Africa	0.60	0.75	0.67	0.58	0.51	0.49	0.46
France	0.43	0.54	0.47	0.42	0.38	0.34	0.27
Australia	0.32	0.35	0.33	0.32	0.31	0.30	0.25

Source: FoES 2015–2016. Results are column percentages.

from Ireland, Australia, and France than from Syria, Pakistan, and Romania. The difference between English and British identifiers, therefore, is in strength of opposition, with greater variation in attitudes towards the different countries among the exclusively English than among the predominantly/ exclusively British. Thus, among the exclusively English, the 2016 mean response varies from 0.33 for immigrants from Australia to 0.66 for those from Romania. At the exclusively British end of the identity spectrum, the mean response varies from 0.25 for Australians to 0.48 for Romanians. The broader range among English identifiers reflects particularly emphatic opposition to the arrival of particular groups.

What is also striking in all of this is the extent to which attitudes towards particular groups among the exclusively or predominantly English, especially, seem to hark back to previous geopolitical relationships. Churchill famously used the phrase 'kith and kin' to refer to the inhabitants of the Dominions and the United States (e.g. Churchill 1940), but the family metaphor was used almost ubiquitously in the same context. That Australian immigrants are viewed so much more positively by the exclusively or predominantly English than any other group of immigrants except those who move to England from other parts of the UK suggests that Australians are still regarded as close, familial relations. This impression is strengthened further by the relatively positive attitude towards Irish immigrants. After all, despite the well-documented anti-Irish bigotry and discrimination that has historically characterized social life across Britain (and not just in England alone), in Churchillian terms Ireland was also a part of the family, even if perceived as errant or wayward and requiring the paternal guidance of the 'stronger island and nation' (cited in Bew 2016: 98). Strikingly, attitudes to French migrants are less positive, despite France having been a close ally of the UK's for many decades—fighting on the same side in two world wars.

Even if parts of the Empire were joined by what Churchill also described as 'ties of blood and history', he did not believe that these strong bonds of kinship extended to the rest of the Empire (James 2016: 321). To the extent that native populations of Britain's African colonies were considered as 'part of the family' they were 'light-hearted, tractable British children' (James 2014: 53). There was certainly no question that they could be considered as deserving of the same treatment or privileges as the inhabitants of what used to be know in more frankly racist times as the inhabitants of the Britain's 'White Dominions'—namely, Canada, Australia, and New Zealand.[4]

---

[4] The 'White Dominions' also included the white population of South Africa, Ireland and Newfoundland. Newfoundland joined Canada after not one but two referendums in 1948, one month

Even if Empire has gone, it seems that many of the attitudes that we have illustrated by reference to Churchill, but that were very widely held in his day, continue to resonate, especially among those who feel predominantly or exclusively English. This group is markedly more negative in its attitudes towards Pakistani or African migrants than it is in its attitudes towards migrants from what we might term the inner circle of Australia and Ireland. That said, attitudes towards Syrian or Romanian migrants are even more negative, suggesting that they are regarded as being more distant still in terms of their relationship with what used to be known (again, almost universally) as the 'mother country'.

To focus more closely on views of migrants in England is, therefore, to expose a more variegated picture that was initially apparent. Yes, predominantly or exclusively English identifiers do tend to hold a deeply racialized view of immigration. But not straightforwardly so, in as much as it does not seem to be the case that those who share a white European heritage are automatically accorded preference or priority. Rather, the views of the predominantly or exclusively English, in particular, appear to expose a hierarchy of relationships firmly rooted in the UK's imperial past. In this view, the problem is not immigrants per se; it is immigrants who are not considered as 'kith and kin' or fellow members of what used to be termed the Anglo-Saxon race.

Distinctive English attitudes towards different groups of immigrants are, moreover, only one of the ways in which history and, more specifically, past geopolitical relationships, continue to impact upon contemporary public attitudes. This is readily apparent when we view the results reported in Table 4.6—namely, the responses to three statements that explore various aspects of these attitudes. The first two may be said to delineate two sides of the same coin: 'As an island, Britain has less reason to belong to the EU than other countries' and 'Britain has a great deal in common with the cultures of other EU countries'. The third, 'Britain's special relationship with the USA makes EU membership less important for it than for other European countries', explores the resonance of perhaps the dominant trope in post-Second World War UK foreign-policy discourse.

---

apart, the second held after the first three-option referendum failed to go the 'right' way. The second referendum resulted in a 52–48 per cent vote in favour of Confederation with Canada. Ireland left the Commonwealth in 1949 with the declaration of the republic. South Africa withdrew in 1961 as a result of opposition from its fellow members states to its policy of apartheid.

Table 4.6 Attitudes towards Britain's place in the world, 2016 (%)

	All	English not British	More English than British	Equally English and British	More British than English	British not English	Other
'As an island, Britain has less reason to belong to the EU than other countries' ***							
Strongly agree	16	34	21	13	9	11	9
Agree	23	27	33	21	19	17	13
Neither	19	19	20	20	16	17	11
Disagree	19	7	15	22	24	23	29
Strongly disagree	14	5	7	14	25	26	31
DK	10	8	5	10	8	7	7
'Britain has a great deal in common with the cultures of other EU countries' ***							
Strongly agree	7	3	3	6	11	13	21
Agree	25	10	19	28	35	31	35
Neither	23	23	24	24	21	19	19
Disagree	24	29	33	24	20	19	12
Strongly disagree	12	27	16	9	6	10	6
DK	10	8	5	9	8	8	6
'Britain's special relationship with the USA makes EU membership less important for it than for other European countries' ***							
Strongly agree	6	14	8	5	3	4	3
Agree	19	23	25	20	17	15	11
Neither	27	31	32	28	20	25	18
Disagree	22	11	20	23	28	25	31
Strongly disagree	12	7	7	11	21	21	26
DK	14	14	9	14	10	10	11
n	5,103	606	1,068	1,892	707	322	237

Source: FoES 2016. Results are column percentages. Asterisks refer to chi square significance tests.
* = p < .1, ** = p < .05, *** = p < .01.

The portrayal of England or Britain as an island nation or again, to cite Churchill, 'island race', has an ancient lineage.[5] The alleged significance of this island-ness is a regular trope in Eurosceptic rhetoric (and note that, while the

[5] *Island Race* was the title of the abridged version of Churchill's four-volume *History of the English-Speaking Peoples* (Churchill 1964). Kathleen Wilson (2002) provides an illuminating discussion of the importance of 'island race' in framing discussions of Englishness in the eighteenth century. In fact, the stress on the significance of 'island-ness' in the context of the culture of this island predates both the English language and the English themselves. Welsh-language literature from the medieval period demonstrates that the Welsh conceived of themselves as an island people, at least in some contexts. In one of the Four Branches of the Mabinogi, 'Branwen daughter of Llŷr', the term 'Ynys y Kedeyrn' (the Island of the Mighty) is used. And the triads used to record and order traditional material are referred to as 'Trioedd Ynys Prydein' (The Triads of the Island of Britain), for example, 'Tri Gwaywrudd Bardd Ynys Prydein' (The Three Red-speared Bards of the Island of Britain).

referent often shifts between 'England' and 'Britain', it seems always to be a singular island: again Northern Ireland is not really 'us' in the same way). Island-ness is regarded as underwriting Britain's role as a global rather than merely a continental player; a 'natural' mercantile power; and so on. Its fundamental island-ness is also taken to mean that Britain is not of Europe in the same way or to the same degree as other EU member states. As can be seen from the responses, this is very clearly the view of predominantly or exclusively English identifiers. This contrasts with the predominantly or exclusively British, where we find a strong plurality of respondents disagreeing with the statement. Among the equally English and British group, agreement and disagreement are evenly matched. Note, too, that among the Other group we find a majority adopting what might be termed the most pro-European position.

Turning to 'Britain has a great deal in common with the cultures of other EU countries', one might perhaps have thought that this would be regarded as a statement of the unobjectionable, even the banal, especially in this era of budget airlines and cheap European holidays. Yet responses to it provide further evidence of the way that Englishness is related to a sense of distance from the UK's continental neighbours. Divisions across identity groups are very similar to those observed in response to the previous statement, but this time with those professing an exclusively or predominantly English identity disagreeing with the statement, and by a decisive margin (the English not British disagree by some 4 to 1). Opinion among the equally English and British is fairly evenly divided, but then decisively flips over in a more positive direction among the more British than English and the British not English. That said, note also that the margin of disagreement towards the most exclusively English end of the identity spectrum is greater than the margin of agreement towards the exclusively British end. Or, in other words, English views are particularly emphatic. Belief in the existence of common cultural ground is, again, strongest among the Other category.

For those who stress their English identity, the cultural distance between south-east England and France appears to be far greater than the twenty-one-mile span between South Foreland and Cap Gris Nez might imply: more chasm than channel. By contrast, physical distance from the USA—four thousand miles and more—is apparently no deterrent to the existence of a close feeling of kinship. Among the English not British, in particular, more agree than disagree with the proposition that 'Britain's special relationship with the USA makes EU membership less important for it than for other European countries'. Support for this view weakens as Britishness becomes more pronounced in our respondents' sense of national identity, with the British not English disagreeing with the statement by a margin of more than 2 to 1. Again, the 'Other' identity group is the most pronounced in its disagreement (by a margin of more than 4 to 1) with a statement that serves to distance Britain from its continental and, indeed, island neighbours.

Another noteworthy finding here is the relatively high proportion of those who emphasize their English identity who neither agree nor disagree with the statement about US relations. While proponents of the special relationship seem to believe that there is a natural kinship between the UK and the USA—London and Washington—there are some who disagree. Enoch Powell, for example, was both a Eurosceptic *avant la lettre* and staunchly anti-American. Does the relatively high proportion of exclusively, strongly, and significantly English-identifying respondents who neither agree or disagree with the statement hint at the continuing presence of a certain ambiguity towards the United States, even among some of those who are staunchly anti-European Union? It is an intriguing possibility.

On every question on this theme, we have found that those who prioritize their English identity consistently adopt more Eurosceptic positions—or positions with Eurosceptic implications—as compared to those who prioritize their British identity. Those in the Other category are the most positive in their evaluation of the linkages between the UK and its nearest neighbours, although we know from Chapter 2 that this category also includes a large proportion of European identifiers and non-citizens, so we can assume that EU nationals are over-represented here. The 'English response' is, moreover, often fundamentally at odds with what had been—until June 2016, at least—the geopolitical trajectory of the UK state, and much of the justification that has been offered for that trajectory. But in relation both to attitudes towards particular groups of migrants and to perceptions of Britain's natural allies, it is a response that appears to be deeply rooted in a particular understanding of the country's past, an understanding of the past that appears to be directly linked to views about the state's current and future place in the world.

It has, of course, already been widely noted that historically derived links with like-minded English-speaking countries—which together form the so-called Anglosphere—has played a central role in the intellectual case for Brexit (Vucetic 2011; Wellings 2012, 2019; Kenny and Pearce 2015, 2018; Wellings and Baxendale 2015; Bell 2017; Campanella and Dassù 2017). Ostensibly a community of common interests and values based on common history as well as a common language, the Anglosphere serves a number of functions in arguments for cutting ties with the UK's external union: it is simultaneously a reminder of past glories; a means of emphasizing the (alleged) fundamental differences between Britain and its nearest neighbours; and a promissory note apparently guaranteeing a bright future outside the EU. Our evidence suggests that the allure of the Anglosphere is felt both at the popular as well as at the elite levels.

But we need to enter two important caveats. First, while some of the intellectual outriders of the Brexit movement have argued that the alleged commonality of interests and attitudes found in the Anglosphere extends to Singapore, the Philippines, and India (see Wellings and Baxendale 2015: 134)—that is, to states that were obviously not numbered among the White Dominions—our analysis strongly suggests that is not the case at the popular level. Rather, recalling the differences in attitudes in England towards different parts of the union discussed in Chapter 3, as well as the data analysed here, it seems much more plausible to suggest the existence of a hierarchy of belonging among the predominantly or exclusively English. First there is England and after that an inner circle that encompasses the rest of Britain but not the UK. So Scotland and Wales but not, it seems, Northern Ireland.[6] Beyond that, there is a slightly larger circle that would appear to include the inhabitants of the 'Old Commonwealth', the US, and, more tentatively, Ireland and Northern Ireland. These are family; the kith and kin of the English. And beyond that? Perhaps castle architecture offers a better metaphor here. Various concentric circles of belonging surround the English keep. But beyond the outer wall that encompasses our 'kith and kin' there lies a moat—a moat that delineates a fundamental gap between 'us' and 'them'.[7]

The FoES was never intended to provide a comprehensive overview of attitudes in England towards every other country in the world, or even all the states that have emerged from the Empire, and there are certainly limits to what we can definitively claim on the basis of the available evidence.[8]

---

[6] Speculatively, given the apparent importance of the English language in underpinning this sense of mutual kinship, it is interesting to consider to what extent the survival of Welsh and Gaelic as important or even, in some places, dominant mediums of communication in parts of Wales and Scotland impact on attitudes in England. Are the emotional ties of belonging with the peoples of these areas less powerful as a result? Given the limitations of our data, we can do more than raise the question.

[7] In this context it is interesting to note Amy Whipple's analysis (2009: 731–3) of a sample from the huge number (100,000 plus) of letters of support received by Enoch Powell in the wake of his infamous 'rivers of blood' speech in April 1968. While previously an ardent imperialist, by 1968 Powell had become contemptuous of the whole notion of the Commonwealth, advocating instead a return to English origins. By contrast, many of his correspondents remained deeply attached to links to kindred 'Old Commonwealth' countries, while supporting Powell in decrying immigration from the 'New'.

[8] Evidence from a survey of British voters (sic) conducted for Chatham House in 2012 points in many of the same directions. So, for example, when asked where Britain should seek its closest ties, 29% of respondents chose the US compared to 25% choosing the EU and 20% choosing emerging economies such as China, India, and Brazil (there was no former-Dominion territory option.) When

Nonetheless, if a hierarchy of belonging of the kind that we have hypothesized and illustrated in these pages does exist, then there can surely be no doubt that it is deeply rooted in Britain's imperial past. Relatedly, there can also be no doubt that it is—here echoing Srdjan Vucetic's analysis—thoroughly racialized. The affective bonds that allegedly bind the countries of the Anglosphere together do not extend beyond the white-dominated societies that emerged from the Empire. (As an aside, one also strongly suspects that there is little awareness of the multicultural reality of contemporary Canada, Australia, and New Zealand.)

The second caveat is that, even as they appear to lead logically to Eurosceptic conclusions, the appeal of these Anglosphere tropes resonates even among many of those who have argued for the continuation of the UK's membership of the EU. Indeed, even if not always articulated in these terms, interrelated assumptions about kith and kin, the continuing ability of Britain to 'punch above its weight', and, of course, the 'special relationship' would appear to be ubiquitous in Anglo-British political discourse. This is not particularly surprising, given the extent to which they have for so long been a largely unchallenged commonplace: it was, after all, Churchill's great rival Clement Attlee who once favourably contrasted the ties that bound the Commonwealth to those of a 'Continentalism' that lacked a shared history or a 'common way of life' (cited by Wellings and Baxendale 2015: 132); Labour's National Executive Committee that argued (in 1950) that 'in every respect we are closer to our kinsman in Australia and New Zealand on the far side of the world than we are to Europe' (cited by Kenny and Pierce 2018: 68); and Hugh Gaitskell (1962), who spoke of Britain as the 'mother country of a series of independent nations', and so on.

As was already pointed out in Chapter 1, these assumptions about Britain's rightful place in the world formed the basis for the case made by leading 'Remainers'—not least David Cameron—in the run-up to the 2016 referendum. The internal logic appears to read as follows: despite the fact we differ from our European partners in fundamental ways because of our proud parliamentary traditions and innate global perspective (that is, our imperial past), remaining part of the European Union is nonetheless vital if Britain is to continue to punch above its weight on the global stage. Unfortunately for the former prime minister, that logic was highly unlikely to resonate among

asked which countries they felt especially favourable towards, Australia, Canada, and the US scored particularly well. Moreover, 56% thought that the UK should 'seek to remain a great power', compared to 25% who thought that the UK should 'accept that it is no longer a great power'. See Knight et al. (2012). Note that there was no breakdown of respondents by national identity.

those who identify as exclusively or predominantly English, in particular, especially in competition with an argument whose own logic is: given how fundamentally we differ from our European partners because of our proud parliamentary tradition and innately global perspective (that is, our imperial past), we need to leave the European Union in order to regain our rightful, leading role on the world stage.

Conclusion

A key theme in Chapter 3 was the emergence in England of a strong sense of grievance about the way that country is treated within post-devolution UK. This sense of grievance is focused on relative levels of public spending and the (pre-EVEL) anomaly of non-English MPs being able to vote on laws that apply only in England, and it is felt most intensely among those who feel most strongly English in terms of their sense of national identity; itself an apparently growing proportion of society (as we saw in Chapter 2). This sense of grievance is accompanied by a strong—if still inchoate—sense that England should be recognized as a unit in its own right within the governmental structures of the UK.

Given that even relatively minor changes to the voting procedures of the House of Commons introduced in 2015 to allow for English votes for English laws (EVEL) were so controversial (as discussed in Chapter 7), some may conclude that such strong support for an explicitly English dimension means that the English no longer care whether the UK survives or not. As Chapter 3 also made clear, there is more truth in this than many proponents of union might like to admit. While it is true the balance of opinion in England remains firmly supportive of the continuation of union with Scotland and Wales, the same is not the case with regards Northern Ireland. Not only that, but support for the union is support for a rather different kind of union than the one with which we are familiar: a union whose constituent units (or most of them) continue to be part of the same state, but nonetheless all enjoy much more autonomy, both fiscal and political, than is currently the case. This is unionism of the conditional rather than wholehearted variety.

English support for radical change in the UK's territorial–constitutional arrangements has become even more apparent in this chapter, as we have turned our attention to English views of Britain's place in the world. The strong and significant relationship between English national sentiment and hostility to the UK's membership of the EU was instrumental in determining the result of the 2016 referendum (Henderson et al. 2017, 2020). Exclusively or predominantly English identifiers are consistently much more suspicious of the supposed benefits of European membership and even more critical of the EU's supposed failings. But this English Euroscepticism does not exist in a vacuum. Suspicion of continental entanglements is accompanied by a hankering after historic ties with at least some parts of what was once the British Empire. In other words, there are both 'push' and 'pull' factors at work. The push elements are most obvious and tangible, of course: leaving and 'taking back control'. But it would appear that there is a desire to use this reasserted control to re-create some kind of arrangement with the 'mother country's' offspring. Not even the faintest outlines of what such an arrangement might entail in practice have actually been put forward. Indeed, one of the most influential advocates of the 'Anglosphere', Robert Conquest, once referred to his own suggestions in this regard as 'a work of cultural and political science fiction' (cited by Wellings and Blaxendale 2015: 132). But this vagueness appears only to heighten the appeal among supporters.

To focus on views in England of the United Kingdom and the European Union, and the view of English identifiers in particular, is therefore to be confronted with support for radical constitutional change, as is now being underlined by the far-reaching and, indeed, traumatic ramifications of the referendum decision to depart the newer of those two unions. But the striking paradox at the heart of this support for fundamental change to territorial–constitutional arrangements is that it is a direct corollary of strongly traditionalist or conservative views about what we might term the appropriate constitution order. While such views would almost certainly have been regarded as wholly unremarkable only fifty or sixty years ago, given intervening development, preserving or otherwise buttressing constitutional arrangements that English opinion seems to regard as legitimate would seem to require wholesale change. Thus, recalling Lampedusa's *The Leopard*: 'if we want things to stay as they are, things will have to change.' But digging deeper into the context of these famous words helps highlight perhaps the most striking characteristic of contemporary English opinion discussed this chapter. In the novel, they are spoken by Tancredi, who responds to the political and constitutional upheavals of the Risorgimento by adapting to and seeking to become a part of the new order—all in order to protect as many as possible of the old privileges. This was, in effect, David Cameron's position. A self-professed 'reluctant European', he nonetheless believed that EU membership was necessary if Britain was to protect as many as possible of its old privileges within the new global order. By contrast, the 2016 referendum seemed to suggest a determination among those who identify as strongly English, in particular, to try to return to the *ancien regime*: 'things must change so that things can return to what we think they were like sixty or more years ago'. What now remains to be seen, of course, is the extent to which this determination can be successfully accommodated to the realities of a world that has been utterly transformed since what were even then the dying days of the British Empire.

5

The English World View

It is not difficult to find the view that England, formerly the land of deference, order, tradition, and squeamish aversion to nationalist excess, has somehow been transformed into a land of right-wing, racist, past-obsessed misanthropes, hellbent on pulling the UK out of a successful economic and political union to satisfy some sort of imperial wanderlust. While there are at least some elements in this negative caricature that have a basis in reality, it is a caricature, nonetheless. There is more nuance in attitudinal and behavioural data about Englishness, and the current form of English nationalism should not simply be dismissed as if it were no more than some nihilistic rejection of contemporary political life. Rather, the following chapter argues that English identity is linked to a set of attitudes that reflect a particular vision of England as a polity with a past, present, and future, and embodies within it a coherent vision of ideal or legitimate governance.

Given the evidence marshalled and the analysis advanced in the previous three chapters, this may seem a surprising turn. After all, we have seen how English grievance about Scotland, in particular, is combined with a strikingly casual attitude towards the territorial integrity of the broader UK state itself. Meanwhile, it is also clear that English Euroscepticism is embedded within a broader set of attitudes about Britain's place in the world that are conditioned by a deep affection for Britain's past, including its imperial history and colonies. All of this might suggest that we are currently bearing witness to the emergence of a militant Englishness that is irredeemably reactionary.

But there are at least two reasons to suggest that jumping to such a conclusion is unwarranted. First and most straightforwardly, even if the relationships between Englishness and attitudes towards the two unions appear to be robust, we have not yet formally demonstrated that they are linked together. That is, we have not shown that those who feel aggrieved at the apparent unfair treatment of England within the UK are the same people who oppose the UK's membership of the EU. Even more importantly, we have yet to establish that attitudes to England's two unions are also linked to English national identity—namely, that it is precisely those who prioritize their Englishness who are most likely to be Eurosceptic or anxious about devolution. There are other possible rival predictors of attitudes, including age, partisan identification, or socio-economic circumstances. We therefore need to demonstrate that attitudes to England's domestic and external unions are linked, and that national identity is significantly related to attitudes towards the two unions even after we have controlled for other possible sources of opinion.

Secondly, even though, as we shall see, national identity does indeed survive control, to conclude on that basis that Englishness is somehow inherently backward looking and reactionary would be facile. Rather, what is required is an understanding of the broader set of social and political attitudes in which these more specific constitutional attitudes are embedded and with which Englishness is so closely associated. The other aim of this chapter is, therefore, to reconstruct the broader world view associated with English identity. By doing so we show that English attitudes towards the two unions are best understood as the outworkings of a set of beliefs or visions about the past, present, and future of the polity, a set of beliefs or visions that coalesce to generate an (at least implicit) understanding of the very nature of legitimate government itself. Of course, observers may decide that aspects of this world view are indeed reactionary, or conclude that the elements of the account of legitimate government to which it gives rise are unsustainable in contemporary conditions. We ourselves will point to some of these challenges in later chapters. That said, it is also important to recognize the internal coherence of this world view as well as the ways in which it is deeply sedimented in the very national identity of those who regard themselves as English. It is this that gives it its common-sense plausibility for so many. In other words, understanding this world view in and on its own terms is a necessary condition for any further engagement.

In order to develop our account of the English world view and demonstrate the political salience of English identity, the chapter proceeds in four steps. First, we explore some of the more historical writing on Englishness and its political implications. Not only does this provide vital building blocks for our own account but it will also serve to remind us that, even if the contemporary manifestations of Englishness seem to have caught many observers by surprise, there are previous discussions on whose insights we are able to draw. Second, we then use our survey data to compare what Englishness and Britishness means to our respondents.

The third step is to compare our own account of English attitudes towards the two unions with the analyses advanced by others and demonstrate that, when modelled, national identity remains significant when compared with those other variables suggested as relevant. In the fourth section of the chapter we demonstrate the existence of an English world view, which, in the final section, we show is closely associated with what political scientists term 'low efficacy'—the sense that the state in uninterested in our views and that we are unable to effect meaningful change. The severing or at least the severe attenuation of the previously close bonds that linked the English to their state (which feature centrally in the more historical writings on the subject) has produced a belief that an English voice has been silenced.

Englishness as Others See it

There is a wealth of research on representations of Englishness in literature from poetry to postcards, and we know a great deal about what the English think of religion, sports, social customs, manners, eccentricity, family life, as well as literature, often in a historical context but also in a contemporary setting (Pounds 1994; Langford 2000; Fox 2004; Rogers and McLeod 2004). By contrast, studies of English political attitudes are comparatively thin on the ground. There is, of course, a substantial literature on political attitudes in Britain and in particularly on territorial divisions within Britain (see, *inter alia*, Curtice 1988, 1992; Miller et al. 1996), but the political attitudes of the English in particular have, until recently, attracted rather less attention. This was not always the case. We see a flourishing of writing in the 1940s, and a second flowering following the advent of social surveys in the 1960s (for the first wave see Brogan 1943; Law 1947; Orwell 1947; Young 1947. Rose 1964 is the outstanding exemplar of the second). Part of the difficulty in studying contemporary English attitudes is that, because they have failed to attract significant attention in recent decades, it is sometimes difficult to identify what is new rather than merely newly discovered. These earlier studies therefore serve as an invaluable point of reference.

Both waves of writing emphasized different themes, although some recur. Those writing on English political life in the 1940s were informed by the observational assessments of the 1930s national character studies, although different authors had different goals, with D. W. Brogan (1943), for example, seeking to evaluate the quality of English democracy, and George Orwell (1947), to cite another example, chronicling the divisions within the English political world and, in particular, divisions across social classes. Within this body of writing we find arguments about attitudes towards the state and the institutions of the state, attitudes to fellow members of the political community and the boundaries of the community, as well as attitudes to outsiders. Overall, two key claims emerge. The first is that Englishness is associated with an attitude that might be termed apolitical (though with qualifications to which we return): a view of the political that is tightly delimited accompanied by a lack of interest in or knowledge of the political system, both of which have tended to result in limited demands for political change. Partly this could be seen as reflecting a fundamental contentedness with the political system. The second, related, argument is that markers of English identity are not political but cultural and, therefore, that English national identity is not a politicized national identity.

Those interested in the English 'national character' argued that the English were characterized by their sense of deference, their fondness for order, their lack of concern about equality, and their apolitical nature, all of which contributed to an anti-revolution conservatism that structured public life (although there is some dispute between authors about the causal ordering of these views or their consequences). Deference manifested itself not as unrestrained support for, or blind obedience to, political elites or institutions but as 'critical loyalty' to the community and low levels of cynicism about politics. For Brogan (1943: 74), the root of this deference was reverence for and loyalty to the sovereign, with the Crown serving the emotional needs of English people in the same way as the Declaration of Independence served the emotional needs of Americans. Orwell (1947: 11), by contrast, linked deference to a general preference for order and a law-abiding temperament, helped in part by the social opiates of religion and sport (or, indeed, betting on sport). This preference for law-abiding orderliness, rather than a prima facie opposition to change as such, is regarded by Orwell as the engine of English conservatism and anti-revolutionary sentiment.

The fundamentally apolitical nature of the English acts as another bulwark of anti-revolutionary sentiment. Orwell (1947: 18) identifies English disinterest in politics as a source of English tolerance: 'The English are not sufficiently interested in intellectual matters to be intolerant about them.'[1] As proof of this disinterest, he cites low levels of political knowledge, not only about key 'isms' but even about such basics as the name of one's MP or constituency, as well as a lack of opposition to a patently unfair electoral system. On this reading, the absence of calls for change could equally be seen as support for conservatism (rooted in a preference for law-abiding order) or

---

[1] This is not, of course, the only view. Brogan (1943: 123) claims that political interest and 'a readiness to take real trouble' were more prevalent in England than in the United States.

as stemming from a fundamental lack of awareness of or interest in politics. This distinction also raises questions about the much-noted English antipathy to nationalism, which could stem from a genuine aversion to a particular 'ism' or serve as yet another by-product of political apathy.

We can discern a fair bit about how the English were perceived to structure their political community, including how they felt about fellow subjects and those who were deemed appropriate to include or exclude. English attitudes to political community were widely regarded as being structured by a characteristically English championing of freedom and a general aversion to—or at the very least a lack of concern for—equality. G. M. Young (1947: 99) claims the Englishman of the nineteenth century was 'a stiff individualist in his attitude to the state', while Richard Law (1947: 33) notes than when Englishmen fight they do so for liberty rather than riches or power: 'his only passion is for freedom, and a threat to his freedom, whether from abroad or from his fellow-countrymen, will always rouse him.' Indeed, Law argues that the history of the English is an 'endless campaign' to preserve freedom, although it should be noted that freedom was interpreted as a right to be extended to the English as individuals. It extended to their politicians, manifesting itself in support for the principle that political candidates need not live in the constituency they seek to represent,[2] but not necessarily for the press (Orwell 1947: 18). This general mingling of deference, order, freedom, ambivalence to equality, and the apolitical nature of those within the English political community coincided with an attitude to 'foreigners'—that is, those outside the community—that ranged from disinterest to outright hostility.

Several authors associate antipathy towards foreigners with an English preference for freedom. Orwell (1947: 13), for example, views English hostility towards foreigners—an aspect of their 'unconscious patriotism'—as a by-product of this broader commitment and, specifically, a sense of outrage at the thought of being ruled by non-English who, by definition, are less committed to freedom than they are. Law (1947: 33) detects a characteristically English attitude of condescending sympathy towards foreigners on the basis that they do not enjoy the same freedoms. Notwithstanding these different emphases, the English view of political community that emerges is a striking one. On the one hand, boundaries are drawn tightly around the domestic population, with a strong sense of 'us and them' pertaining to foreigners. But,

---

[2] Indeed, curbing this would violate two freedoms, those of representatives to live where they wish, and those of voters, who would be denied the freedom of political choice by such a restricted approach to candidature (Brogan 1943: 71).

on the other hand, the bonds within the community are perceived to be relatively loose, with a strong vertically defined class system inhibiting different social groups from knowing each other. This particular form of order—the order of the class system—has implications for national cohesion. For Brogan (1943: 156): 'England will not be a full or anything like a full democracy as long as one of the kindliest and most united peoples in the world is internally divided in a fashion that so impoverishes the national life.' As for Orwell (1947: 8), even as he lauds the English traits of kindliness and gentleness, his examples are in the individualized form of helping strangers (helping a blind person on a bus) rather than a commitment to national solidarity (viewed, one would assume, as a decidedly French trait), or to public policy that would assist fellow citizens.

Given the preponderance of references to the Second World War as a unifying experience and a touchstone for contemporary English nationalism, it is perhaps not surprising that the Second World War features in early accounts of English political culture. The Blitz is credited with generating a priority for national community over intra-class solidarity, and indeed the English reaction to the war is seen as a proof of support for freedom and a source of pride: 'The amount of liberty, intellectual or other, that we enjoy in England ought not to be exaggerated, but the fact that it did not markedly diminish in nearly six years of desperate war is a hopeful symptom' (Orwell 1947: 20). Brogan anticipated a permanent post-war shift in English national sentiment and a greater priority for national solidarity. Orwell was less sanguine, assuming that class sentiment and and ambivalence towards equality were likely to reassert themselves when the immediate danger had passed. In a sense, Brogan was right: one need only look to the rich literature on the development of the post-war welfare state that was rooted in and then sought to sustain bonds of social solidarity among residents of the UK. Contemporary manifestations of this view, including references to the bulldog spirit or Blitz spirit, or the 'one world cup and two world wars' approach to English accomplishment, are not difficult to find.

Two decades later, the political scientist Richard Rose returned to what he thought to be the traits of English political culture. Rose's examination was wide-ranging, covering attitudes to the political community and its boundaries, attitudes to the wider state and political system as a whole, norms about roles for citizens and governments, and the boundaries of what was considered to be political or not. The scope of this endeavour was much larger than that attempted by authors in the 1940s, and, in many ways, it remains the most comprehensive survey research-based attempt to map the political culture of England.

Unsurprisingly, given that his book is over half a century old, some of his assessments are dated: there were, he reported, very few divisions on political attitudes even on religion, not just in England but even in Northern Ireland. England had yet to assimilate large numbers of migrants, and so some of the challenges faced in other migrant countries such as Canada and Australia were yet to be felt in England. It would not be very long before such observations, however accurate they were at the time, would no longer apply. Some of the findings, however, remain as pertinent as ever. For example, his observation that the UK government 'has never adopted a consistent policy in differentiating the parts of the British Isles' not only captures the post-devolution arrangements for the constituent units of the UK but applies equally to the internal governance of England today (Rose 1964: 25).

Rose's discussion encompasses the values that define an English political culture as well as its structure and coherence; the way attitudes align with English national identity as well as perceived sources of change in attitudes. The types of shocks that were seen at the time to be prompting a reconfiguration of dominant attitudes have their contemporary parallels.

In his discussion of values, Rose (1964: 39) echoes many of the themes highlighted by the earlier generation of writers. Deference and pride in political institutions, notably parliament and the sovereign, are all cited, as is a valorization of freedom and a lack of regard for social equality: 'In no society is social equality fully achieved; in England, it is often not valued as a goal.' Rose references deliberate attempts to shore up national unity during the Second World War and its aftermath, as well as the role of the welfare state as a tool of social solidarity. He regards attachment to the status quo and a 'traditional English way of life' as ends in themselves, and central not only to anti-revolutionary sentiment of English political culture but present well beyond the political sphere itself. Those who sought to challenge the constitutional status quo were perceived to be few in number, and, to the extent that they existed, they could safely be regarded as eccentrics or crusaders. Rather, '[t]he great implicit major premise of the English political culture would seem to be that all necessary and desirable changes can be assimilated into the existing political system' (Rose 1964: 57). This preference for the status quo—whether rooted in deference or order or in an a priori antipathy to change—is particularly striking when compared to the upheavals of contemporary calls for change. But, as already discussed in the Chapter 4, an alternative reading of both anti-devolution and Eurosceptic sentiment is as expressions of support for the status quo ante. Here, change is not change, but a resetting of the entire political system to its original root: English conservatism at its most muscular.

If previous authors suggested a lack of English nationalist sentiment could be attributed in part to divisions across class lines, Rose sought to map the points of agreement and disagreement. Deference (accompanied by a suspicion of unnecessarily 'clever' leaders (Rose 1964: 47)) obviously features, as does the separation of church and state, the role of the welfare state (despite disagreements on its particular form), trust in political institutions, as well as support for the status quo tied to a preference for muddling-through gradualism. Key areas of disagreement were the role of the military and the role of the state in social life, but these fault lines were perceived to be partisan rather than class based or regional; territory generating variations in 'dialect, speech and life styles' but not in political attitudes (Rose 1964: 32).

If Rose's account chimes with earlier writings, and if we can also observe clear parallels in contemporary political life, an obvious question to ask is how and to what extent does change ever occur in English political attitudes? Rose argues that political culture—in England as elsewhere—has been influenced by a mix of traditional norms, wider historical processes such as industrialism and imperialism, as well as specific leaders, events, and circumstances. As a result, and notwithstanding a general preference for the status quo, English political culture cannot be static. Rose is clear that marked shifts arose often in reactions to crises. Indeed, he identified a pattern whereby government efforts to head off possible crises or significant change tended to produce legislation or programmes that themselves introduced seismic shocks to wider political culture. The 1832 Reform Act, portrayed as an 'adaptation of political institutions in keeping with changes in society and in the political culture', was, in part, a Whig effort to head off 'dangerous and uncontrollable innovation' (Rose 1964: 32). The Liberal government of 1906–14 similarly found itself seeking institutional responses that might head off more radical social change. These reformist efforts, bitterly resisted by the House of Lords and the monarch, were stopped by the outbreak of the First World War, at the cost of a fractured state and a permanently enfeebled Liberal Party. To this list one might be tempted to add the Conservative Party's commitment to hold a referendum on Europe in an effort to see off defections in electoral support to UKIP. Viewed in this way, Rose's research remains useful not only because of its account of public attitudes and the key values characterizing English political life, but also because of the way it outlines the mechanisms by which shifts in the English political culture can occur.

This review of writing on English political attitudes highlights three themes relevant to contemporary debate. The first is the extent to which English views about the political system could be characterized as apolitical. While there is some evidence in the earliest national character studies of a general antipathy to politics, by the time Rose was analysing survey data about English preferences this appears to have disappeared. The second is the presence of competing understandings of England and Englishness. These differences are sometimes matters of nuance—about the origins of a preference for tradition, for example—but at other times offer almost entirely contradictory understandings of 'typical' English values. Part of understanding English attitudes is, therefore, not only identifying prevailing views but also identifying who holds them and who holds rival visions. The third theme relates to how changes in political culture occur, and in particular how incremental change—often intended to off more radical revision—has the capacity to transform attitudes and preferences.

The Meaning of Englishness

Given that decades have elapsed since these earlier writers pondered the nature of the English, it is possible that the England they describe no longer exists: whither, in more recent times, deference, order, or loyalty? And yet we find that contemporary writing on England echoes previous claims. Frank Bechhofer and David McCrone (2013), for example, distinguish between English identity, which draws on predominantly cultural markers, and Scottish identity, which is more aligned with political markers, a claim that sits well with earlier pronouncements about the apolitical nature of Englishness. What is less clear is how the themes raised by previous writers fit with the ways that individuals choose to describe Englishness in their own words. In addition, we know from Chapter 2 that respondents tend to elide markers of English and British identities. This raises the prospect that individuals do not distinguish the traits they associate with Englishness and Britishness.

In our 2016 survey, we asked respondents what made them proudest to be English or British. The response options that we provided were discussed in Chapter 2, but here we focus on the open-ended responses that were also provided by respondents—that is, those things that were mentioned without our prompting. While the general range of responses is interesting in its own right, we are particularly keen to determine whether politics or political values feature at all and, to the extent that they do, whether we see reflections of the markers of English political culture raised in earlier writing, or indeed those factors that we have seen associated with Englishness in our earlier chapters.

Of the 5,103 respondents in our 2016 survey, 3,846 were asked the closed-ended version of the question, either about England or about Britain. Of the remainder, half were asked what makes them most proud to be English, while the other half were asked what makes them most proud to be British. In total, 498 offered no answer.

Of those asked what made them 'most proud to be English', 759 responded. Some respondents mentioned multiple things, and we have coded each separately, resulting in 970 items. The full results of the coding scheme are found in Figure 5.1. We have clustered responses into broader themes of values, history, institutions, habits or traits, geography and the built environment, culture, and so on. These allow us to determine how important institutions or values are relative to, say, food, symbols, or sport. In particular, this helps us to understand the relative importance as well as the nature of any political dimensions. As it stands, the political dimensions of Englishness— combining values, institutions, societal structure, state architecture, and policy—represent over one-third of all things cited. The largest among them is political values, either in general (28) or specifically, with the most references to tolerance (45), freedom (35), and fairness (30). The earlier writings on political values, which pointed to a general lack of concern for equality, are reflected in the comparatively little attention to this (6) relative to freedom. Not a single respondent mentioned deference, although we should perhaps be cautious before reading too much into this. There is, after all, an obvious difference between believing something to be a core trait of an identity and listing it as a source of pride.

With respect to political institutions, not a single respondent referred to parliament, the House of Commons, or the House of Lords when explaining what made them proud to be English. As many people mentioned scones (2) as mentioned 'being part of Britain' (1) or the constitution (1). The most oft-cited political institution is the Head of State, although the reference is often to the royal family as a whole. Other references to state architecture or government policy include the education system and welfare state.

The areas of dissensus identified in the work of earlier writers have their contemporary echoes. We see a tension between those who cite traditional or family values as that which makes them proudest to be English and those who cite liberal values or gay rights as a source of pride.

References to the past are frequent, both with respect to England's history and heritage, but also its role in previous wars or its colonial past. Also relevant is that more than one in ten felt that there was nothing that made them proud to be English. Many deliberately contrasted a glorious past with a less than ideal

NOTHING 93
Blank 1
Nothing 45
Nothing I am British 5
Nothing I am [something else] 11
I am not English 14
I am not proud 18

VALUES 176
Values general 28
Tolerance 45
Freedom 34
Fairness/fair play 30
Compassion/charity/generosity 19
Traditional values/family values 8
Liberal values 7
Equality 6
Openness 7

HISTORY 162
History general 104
Heritage 14
Tradition 30
Past general 4
War/undefeated 8
Empire 2

INSTITUTIONS 126
Institutions general 1
Queen/royal family/monarchy 92
NHS 11
BBC 4
Church of England 1
Democracy 12
Law/legal system 5

HABITS/TRAITS of ENGLISH 93
People 10
Humour/sarcasm 23
Gentleness 28
Politeness 17
Decency/honesty 5
Friendly/hospitality 2
Civilized 2
Chivalrous 1
Kind 1
Peace and order 29
Queues 7
Respect 7
Level headed 3
Stiff upper lip 2
Hardworking 2
Resilience 9

Unity 3
Community 3

GEOGRAPHY/BUILT ENVIRONMENT 70
Rural/countryside 54
Island 4
Architecture/infrastructure 4
Weather 2
Specific places 7
London 4
Cornwall 1
Midlands 1
Yorkshire 1

CULTURE 60
Culture general 31
Literature/language 22
Music 4
Intellectual life 3
Celebrities 1
Pomp 2

GOOD THINGS 56
Just because/can't explain/I just am 25
Way of life/atts/behaviour 9
Everything 3
Patriotism 4

'accomplishments' 3
Uniqueness 3
We're lucky things are lovely 1
Country is well run 1
Peaceful/stable/safe 7

SOCIAL STRUCTURE 33
Multiculturalism/multi-ethnic/multiracial/diversity 20
Innovation/invention 11
Opportunities 2

PUR LAINE 24
Place of birth 10
Ancestry 9
Whiteness/race 3
Christianity 2

INTERNATIONAL ORDER 22
Viewed positively on world stage/force for good 14
Independence/indep from EU/Brexit 8

FOOD 17
Food general 1
Fish and chips 6
Tea 6

Scones 2
Yorkshire puddings 1
Cucumber sandwiches 1

SPORT 15
Sport general 7
Football 2
Rugby 3
Cricket 2
Sporting arenas 1

STATE ARCHITECTURE AND POLICY 10
Education system 3
Welfare state 2
Infrastructure/economy 2
Constitution 1
Being part of Britain 1
Military 1

SYMBOLS 8
Union Jack flag 1
Red rose 1
St George flag 4
St George 1
Pound 1

OTHER 5
Could be great in future 5

Figure 5.1 What makes you especially proud to be English?
Source: FoES 2016.

present, attributed to declining morals, a lack of opportunity for the country to prove itself on the world stage, or a perceived 'dilution' of English culture.[3] For these respondents, England's best years lie—emphatically—in the past.

We can compare these responses to those of the people asked what made them 'most proud to be British' (Figure 5.2). In this case, we have 1,220 separate sources of pride. As with the responses on Englishness, we have ranked them from most often cited to those least cited and employed the same general headings used in Figure 5.1.

A comparison between Figures 5.1 and 5.2 highlights some interesting differences. Those describing what makes them proudest to be British are even more likely to refer to history than those describing what makes them particularly proud to be English. Values, by contrast, are relatively more important for Englishness than for Britishness. The overwhelming impression, however, is how similar the responses are, even when the prompts—English or British—are different. Thus, even while values might be proportionately more important to Englishness than to Britishness, it is nonetheless the same sort of values (tolerance, freedom, fairness, compassion) that people have in mind when they think of what makes them proudest to be British. Similarly, while institutions would seem to be proportionately more important to Britishness than to Englishness, it is the nonetheless the same institutions that tend to be cited: the monarchy, the (in fact, devolved) NHS; the (partially regionalized though not devolved) BBC, and so on. Does this suggest that people conceive of Englishness and Britishness in the same way? Not in the case of all our respondents, some of whom—regardless of the prompt they were offered—chose to contrast explicitly what they thought of England and Britain. This can perhaps be best summarized by the following two quotes:

The word English sounds very gentle. British to me is rough around the edges, violent and selfish. An injection of Englishness into Britishness could encourage much needed kindness. (63-year-old female, English not British, Leave voter, South-East)

Nothing—I'm proud to be British but being saying you are proud to be English makes me think of racist biggots [*sic*] and football hooligans.

(34-year-old female, British not English, Remain voter, North East)

---

[3] In the words of two respondents: 'Nothing. 90% people are bitches, no values, a lot of alcoholics and people on benefits, will be Islamic country soon' (34-year-old male, Other—Polish, Remain voter, London); 'I used to be proud but no longer. We are now appeasers & followers not world leaders' (64-year-old female, English not British, Leave voter, South-West).

NOTHING 102
Blank 2
'Nothing' 60
Nothing am English 11
Nothing am [something else] 1
I am not English 8
I am not proud 20

HISTORY 247
History general 127
Heritage 59
Tradition 43
Past general NONE
War/undefeated 11
Empire 7

INSTITUTIONS 205
Institutions general 1
Queen/royal family/monarchy 124
NHS 25
BBC 6
Church of England 1
Democracy 29
Law/legal system 18
Parliament/system of government 1

VALUES 201
Values general 32
Tolerance 35
Freedom 43
Fairness/fair play 39
Compassion/charity/generosity 12
Traditional values/family values 6

Liberal values 1
Equality/social justice 16
Openness 17

HABITS/TRAITS of BRITISH 98
People 5
Humour/sarcasm 23
Gentleness 27
Politeness 6
Decency/honesty 13
Friendly/hospitality 2
Civilised 3
Humility 1
Kind 2
Peace and order 29
Queues 2
Respect 6
Honour/dignity 3
Level headed 8
Stiff upper lip 3
Hardworking 1
Resilience 6
Unity 8
Community 5
Public duty 1

GEOGRAPHY/BUILT ENVIRONMENT 49
Rural/countryside 25
Island 6
Architecture/infrastructure 7
Weather 5
Specific Places general 1

London 2
Cornwall 1
Midlands NONE
Yorkshire 1
'The North' 1

CULTURE 73
Culture general 40
Literature/language/poetry 11
Music 10
Intellectual life/intellectuals 4
Celebrities NONE
Pomp 3
Tv/tvshows/film 4
Theatre/dance 1

GENERIC GOOD THINGS 64
Just because/can't explain/I just am 23
Way of life/atts/behaviour 6
Everything 12
Patriotism 7
"accomplishments" 6
Uniqueness 3
We're lucky things are lovely NONE
Country is well run NONE
Peaceful/stable/safe 7

DYNAMISM 46
Multiculturalism/multi-ethnic/multiracial/diversity 31
Innovation/invention 14
Opportunities 1

PUR LAINE 33
Place of birth 15
Ancestry 15
Whiteness/race 2
Christianity NONE
Heterosexual 1

INTERNATIONAL ORDER 43
Viewed positively on world stage/force for good 26
Independence/indep from EU/Brexit 9
Commonwealth 2
Being part of EU 1
Strong country 5

FOOD 16
Food general NONE
Fish and chips 3
Lemon curd 1
Tea 1
Crisps 2
Sausages 2
Beer/real ale 2
Toasted cheese 1
Roast dinner 1
Cooked breakfast 1
Pubs 2
Scones NONE
Yorkshire puddings NONE
Cucumber sandwiches NONE

SPORT 9
Sport general 6
Football NONE

Rugby 1
Tennis 1
Cricket NONE
Sporting arenas NONE
Sporting events 1

STATE ARCHITECTURE AND POLICY 27
Education system 3
Civil human rights law 3
Welfare state NONE
Infrastructure/economy/standard of living 2
Constitution 1
Being part of union of Sc/NI/W 2
Military/armed forces 11
Gun laws 5

SYMBOLS 7
St George flag NONE
St George NONE
Union Jack flag 1
Red rose NONE
Pound 5
Passport 1

Figure 5.2 What makes you especially proud to be British?
Source: FoES 2016.

The contrast between Englishness as gentleness versus Englishness as insularity pointed to in the earlier writing clearly lives on.

All that said, two main findings emerge from these survey responses. First, when similar cross sections of respondents in England attempt to describe the markers of Englishness or Britishness that make them proud, they overwhelmingly refer to the same things. Not only that, but, contra both older and more recent claims that Englishness is somehow a cultural rather than political identity, there are clear political dimensions to Englishness too.

England's Two Unions: National Identity and Constitutional Attitudes

Other more recent research has also linked Englishness to political attitudes or evaluations of contemporary politics. It has been seen, variously, as a form of nationalism fundamentally reactive to devolution, tied primarily to anti-European sentiment, linked to imperial decline, or seen as the expression of a dominant ethnicity and thus aligned with attitudes towards multiculturalism and migration (Kumar 2003; Kaufman 2004; Loughlin 2011; Wellings 2012). Previous chapters have shown that English national identity correlates with attitudes to the domestic union, and specifically to a sense of English national grievance, particularly as it relates to Scotland, and to the UK's external union with Europe. Each of these has been portrayed by others as rival features of Englishness or English nationalism. In a departure from—or at least a development on—other contributions, we regard all of these attitudes as related to each other (an argument we first outlined in Wyn Jones et al. 2013).

In order to demonstrate this more formally, we take two interrelated steps. First, we show that the attitudes towards the domestic union outlined in Chapter 3 are indeed related to the attitudes to the (former) external union outlined in Chapter 4. In other words, having treated the domestic and external dimensions separately, we demonstrate that, in England, those who are most negative in their assessments of the place of England within the UK are precisely those who are most negative about the EU, and that these attitudes are correlated with English national identity. Secondly, and even more fundamentally, we demonstrate that these attitudes remain positively correlated with English identity, even when other potential explanations are considered.

Table 5.1 provides a quick initial overview of the relationship between attitudes to the two unions. Even if asking whether 'the UK's membership of

Table 5.1 Attitudes towards England's Two Unions (%)

	EU bad thing	EU good thing
Reduce Scottish spending	81	55
Scottish MPs shouldn't vote on England-only laws	63	39
Scotland more than fair share	53	30
England less than fair share	44	19
Scottish Parliament made things worse	37	17
Wales more than fair share	22	12
Welsh Assembly made things worse	21	10
UK governs not in England's interests	19	38

Source: FoES 2016. Results are column percentages.

the European union is a good thing or a bad thing' hardly exhausts the various dimensions of Euroscepticism, this simple question nonetheless discriminates among respondents fairly easily. Those most negative about the EU are markedly more likely to express dissatisfaction with the domestic status quo, and more likely to take a dim view of devolution and, in particular, Scottish devolution. With respect to attitudes to England, those with less positive attitudes to the EU are twice as likely to believe England is getting less than its fair share, and are half as likely to say that the UK government will function in England's long-term interests.

The panels in Figure 5.3 demonstrate the relationship between attitudes to the two unions and national identity in a more sophisticated fashion. It is based on two indices, one of devo-anxiety and another of Euroscepticism.[4] Our devo-anxiety index uses the eight items listed in Table 5.1, while the Euroscepticism index comprises the eight items of our Euroscepticism battery as already outlined in Chapter 4. Onto this we have plotted the responses of our individual survey respondents, distinguishing among respondents by the national-identity labels they selected on the Moreno scale.

Three key findings emerge. First, the two concepts—devo-anxiety and Euroscepticism—are related, with a significant positive correlation of. 51 across the sample as a whole. As anxiety about devolution increases, so too does Euroscepticism. Secondly, those who describe themselves as English not British occupy the top right of the graph, with most expressing high levels of both devo-anxiety and high Euroscepticism. Thirdly, the British not English group is more evenly distributed across the graph, with a clearer positive trend, with those low on anxiety also low on Euroscepticism, or high on both.

---

[4] The relevant alpha scores for the indices are 0.909 for Euroscepticism and 0.727 for devoanxiety.

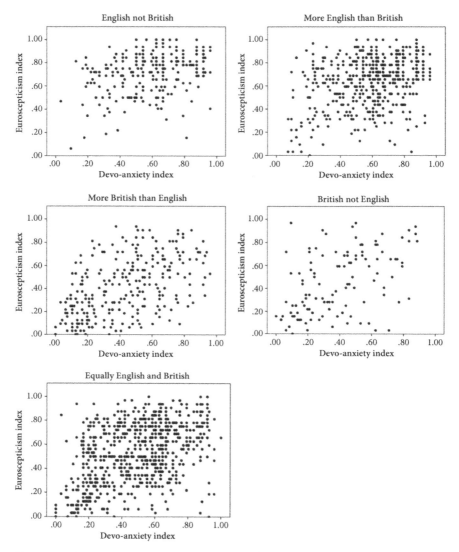

Figure 5.3 Devo-anxiety, Euroscepticism, and national identity in England
Source: FoES 2016.

This is reflected in the higher correlation scores for British respondents (0.52 versus 0.37 for English not British respondents). Part of the reason for the lower correlations among English identifiers is that those who describe themselves as English not British are so Eurosceptic that there is markedly less variation on this index for us to assess the relationship between attitudes to devolution and attitudes to Europe. The key point, however, is clear:

English national identity, devo-anxiety, and Euroscepticism are all linked together. This also suggests that English national identity, far from being a depoliticized construct, is closely connected to evaluations of the current political system.

It is one thing to show that attitudes to devolution and the European Union vary with national identity; it is quite another to suggest that this relationship is central to understanding current constitutional attitudes in England. What we have presented here is our estimation of the things that matter when trying to understand contemporary politics, but it is possible that this reflects our perceptions, informed by years of writing on territorial politics, both in Scotland and Wales but also in a wider comparative setting. To test whether this is an artefact of our own 'territorial' interpretation or is reflected in the data more widely, we must evaluate it in the light of other possible explanations for why people hold these views.

Identifying alternative explanations for Euroscepticism is relatively straightforward. They are in fact multiple and include, *inter alia*: value cleavages, with populism versus pluralism increasingly being considered alongside the more familiar axes of left–right and authoritarianism–liberalism (Tilley 2005; Stubager 2008; Kriesi 2014; Goodwin and Eatwell 2018; Norris and Inglehart 2019); social class, whereby those 'left behind' by globalization are regarded as being more sceptical of large supra-national organizations (Ford and Goodwin 2014); age, where those with longer memories are seen as more likely to identify with the status quo ante where sovereignty was not shared; economic views, and in particular opposition to the global capitalist system of which the EU is a part (Charalambous 2011; March and Rommerskirchen 2015); objections to public services under pressure and concerns about the migrant and/or refugee populations perceived to be taking them to breaking point (Evans and Mellon 2019); exposure to particular media narratives (Foos and Bischof 2018; Gavin 2018); and membership of political parties that provide particular 'cues' in terms of proposed problems and solutions (Hobolt 2007; Clarke, Goodwin and Whiteley 2017b).

It is harder to identify alternative explanations for attitudes towards devolution, in part because, after the initial flurry of research in the immediate post-devolution period, there has been considerably less attention to English evaluations of how the UK functions as a state. Indeed, the Future of England Survey (FoES) was established precisely because we lacked sufficient data about how the population of the largest constituent unit of the UK viewed the state. For the most part, our subsequent argument that national identity matters—and, in particular, that Englishness is related to discontent about the post-devolution constitutional status quo—has been accepted by others (e.g. The McKay Commission 2013; Kenny 2014). Identifying rival explanations is, therefore, a rather more difficult task, but it is potentially the case that those most likely to express anxiety might include: those most affected by pressure on public services, such as respondents who are older or have lower incomes, and who might therefore be less sympathetic to policy variation that in their eyes puts them at a disadvantage vis-à-vis Scotland and Wales; supporters of a smaller state who hold principled objections to devolution as a source of extra layers of government—an attitude that could also be associated with partisan preference; or older voters, who might hanker after a pre-devolution era in which the bonds of social solidarity appeared simpler.

Clearly, some of these explanations are potentially compatible with an explanation that focuses on national identity and related nationalism. For example, national identity can provide a way of demarcating ingroups and outgroups. Thus, attitudes towards immigrants may well connect. It is, therefore, important to be clear that our contention is not that the various rival explanations for Euroscepticism or devo-anxiety are necessarily incorrect, but that they are missing a key, and typically underexplored, phenomenon in England—namely, the salience of nationalism and national identity. Indeed, and specifically with respect to Euroscepticism, some of the 'rival' explanations are in fact part and parcel of the rise of an English interpretation of the unions of which England has been or remains a part.

Bearing all this in mind, and in order to compare these various potential explanations with our own, we have constructed two models of devo-anxiety and Euroscepticism. Such models help us to identify a range of possible causal factors. They have been used to demonstrate how, for example, age affects vote choice, or how gender affects attitudes to policies. This causal relationship can be misleading. With age, gender, and vote choice, for example, it is possible for us to know which came first. Gender and age cannot be affected by attitudes and behaviour. When we are looking at attitudes in general, however, the causal relationship is less certain. For the moment we are less interested in whether an individual's sense of national identity influences his or her attitudes to either union or vice versa and are merely attempting to show that they are related, and related even when we control for other things.

Our analysis uses the same indices for devo-anxiety and Euroscepticism used in Figure 5.3 and the models include a range of standard variables such as age, gender, education, and income, measures of national identity, as well as variables that are linked to wider explanations that have just been canvassed. For social solidarity explanations, we include a social capital index and measure of religiosity. Social capital captures how involved an individual is in various social groups. Religiosity is a measure of religious observance—the frequency with which someone visits a place of worship rather than a particular religious denomination or view of God. Both are measures of embeddedness and engagement within wider communities. For attitudes to a small state, we include a left–right index and a state intervention index. For populism, we use very rough proxies via a low efficacy index and a generalized trust index. (In political science terms, an individual with low efficacy has little faith in his or her ability to make any meaningful difference to the actions of government, either because the government is not interested in his or her views (low external efficacy), or because he or she is not capable of making those views known (low internal efficacy).) Finally, to explore the significance of cues, we include whether the respondent reads a pro-Brexit newspaper[5] as well as whether he or she intends to vote for UKIP, the Conservative Party, or Liberal Democrats—namely the parties with the clearest cues on the issues in which we are interested (although, as Chapter 1 made clear, there was obviously more than one view within the Conservative Party on Brexit). The inclusion of the Liberal Democrats also allows us to include a party that champions a federal UK, supporters of which would presumably receive pro-devolution cues.

Some of these socio-economic and demographic variables were included in the modelling presented in Chapter 2 as possible predictors of national identity. They are included here to determine whether national identity has a significant relationship with Euroscepticism and devo-anxiety, even after we control for other sources of attitudes. To repeat, we are neither expecting nor hoping to find that other explanations carry no weight, but rather to see whether national identity remains significant. Given our previous findings, we would expect both English and British identity to be related to both anxiety and scepticism, with English identifiers more anxious and sceptical and British identifiers less so. For this reason we use the separate national-identity strength variables rather than categories of the Moreno scale as our variables of interest.

As Table 5.2 makes clear, the results show that both English and British identity are significantly related to Euroscepticism and devo-anxiety, and critically that this remains the case even after we control for a range of other factors. Indeed, for devo-anxiety, relatively few other variables reach

---

[5] A Reuters Institute for the Study of Journalism research report shows that five newspapers contained the most pro-Leave articles: *Daily Mail, Daily Express, Daily Star, Sun,* and *Daily Telegraph.* Press release at www.ox.ac.uk/news/2016-05-23-uk-newspapers-positions-brexit#.

Table 5.2 Modelling devo-anxiety and Euroscepticism

	Devo anxiety			Euroscepticism		
Constant	0.45 (0.05) ***	0.38 (0.06) ***	0.26 (0.09) ***	0.38 (0.04) ***	0.39 (0.04) ***	0.16 (0.05) ***
English identity	0.23 (0.04) ***	0.20 (0.04) ***	0.15 (0.04) ***	0.32 (0.03) ***	0.28 (0.03) ***	0.15 (0.02) ***
British identity	-0.11 (0.05) **	-0.14 (0.05) ***	-0.10 (0.05) **	-0.11 (0.04) ***	-0.13 (0.04) ***	-0.07 (0.03) **
Age		0.22 (0.06) ***	0.17 (0.06) ***		0.17 (0.04) ***	0.11 (0.04) ***
Gender		-0.01 (0.02)	0.01 (0.02)		-0.03 (0.02) *	-0.10 (0.01)
Education		-0.02 (0.02)	0.00 (0.02)		-0.09 (0.02) ***	-0.04 (0.02) **
Income		0.03 (0.04)	0.03 (0.05)		-0.02 (0.03)	-0.02 (0.03)
Town & fringe		0.02 (0.03)	0.02 (0.03)		0.01 (0.03)	-0.01 (0.02)
Rural		0.05 (0.03)	0.05 (0.03)		0.02 (0.03)	0.00 (0.02)
Religiosity			0.01 (0.04)			-0.03 (0.02)
Social capital index			-0.02 (0.08)			-0.06 (0.05)
Right wing			0.10 (06)			0.27 (0.04) ***
State intervention index			-.08 (.06)			-0.02 (0.04)
Trust			-0.01 (0.06)			-0.12 (.03) ***
Low efficacy			0.13 (0.05) **			0.22 (0.03) ***
Newspaper			0.01 (0.02)			0.05 (.01) ***
UKIP			0.12 (0.03) ***			0.22 (0.02) ***
Conservative Party			0.03 (0.03)			0.10 (.02) ***
Liberal Democrat			0.04 (0.04)			0.00 (0.03)
Adj R²	0.07	0.10	0.16	0.13	0.19	0.54

Source: FoES 2016. Results are unstandardized coefficients from OLS regression with standard errors in parentheses. * = p<.1, ** = p<.05, *** = p<.01.

significance. Among the range of possible attitudinal drivers of attitudes to the union, only low efficacy and an intention to vote for UKIP are significant, while, among the demographic or socio-economic explanations, only age is relevant: older people are more likely to feel anxious about devolution.

The assembled possible explanations for Euroscepticism do a better job of accounting for the variation we see in our dataset. Much of this is down to the attitudinal variables, where low efficacy and being right wing are both positively related to Euroscepticism, and trust has the opposite relationship: those with higher levels of general trust are less sceptical of the European Union. Among the demographic and socio-economic variables, older people are more sceptical of the EU, while the opposite is true of those with university degrees. Although religiosity and social capital are both negatively associated with Euroscepticism, this relationship holds only until we add measures of partisan support. Using the perhaps crude labels of cues, ideology, solidarity, populism, and economic circumstance, we appear to have stronger findings on cues and populism and mixed findings on ideology. But, even when we control for all of these, national identity remains a significant explanation. Not only that, but, critically, it is working in the expected direction, with English identifiers sceptical of the EU, while the opposite is true of British identifiers.

What, then, are we to make of this? Two of the key themes that emerged from our survey of earlier literature on Englishness were support for the status quo and a certain (critical) deference towards the political class. Yet we have now shown that, in more recent years at least, radicalism has replaced the constitutional caution of old. Not only is English national identity strongly linked to devo-anxiety and Euroscepticism separately, but all three are linked together. Furthermore, identity remains a significant predictor of attitudes towards England's two unions even after we consider other possible explanations. National identity is as important as other possible explanations in the case of Euroscepticism and far outstrips any other when it comes to attitudes to the domestic union. To understand the wider set of attitudes and values in which these constitutional attitudes are located, and in which they would appear to make sense, we shall now attempt to reconstruct the broader world view associated with contemporary English identity. In other words, bearing in mind possible patterns of continuity and change since the 1940s and 1960s, we will seek to delineate the contemporary English world view. This, in turn, allows us to begin to identify possible explanations for why we see what we see in England today.

The English World View

In previous sections we have outlined how our findings compare to what we know from earlier writings on English 'national character' or 'political culture' and how it connects to wider evaluations of contemporary politics. While all of this has descriptive value, in that it helps to outline the contours of what we are seeing in England today, it offers less by way of explanation for why English identity relates to particular attitudes in the way that it does. Furthermore, it does little to explain the seemingly contradictory findings about Britishness—Namely that these those who hold different identities have different attitudes to England's two unions but do not appear to conceive of Englishness and Britishness in fundamentally different ways. It is to a very significant extent the same institutions, values, attitudes, and cultural markers that are evoked by both terms—and yet those who prioritize an English versus a British identity appear to have near opposite views on the two unions of which England is a part. The following section allows us to a take a step towards unravelling these puzzles by identifying the underlying dimensions of an English world view.

By this point, readers will be well aware that our surveys have included a range of questions not only on Europe and devolution, but also on attitudes to the UK state as well as to Britain's past and (potential) future, on British and English identity, and so on. Many of the questions probe similar themes that we have identified beforehand, but there are statistical techniques available to us that help us to determine whether responses to certain questions group together in a meaningful way. To uncover this, specifically to identify what we might describe as the underlying latent structure in certain questions of interest, we can employ a technique called factor analysis. In what follows, we have used data from our 2016 survey to construct such an analysis and then verified that the results hold for different years. As will become clear, in this way we have been able to identify the various elements that combine to form this English world view.

Factor analysis allows us to list the possible variables that we believe might be related to an English world view. This includes measures of English identity (measured here as strength of identity from 0 to 1), previously employed measures of Euroscepticism, and measures of devo-anxiety, as well as British identity, European identity, and attitudes to England's place in the world, its past, and its future. We have therefore disaggregated the variables used to create the indices of Euroscepticism and devo-anxiety. This allows us to distinguish between, for example, attitudes to devolution in principle or in practice, or attitudes to devolution in different parts of the state. We include additional variables, such as attitudes to newcomers (whether it is bad for England if new people come to live in it), whether young people today respect British values, attitudes to fair access to resources, assessments of the Scottish-English relationship (specifically whether the two will continue to drift apart), and whether English values are different. We include explicitly political as well as cultural indicators (including, for example, whether English culture is valued as much as other cultures and whether St George's Day should be a public holiday). Most of the variables are fairly self-explanatory. The only variable we have modified is 'attitudes to English governance'. This is a measure that is coded as 1 if the respondent wanted something other than the status quo in terms of how to accommodate English governance and 0 otherwise. It is, therefore, best interpreted as a 'something needs to be done about England' variable.

In general, the factor analysis of these variables serves two purposes. It allows us to identify those indicators that hang together in a meaningful way (allowing us to distinguish, possibly, between attitudes to devolution in principle and in practice) but also to identify those indicators most related to English identity. In so doing we can see whether British identity attaches to the same indicators or to different ones. It loses the causal assumptions of regression—namely, that certain attitudes cause other attitudes—and helps to uncover those that are more closely aligned.

The results of our analysis, contained in Table 5.3, suggest that we can identify six distinct dimensions of an English world view. The individual variables (most of them familiar from previous chapters) are listed in the first column. How they relate to each other—or how they 'load' onto latent underlying dimensions—appears in the columns and are labelled components 1 through 6. We can, for example, separate out attitudes of national grievance (component 4)—including the perceived fair share questions about Scotland, England, and Wales—as well as attitudes to the impact of the devolved assemblies on the governance of the UK as a whole (component 3). This dimension—on the impact of devolution on the UK—is distinct from attitudes to what the Scottish Parliament is doing and how it should develop, including the ability of the Scottish Parliament to control its own taxation powers and its own welfare policy (component 5). In addition, we see a grouping of attitudes that relate purely to Europe (component 1), which includes various items in our battery of Euroscepticism, as well as European identity. The largest grouping (component 2), however, includes attitudes aligned with English national identity. These include attitudes to England—a

Table 5.3 The dimensions of an English world view

	1 Euroscepticism	2 Englishness	3 Devolution	4 Grievance	5 Scotland own way	6 Britishness
EU has no benefit	0.771					
EU offers no freedom	0.707					
No common culture across EU	0.697					
European identity	-0.645					
EU not needed because UK island	0.667	0.456				
EU has too many regulations	0.582	0.466				
EU has made migration too easy	0.508	0.504				
US special relationship makes EU less important	0.409	0.413				
English culture is not as valued as other cultures		0.654				
Make St George's Day a holiday		0.587				
Young people no respect British values		0.523				
Scottish MPs shouldn't vote on English issues		0.475				
English values are different		0.471				
Britain's best moment was in the past		0.328				
Reduce Scottish public spending		0.424		0.311		
Change English governance		0.343			0.326	
English identity		0.317				0.564
Welsh Assembly made UK governance worse			0.914			
NI Assembly made UK governance worse			0.729			
Scottish Parliament made UK governance worse			0.604			
Scots more than their fair share				0.735		
England gets less than its fair share				0.545		
Wales gets more than its fair share				0.510		
Scottish Parliament should control tax policy					0.835	
Scottish Parliament should control welfare policy					0.748	
British identity						0.652

Source: FoES 2016. Results are factor loadings from principal components analysis.

sense that its values are different from elsewhere in the UK and that English culture is not as valued as other cultures—but also attitudes to Scottish public spending and Scottish influence over England, measured here as attitudes to the influence of Scottish MPs on legislature related only to England, as well as attitudes to Britain's past. They also include support for recognition of St George's Day as a holiday, as well as a sense that young people today have no respect for British values.

For some, no doubt, the set of attitudes that coalesce around a sense of English identity will appear to represent no more than a list of grievances: political Englishness seen as a kind of communal rage against the dying of the light. And it is certainly hard to deny that grievance is part of the story, although it is worth noting that the explicit questions probing grievance about the distribution of resources load separately. But a more plausible interpretation is a more rounded one. As we have sought to demonstrate in Chapters 3 and 4, devo-anxiety and Euroscepticism are clearly related to a more positive political programme (or potential programme). The variable directly testing calls for change in English governance loads with attitudes to the development of devolution in Holyrood. This suggests that what might be perceived as sour grapes about Scottish fiscal largesse is in fact directly related to the absence of more positive recognition of England itself within the state. Euroscepticism is strongly related to a sense that Britain's true friends do not lie on mainland Europe but further afield in the Anglosphere, or at least certain parts of it, as well as a valorization of a particular understanding of self-government ('a sovereign parliament'). It should be clear that these views combine evaluations of the past, present, and the potential futures of England and Britain and—at least implicitly—an understanding of what is legitimate and fair in terms of governmental arrangements and what is not. Moreover, as this chapter has made clear, all of these views are related—not only in the general sense that devo-anxiety and Euroscepticism are related and closely tied to English national identity but, as Table 4.3 has demonstrated, in the narrower sense that factor analysis uncovers a latent structure underpinning a series of key indicators, distinguishing in particular among the different components of devo-anxiety, and tying them to English identity.[6]

In striking contrast, British identity does not connect with any of these attitudes. We know from our earlier analysis that those who prioritize their

---

[6] Moreover, when we repeat the factor analysis for 2015, we see similar results. English identity loads with a blend of attitudes to devolution (Scottish devolution in particular), attitudes to Europe, as well as attitudes to England. Other attitudes related to Europe—including European identity and perceiving the EU as a good thing or a bad thing—load, as in 2016, in a separate dimension.

British identity are less likely to be Eurosceptic and are less hostile to devolution, and yet, were the identity a salient one, relevant to evaluations of contemporary politics, we would expect to see these various questions load negatively with British identity. Instead we find that British identity is related to English identity but to nothing else. This is consistent with what we have discussed earlier—namely, the general elision between England and Britain as well as the similarity in markers of Englishness and Britishness. It relates also to our discussion in Chapters 2 and 3, that those most nationalist about the British state are English identifiers, nor British identifiers. The strength with which one feels British does not connect with any of the attitudes related to evaluations of contemporary political life in England. Britishness is, in this respect, something of an empty vessel in England. Our earlier modelling, which shows that English and British identifiers typically have opposite views of Europe and devolution, remains relevant, but the factor analysis suggests that it is Englishness that underpins a politicized national identity that helps to explain political views in England. All of this serves to underline the fundamentally different ways in which English identity and British identity (detached from Englishness) operate in England.

The second section of this chapter illustrated the very close alignment between understandings of Englishness and Britishness. It is the same institutions and values—the same markers—that are referred to when people in England are asked to say what makes them proud to be English or British. But, as we have gone on to demonstrate, even if the public do not differentiate clearly between Englishness and Britishness, this does not mean that Englishness and Britishness are equally meaningful. It is rather those who feel English who tend to have strong views about the governance of England and Britain. British identifiers without a strong sense of English identity do not. Our factor analysis has underlined the existence of an English world view whereby English identity clusters with a specific set of understandings of the past, present, and future of the British state, combining both affective and evaluative elements. To reduce this world view to 'grievance politics' is gravely to misunderstand as well as to underestimate its basic common-sense plausibility for those who share it.

As a final step in this discussion we will turn to a more careful examination of the question: who shares this English world view? It will become clear that the answer may well help us to understand the transition that has taken place from the basic (constitutional) contentment and even deference that features so centrally in earlier discussions of Englishness to the discontent—and resulting turmoil—that characterizes the present.

Efficacy and the English World View

Previously we identified those individuals who were most likely to feel their English or British identity strongly, and those who were likely to prioritize an English identity over a British one. Since then we have outlined how these identities interact with the different evaluations of the unions of which England was or is a part. These different dimensions are all components of an English world view. As a final step in our analysis, we return to those different predictors of attitudes to determine whether those individuals who, for example, score strongly on the Englishness dimension also score highly on, for example, a sense of grievance, negative attitudes to the union, or Scottish self-sufficiency (such as support for Scotland to set its own policy but also to pay for it). We deliberately return to demographic predictors such as age, gender, and education as well as various measures of embeddedness within England, including place of birth, length of residency, citizenship, and measures of social capital.

The results (given in Table 5.4) show that many of the variables tied to broader English identity cannot help to explain higher scores for the dimension that we are calling 'Englishness' as such. Instead, what we find is that three things tend to matter: gender, place of birth, and efficacy. Women are less likely to score highly on the Englishness dimension. This is also true of those born in the rest of the UK (though, interestingly, this is not true of those born outside the UK). Among the range of attitudes that we include as possible predictors, only efficacy matters. The lower one's sense of efficacy, the more one scores highly on the 'Englishness' dimension of the world view. The implication appears to be that the less one believes in an ability to influence politics—the less voice one feels one has—the greater the appeal of this particular vision of England as a political community.

While it is all very interesting to look at the 'Englishness' factor alone, for comparison we have conducted the analysis for other dimensions that emerged from our factor analysis (Table 5.3). The results differ from the predictors of Englishness. Efficacy does not matter for any of them. In terms of demographic predictors, university education is associated with lower scores for the Euroscepticism and Britishness dimensions, but a higher sense of grievance. Older respondents are more likely to score highly on Scottish self-sufficiency and Britishness. Those who were born in the rest of the UK are less likely to feel a sense of grievance about inter-regional transfers, but they are also less likely to score highly on both Englishness and Britishness. Inter-regional mobility appears related to general support for inter-regional

Table 5.4 Who holds the English world view?

	Englishness	Euroscepticism	Devolution	Grievance	Scottish self- sufficiency	British–English elision
Age	0.24 (0.42)	-0.91 (0.53) *	0.05 (0.66)	-0.30 (0.49)	10.50 (0.59) **	1.00 (0.31) ***
Gender	-0.30 (0.12) **	0.27 (0.09)	0.05 (0.19)	0.09 (0.14)	0.02 (0.17)	0.03 (0.09)
Education	0.09 (0.14)	-0.46 (0.18) **	0.08 (0.22)	0.25 (0.17) **	-0.22 (0.20)	-0.22 (0.11) **
Income	0.42 (0.28)	-0.77 (0.35) **	-0.52 (0.44)	-0.43 (0.33)	0.50 (0.39)	0.36 (0.21) *
Non-white	-0.11 (0.51)	1.72 (0.64) ***	-1.56 (0.80) *	0.10 (0.60)	0.17 (0.72)	-0.59 (0.38)
Non-Christian	-0.37 (0.40)	-1.08 (0.50) **	0.88 (0.63)	-0.10 (0.47)	0.68 (0.56)	-0.24 (0.30)
Non-citizen	0.13 (0.55)	-0.55 (0.69)	-0.58 (0.86)	1.45 (0.64) **	0.66 (0.77)	-0.56 (0.41)
Born rUK	-0.26 (0.14) *	-0.03 (0.17)	-0.05 (0.22)	-0.30 (0.16) *	0.17 (0.19)	-0.41 (0.10) ***
Born outside UK	0.05 (0.31)	-0.22 (0.39)	0.07 (0.49)	0.57 (0.36)	-0.18 (0.44)	-0.37 (0.23)
England < 5 years	-0.90 (0.78)	-0.18 (0.99)	-0.44 (1.24)	0.24 (0.93)	-0.01 (1.1)	-0.42 (0.59)
London	0.26 (0.23)	-0.27 (0.30)	0.47 (0.37)	-0.33 (0.28)	-0.17 (0.33)	-0.30 (0.18) *
South-East	0.16 (0.20)	-0.25 (0.25)	0.144 (0.32)	-0.33 (0.24)	-0.13 (0.28)	0.21 (0.15)
Midlands & East	-0.04 (0.19)	-0.23 (0.24)	0.12 (0.30)	-0.35 (0.23)	0.05 (0.27)	0.31 (0.15) **
North, Y & Humber	-0.02 (0.18)	-0.19 (0.23)	0.26 (00.29)	-0.27 (0.21)	0.37 (0.25)	0.09 (0.14)
Town & fringe	-0.03 (0.18)	-0.07 (0.23)	-0.32 (0.29)	0.40 (0.22) *	0.02 (0.26)	0.17 (0.14)
Rural	0.11 (0.16)	0.05 (0.20)	0.18 (0.25)	-0.10 (19)	-0.26 (0.23)	-0.01 (0.12)
Social capital	-0.04 (0.43)	-0.32 (0.55)	0.41 (0.69)	-0.92 (0.51) *	-0.00 (0.61)	-0.24 (0.33)
Religiosity	-0.04 (0.23)	-0.13 (0.29)	0.07 (0.36)	-0.38 (0.27)	-0.20 (0.32)	0.06 (0.17)
Political Interest	32 (0.23)	-0.74 (0.29) **	0.28 (0.37)	1.20 (0.28) ***	0.42 (0.33)	0.19 (0.18)
Trust	0.18 (0.36)	-0.99 (0.45) **	-0.95 (0.57) *	-0.45 (0.43)	0.12 (0.51)	1.21 (0.27) ***
Right wing	0.51 (0.35)	0.74 (0.44) *	1.16 (0.55) **	-0.56 (0.41)	1.06 (0.49) **	0.31 (0.26)
Low efficacy	1.18 (0.33) ***	-0.20 (0.42)	0.06 (0.52)	0.24 (0.39)	-0.35 (0.47)	-0.16 (0.25)

State intervention	-0.20 (0.33)	-0.23 (0.42)	-0.22 (0.53)	-0.62 (0.39)	1.09 (0.47) **	0.30 (0.25)
Moral conservatism	0.48 (0.31)	0.22 (0.40)	0.43 (0.49)	0.28 (0.36)	-0.11 (0.44)	0.14 (0.24)
Inter-regional solidarity	-0.01 (0.27)	0.49 (0.34)	-0.21 (0.43)	0.12 (0.32)	0.04 (0.38)	0.45 (0.21) **
Civil liberties	-0.31 (0.27)	0.15 (0.34)	0.14 (0.42)	-0.61 (0.32) *	0.23 (0.38)	0.02 (0.20)
Atts to Islam	0.30 (0.20)	0.47 (0.25) *	0.06 (0.32)	0.02 (0.24)	0.01 (0.28)	-0.02 (0.15)
Constant	-1.66 (0.70) **	2.14 (0.89)	-0.29 (1.11)	0.68 (0.83)	-2.51 (0.99) **	-1.99 (0.53) ***
Adj R²	0.39	0.33	0.04	0.16	0.01	0.52

Source: FoES 2016. Results are unstandardized coefficients from OLS regression with standard errors in parentheses. $*$ = p < .1, $**$ = p < .05, $***$ = p < .01.

resource distribution, but does not appear to generate a strong sense of Britishness in England. There are some obvious dogs that did not bark, not least the near total inability of regional or urban–rural location to predict much of anything.

When we turn to the attitudinal predictors, we see that political interest is negatively associated with Euroscepticism and positively associated with grievance. Those who are most interested in politics are most likely to feel that England gets less than its fair share while others get more. Right-wing respondents are more likely to feel that devolution has been bad for UK governance and that the Scottish Parliament should have more autonomy. Those who feel a strong sense of inter-regional solidarity in principle are not less likely to feel a sense of grievance about resource distribution, but they are more likely to be British, so there is clearly more digging to be done on the relationship between inter-regional mobility, inter-regional solidarity in principle, and the day-to-day evaluations of whether certain regions get more than their fair share. Efficacy, while key to understanding the Englishness factor, appears not to play a role in any of the other dimensions of the world view.

The link between a low sense of efficacy and the Englishness dimension provides a striking contrast to English attitudes towards the political system that emerged from our discussion of earlier treatments of the subject in the first section of this chapter. A central theme—perhaps the central theme—of this was the basic constitutional contentment of the English. Institutions were venerated. Not only was the political process respected, but political elites were regarded as 'reasonably truthful, brave and honest'. Brogan, it will be recalled, lauded a characteristically English sense of 'critical loyalty to the community': the Englishman believed 'that was his country does is his business'. Our discussion of these arguments brings to mind Almond and Verba's famous treatment of civic culture (1963). If we follow the arguments from the 1940s and 1960s, then it is plausible to argue that, in that period at least, the English enjoyed something like the ideal combination of deference and efficacy for a representative democracy—that is, they felt a sufficient sense of efficacy to believe that the state was interested in them and their welfare and that they could effect change if required, but at the same time felt a sufficient sense of deference to enable political classes to get on with things without having constantly to guard against what we might now term populist insurgency. If that was the case then, our analysis suggest that things are very different now.

Some caution is clearly required here. The political science concept of efficacy post-dates those writing about Englishness in the 1940s and did not feature in Rose's later treatment. Neither do we have comparative data that might allow us to measure or model the levels of efficacy in the English population of the time. Even so, it seems plausible to suggest that high efficacy was then a characteristic of English political culture, whereas the opposite—low efficacy—tends to be a characteristic of those who score highly on Englishness. They are a part of the population that simply does not believe that the state is interested in them or that they can effect meaningful change to its direction. It is also possible that low levels of individual efficacy are related to what are perceived to be low levels of collective efficacy for England as a whole: a nation less able than it once was to effect the change it wants on various stages, with an international system unresponsive to its broader wishes.

If so, then it would seem that this is the point at which the various strands of our analysis link up. Rose argued that attention to the past, indeed veneration of the past, and a desire to preserve the past through institutions (the preservation of which was also an end in itself) have long featured in English political culture. In many ways, the politicized English identity that we have explored in this book would appear to be a direct continuation of this culture, given that so many of its key elements can be plausibly regarded as a desire to return to the past. Its potentially radical implications are fuelled by a hankering for the status quo ante or at least its approximation ('English votes for English laws'), rather than support for change for its own sake. This is still a fundamentally anti-revolutionist sentiment, even if in the contemporary context it has revolutionary implications.

It is, moreover, a sentiment anchored in a world view that has a coherent internal structure embracing both affective and evaluative dimensions; a world view associated with a particular sense of past, present, and (potential) future in which the current (or at least, recent) orientation and operation of the state leave a significant proportion of those who identify as English feeling that it is not interested in them and their views and that they are unable to effect meaningful change. Hankering for a return to the past, or at least its best approximation, is also, therefore, a hankering for a time in which it was felt that they (or people like them) actually mattered; a time in which the English felt valued in England and Britain, and an England-dominated Britain knew its proper (elevated) place in the world—and, naturally, the rest of the world knew it too. Seen in this light, the link between (low) efficacy and Englishness is key to understanding much of its current salience and power.

Conclusion

In the early years of devolution, those searching for an English backlash suggested that the asymmetrical nature of devolution was likely to result in an 'and us' growth in support for institutional change, a rise in English national identity, and a desire to see an end to perceived privileges for Scotland. On the basis of data collected in the first FoES, we suggested that this had eventually manifested itself as 'the dog that finally barked': strong English national identity, a sense of grievance at (perceived) fiscal largesse elsewhere, and tepid support for the constitutional status quo (Wyn Jones et al. 2012). Upon further investigation, we found that dissatisfaction with the domestic union was linked also to Euroscepticism, and that these two correlated strongly with English national identity (Wyn Jones et al. 2013). The findings in this chapter add more flesh to the bones of this 'two-unions' argument. They suggest that English identifiers draw on the imagery of the British state as a source of pride; those with strong English national identities are, strictly speaking, British nationalists rather than or as well as English nationalists. Their attitudes to governance, while obviously reflecting a sense of grievance about Scotland, are more than merely reactive but an expression of absent English voice—or, even more potently, perhaps, a sense of a voice lost or silenced. Understanding this not only helps us to explain the difference between English and British identifiers (as found in Chapter 2), but allows us to distinguish between those who subscribe to the forms of Englishness we have identified. It is efficacy, or rather a lack of efficacy—not deference or tolerance or a dislike of outsiders—that explains the differences between English and British identifiers and their relative world views.

The last two chapters of this book will consider the implications of this analysis of Englishness both for the UK state itself and for the political analysis of the state. Before that, however, we will concentrate on a crucial question that we have so far left unaddressed—namely, how do the senses of national identity that we have discussed in the context of England (namely, Englishness and Britishness) relate to the senses of national identity (including Britishness) found in the rest of Britain beyond England's borders?

6

England, Scotland, and Wales Compared

It is tempting to assume that the rise of a politicized English national identity is an English response to what has already occurred in Scotland and Wales. On this reading, the rise of Scottish and Welsh nationalisms has pushed the English electorate into a kind of 'catch-up nationalism', encouraging them to view their governance arrangements through a sub-state lens in the same way that voters in Scotland and Wales already do. In part, this may well be true: Scottish and Welsh nationalisms—which includes distinctly Scottish and Welsh interpretations of the union—have clearly had an impact on the structure as well as the tone of British politics; English nationalism is, in part, a reaction to that. But, as has already been intimated, to reduce English nationalism to a response to, let alone an aping of, Scottish and Welsh nationalism—to view it as merely the latest sub-state nationalism within the UK—is also to miss much that is distinctive and different about England. After all, if this were the case, we would expect English nationalism to share many features of nationalism in Scotland and Wales, and this is not in fact the case. English national identity, and English nationalism, are different from that found in Scotland and Wales. We demonstrate this in the following chapter by exploring three facets in turn.

English national identity is different from national identity in Scotland and Wales partly because those outside England are more likely to prioritize their sub-state national identity, and partly because different types of people choose to emphasize a sub-state identity across the three territories of Britain. Second, not only are the socio-economic and demographic characteristics of those with strong Scottish, Welsh, or English identities different, but those national identities align with completely different understandings of the state. So those who describe themselves as English have different—at times polar opposite—views from those who describe themselves as Scottish or Welsh. When we turn to Britishness, we see also that this identity aligns with different views inside and outside England. Those who identify as British in England are not like the self-described British in Scotland or Wales. Indeed, British identifiers in Scotland and Wales are very like those who describe themselves as English in England. Third, notwithstanding this general arrangement, which implies that individuals in different parts of the union have different preferences for the future of the union and different visions of its ideal structure, this is not a state in which individuals have high levels of knowledge about other parts of the state. In fact, we might characterize it as a union of ignorance. Individuals in each territory are happy to have opinions about their own part of the UK and its relationship with England (or, in the English case, about the apparent iniquitous aspects of England's relationship with Scotland), but are less likely to have strong views about other parts of the state. All of this serves to feed an interpretation of the union not as a four-way partnership but as a series of bilateral relationships with England or even, at times, with Westminster and Whitehall (an interpretation that chimes with Mitchell 2009).

In order to explore these themes, we have devised surveys for Scotland and Wales, allowing us to compare findings from our English survey and explore English nationalism in light of attitudes in the rest of Britain. This chapter draws on these parallel surveys.

National Identities

When we compare patterns of national identity across Britain, we are interested in the relative levels of identification with different identities, as well as the type of person who is likely to choose one identity over another. We begin with the Moreno measure of nationality. As argued in Chapter 2, it is an imperfect measure, but it nonetheless provides us with a useful starting point for comparing relative state and sub-state identities across the three territories. Our findings, summarized in Table 6.1, are broadly consistent with

Table 6.1 National identity (Moreno) in Scotland, Wales, and England (%)

	Scotland	Wales	England
x not British	24	14	11
x more than British	26	24	20
x and British equally	29	27	41
British more than x	6	12	12
British not x	7	17	6
Other	5	5	4
Don't know (DK)	3	2	5
n	1,014	1,027	3,695

Source: FoES 2014. Results are column percentages.

other data in the British Election Study (BES) and the British Social Attitudes Survey (BSAS). Four general trends are identifiable. When we look at those who hold two identities, the degree to which one prioritizes the sub-state identity over a British identity is fairly similar in Scotland and Wales. They are, on balance, equally likely to claim they hold a sub-state identity label as strongly as British one (29 per cent and 27 per cent respectively), and equally likely to claim they hold such an identity more than a British one (26 per cent and 24 per cent respectively). Those in England, however, are more likely to hold both identities equally and less likely to prioritize a sub-state identity than those in Scotland and Wales. When it comes to those who hold only a sub-state identity, almost double the proportion of Scots say they feel Scottish when compared to the equivalent identity in Wales or England.

If we look at the British end of the scale, those prioritizing a British identity are more prevalent in Wales than they are in either England or Scotland, a fact that may reflect the high number of residents born in the rest of the UK (and specifically in England) in Wales as compared to Scotland, a point to which we will return. Almost 30 per cent of those in Wales describe themselves as British only or British more than Welsh, but the figures are lower in Scotland (13 per cent) and England (18 per cent). England stands out as the place where sub-state identities are prioritized least (although the gap with Wales is not particularly large) but also where the proportion of those describing themselves as predominantly British is not particularly high. The most popular identity category in England is an equal regard for Britishness and Englishness, with a more than ten-point gap over the equivalent identity in Scotland and Wales. We can distinguish, therefore, those areas where sub-state identities are strong (Scotland), simultaneously strong alongside identities prioritizing Britishness (Wales), and strongest *only when* combined with Britishness (England). In some respects the interesting results from these data are not the prevalence of sub-state identities but variations in the way that Britishness interacts with other identities across Britain.

Asking the Moreno question in different parts of the UK assumes that the identity poles in the answer options are the two most relevant ones for individual respondents. As we can see, approximately one in twenty believes that none of the identity labels is meaningful. In Wales, of the fifty respondents who listed their identity as 'Other', more than half mentioned that they felt either exclusively English or some combination of English (or a region of England) and British: 'English Briton living in Wales (and loving it),' as one respondent put it. Of the forty-one respondents who selected the 'Other' category in Scotland, just under one-third mentioned an identity related to Englishness: 'English and British (and a little bit Scottish).'

These open-ended responses offer insights into the different ways that national, identity questions are interpreted. Some view the identity labels as an indicator of citizenship ('Dual citizen—South African & British'), a measure of ethnicity ('half English half Welsh'), or subject to various birth or residence strictures ('More English than British—I wasn't born and bred in Wales'). Thus, while the overwhelming majority of respondents feel able to locate themselves within the two identity poles provided, it is worth remembering that this is not universally true and that the identity labels are not necessarily interpreted as labels of *national* identity.

Some of this is consistent with what we know from previous research on national identity, although it is worth noting that much identity research examines a single nation within the UK (or two, at most) and does not engage in a three- or four-nation comparison across Britain or the UK. Moreover, those works that examine more than one part of Britain tend to focus on British identity, rather than sub-state identities. We have discussed the research on English and British identities in a previous chapter, so we focus here on the research about Scottishness and Welshness (and Britishness in Scotland and Wales).

There are obviously multiple ways to examine national identity. We could examine the policing of its boundaries by elites, including political parties and politicians, who might seek to pronounce on who belongs in a particular place. We might be interested in the way that individuals make claims about the identities they use and what they mean to them. Or we might be interested in how individuals evaluate the identity claims of others.[1] Together these can offer contradictory understandings of identity and belonging. Indeed, they can operate as another form of a hierarchy of belonging (Henderson 2007)—different from that discussed in Chapter 4—where individuals manoeuvre between the claims they would seek to make about whether certain labels apply or whether they belong, and the claims they think will be accepted by others. In addition, elite pronouncements and public understandings of who belongs can differ. The overtly welcoming messages about Scottish national identity from the Scottish National Party (SNP), for example, stand at odds with public interpretations of national belonging that rely on birth, accent, and religion (Henderson 2007). Frank Bechhofer and

---

[1] There are also other possibilities, not least we could examine the etymology of the identity labels themselves (Pryce 2001).

David McCrone (2014a) argue that, while Scots and English used to employ the same checklist of necessary characteristics for national belonging, this has changed since 2010. Individuals are more likely to accept that people belong in Scotland if they were educated there, whereas in England, they claim, being white still matters. It is worth noting, however, that the debate about racism and national belonging in Scotland is a live one (Davidson et al. 2018; Hunter and Meer 2018) and calls into question any easy labelling of Scotland as more inclusive and welcoming than England.

We know that minority ethnic groups tend to describe themselves as British rather than to employ sub-state identities (Bond 2017), but this occurs within a debate in which certain groups opt for 'post-British' identities. The often hyphenated and hybrid national-identity labels employed by, for example, Glasgow teenagers of Pakistani descent would challenge the simple categories of the Moreno question (Saeed et al. 1999). Racial and ethnic diversity are often associated with newer arrivals, but linguistic diversity within a domestically born population—which in other contexts is referred to as the *pure laine* population—can likewise influence identity labels (Bechhofer and McCrone 2014b).

With respect to the political salience of national identities, Bechhofer and McCrone (2012) suggest that Scottish identity is more politicized than a predominantly 'cultural' English identity, and certainly there are research findings that suggest that national identity is linked to domestic constitutional preferences, including to the 2014 independence referendum (Bond 2015). But the effect is not uniformly strong across contexts and over time. So, for example, as devolution became more widely accepted across Welsh society, national identity played a weaker role in the 2011 referendum on the extension of powers to the National Assembly for Wales than it had done in the 1997 referendum on the establishment of a devolved legislature (Wyn Jones and Scully 2012). There is, in addition, a separate and lively academic debate about the relationship between national identity and party preference in both countries. Eichhorn (2015), for example, suggests the rise of the SNP can be viewed as a sign of the depoliticization of Scottish national identity. In Wales, Bradbury and Andrews (2010) attribute this connection—between national identity and partisan preference—to a form of civic Welshness that has developed since devolution, but note that a rise in Welshness has not occurred at the expense of Britishness, nor has it translated into increased support for Welsh independence. McGrattan and Williams (2017) agree, noting that devolution has created a civic space to articulate the meaning and salience of different national identities.

As we have seen, there are variations in the way that Britishness operates across Scotland, Wales, and England. There are several different possible explanations for this variation (some, perhaps, likelier than others). It could be that identities are aligned with particular political attitudes that are more or less prevalent across Britain. These could include attitudes towards the state and its constitutional structure, or a perceived sense that a particular national community is a better fit for one's political values than another. It could also be that national identities are aligned with particular demographic groups. Two possibilities flow from this. First, if we find that certain demographic or socio-economic groups occur unevenly across Scotland, Wales, and England, and if we know that membership of those groups is related to whether one feels British or not, then we might find variations in the levels of those who describe themselves as British across Scotland, Wales, and England. Alternatively, we might find that certain demographic or socio-economic characteristics are aligned with identities in one part of Britain but not in another. To explore these various possibilities, we have developed models similar to those used in Chapters 2 and 5. This allows us to see whether the determinants of national identities are common across Britain or vary across the constituent nations. As in the previous chapters, we build our models using a national-identity measure that captures strength of identification. We first examine the state and sub-state identities in isolation, using a 0 to 10 scale where people are not at all attached (0) or very much attached (10) to Britishness and to either Scottishness, Welshness, or Englishness.

We include as possible predictors age, gender, education, income, and religion, as well as whether one is a visible minority. In addition, we include measures that speak to the embeddedness of an individual within the territory or state. This includes measures of place of birth (both whether a respondent was born in the UK but also whether he or she was born in that particular territory), length of residence in the territory, and citizenship. We tap two other measures of social embeddedness: religiosity, measured here as frequency of religious observance; and social capital. We have added political interest as a measure of political engagement.[2]

We might assume that, across the territories, older residents would feel a greater attachment to British identity. Given what we know from the literature on migration and sub-state nationalism, we might likewise assume that non-citizens, those born outside the UK and those resident in the territory

---

[2] Note that our 2014 surveys in Scotland and Wales were not as extensive as our English survey and so lack some of the other questions utilized in Chapters 2 and 5.

for less than five years, would hold weaker identities in general, but that they would tend to have stronger state-level than sub-state identities. Likewise, we might assume that individuals who are more embedded in their particular society are likely to have stronger identities regardless of the territorial frame of that identity, while those with ties to other parts of the UK—such as having been born outside the current region of residence—would hold a stronger statewide identity rather than a sub-state one.

The results of the model are presented in Table 6.2. We can immediately observe variations in terms of the performance of predictors for state and sub-state identities. Across Britain, the assembled variables do a better job of explaining Scottishness, Welshness, and Englishness than they do of explaining Britishness. In fact, the model fit statistics are three times better for the sub-state identities than they are for Britishness. This in itself is interesting, because it suggests we are better able to predict when people will feel strongly attached to their sub-state territory (or nation) using various embeddedness variables but not to the state identity. In addition, the direction of variables changes depending on whether we focus on state or sub-state identities. Having been born outside the region or outside the UK makes one less likely to hold a territorial identity strongly, and this is true in Scotland, Wales, and England. Outside England, having been born in another part of the UK makes one more likely to have a stronger British identity, although the relationship as a whole is slightly weaker. And, while having been born outside the UK makes one markedly less likely to hold a territorial identity, with the exception of England this does not affect Britishness at all. This is consistent with what we know from the social psychology literature, that 'bi-cultural' individuals—in our example those with experiences from multiple parts of the UK— are less likely to feel a strong sense of identification with only one of those (Hong et al. 2000). A British identity could well be a way of navigating this. In addition, the lifecycle forms of embeddedness (place of birth, length of residence) exert a greater impact on sub-state identity than on Britishness, although we see that in England having been born outside the UK results in weaker British and English identities. Age, as anticipated, makes one more likely to subscribe to a British identity across the three nations (and in England it is also a significant predictor of a strong English identity). In general, though, the demographic and socio-economic variables offer us fewer consistent messages across state and sub-state identities.

We also see variations in the performance of predictors across territories. Citizenship appears most relevant in England, where not being a citizen of the UK makes one likely to have a weaker English and British identity. If we

Table 6.2 Predictors of Britishness and sub-state identity in Scotland, Wales, and England

	British identity in…			Scottish identity	Welsh identity	English identity
	Scotland	Wales	England			
Age	0.25 (0.07) ***	0.28 (0.06) ***	0.10 (0.03) ***	0.07 (0.05)	0.04 (0.06)	0.12 (0.02) ***
Female	-0.03 (0.03)	0.01 (0.03)	0.03 (0.01) **	0.07 (0.02) ***	-0.03 (0.03)	0.02 (0.01)
Education	-0.03 (0.04)	-0.05 (0.03)	0.01 (0.01)	00 (0.03)	0.05 (0.03)	-0.03 (0.01) **
Social class ABC1	0.09 (0.04) **	-0.07 (0.03) **	0.02 (0.01)	-0.07 (0.03) ***	-0.02 (0.03)	-0.02 (.01) *
Non-white	-0.14 (0.08) *	0.02 (0.08)	-0.02 (0.03)	0.00 (0.06)	0.00 (0.08)	-0.11 (0.03) ***
Non-Christian	0.12 (0.06)*	-0.04 (0.04)	-0.02 (0.02)	-0.06 (0.04)	0.01 (0.04)	0.01 (0.02)
Non-citizen	-0.16 (0.12)	-0.45 (0.13) ***	-0.48 (0.05) ***	0.00 (0.08)	-0.12 (0.14)	-0.38 (0.04) ***
Born rUK	0.14 (0.05) ***	0.14 (0.03) ***	0.00 (0.03)	-0.47 (0.03) ***	-0.59 (0.03) ***	-0.53 (0.03) ***
Born outside UK	-0.09 (0.08)	0.00 (0.08)	-0.08 (0.03) ***	-0.19 (0.06) ***	-0.52 (0.08) ***	-0.24 (0.02) ***
In region < 5 yrs	0.08 (0.09)	0.08 (0.06)	-0.03 (0.08)	-0.37 (0.06) ***	-0.16 (0.06) **	-0.20 (0.07) ***
Political interest	-0.15 (0.06) **	0.05 (0.05)	0.05 (0.02) **	0.01 (0.05)	-0.03 (0.05)	0.02 (0.02)
Religiosity	0.05 (0.05)	-0.00 (0.05)	-0.05 (0.02) **	0.05 (0.04)	-0.05 (0.05)	-0.08 (0.02) ***
Social capital	-0.10 (0.12)	-0.11 (0.10)	-0.08 (0.04) *	-0.09 (0.08)	0.18 (0.11) *	-0.07 (0.04) *
Constant	0.62 (0.06) ***	0.63 (0.05) ***	0.79 (0.02) ***	0.88 (0.04) ***	0.91 (0.05) ***	0.86 (0.02) ***
Adj R²	0.14	0.17	0.12	0.52	0.56	0.39

Source: FoES 2014. Results are unstandardized coefficients from OLS regression. * = p < .1, ** = p < .05, *** = p < .01.

consider that the full run of the identity scale is from 0 to 1, then having been born outside the UK causes a substantial drop in the strength of identity. We should be mindful of the causal arrow here: we are hypothesizing that our independent variables in the first column have an impact on identity. It could well be that someone with a weak degree of attachment does not choose to take out UK citizenship if he or she is eligible. As we did not ask about eligibility, this is something we cannot determine. Race appears to matter little, although, in England, non-white respondents were likely to have a weaker English identity and, in Scotland, were less likely to feel strongly British. With respect to religion, there appears to be no denominational relationship to identity if we are interested in a Christian/non-Christian division of the electorate, except in Scotland, where non-Christians are likely to hold stronger British identities. We know in Scotland that there are denominational differences among Christians, with Catholics likely to hold weaker Scottish identities. As this division is less salient across Britain, we have chosen not to model it here.

The behavioural measures of embeddedness—interest, religiosity, and social capital—appear to matter less than the lifecycle measures of embeddedness or the more 'ethnic' measures of race and religion. To the extent that they matter at all, they are more relevant for explaining identity in England, where those with greater degrees of religious observance, and with higher levels of social capital, have weaker English and British identities. This might well suggest that territorial identities are tapping some measure of wider alienation than is the case in Scotland or Wales. Certainly, this would be consistent with the way that low efficacy is aligned with the English 'world view', as discussed in Chapter 5. In Scotland and Wales, however, these behavioural measures of embeddedness seem to matter less, and, when they do matter, the relationship is not consistent. In Wales, for example, those with higher levels of social capital are likely to hold stronger sub-state identities. This suggests that those who are more active in their communities and have greater connections with other individuals are more likely to hold sub-state identities in Scotland and Wales, but in England it is those who are more isolated who are more likely to feel a stronger sense of sub-state identity, although the strength of the relationship should not be overstated. While the data allow us only to speak of the relationship between social capital and identity, the results point to possible explanations for why these relationships might exist. It appears that English identity is related to a sense of dislocation and alienation that we simply do not see in Scotland and Wales.

We know from Chapter 2 that examining the strength of state and sub-state identities and how they relate to each other provides us with more detailed information than is available from the Moreno question alone. Those who describes themselves as 'Equally Scottish and British', for example, could have rated both Scottish and British identities as 10 out of 10, or both identities as 1 out of 10. Likewise, someone 'More Welsh than British' might judge the strength of those two identities to be one point apart (3/10 Welsh and 2/10 British, or indeed 9/10 Welsh and 8/10 British) or eight points apart. In order to explore these relationships, we plot the relationship between the strength of state and sub-state identities in Scotland, Wales, and England.

To explore this in greater depth, we have constructed a measure of relative identity, used in Chapter 2 and deployed elsewhere (Henderson et al. 2013, 2020), that captures the distance between sub-state identity and state identity in Scotland, Wales, and England; in short, we subtract the strength of British identity from the relevant sub-state identity. When we examine the distribution of responses across Britain, we can see that, while in all three places those assigning equal strength to state and sub-state identities form the largest group, Scots are more likely to prioritize a sub-state identity, respondents in Wales are more likely to prioritize a British identity, and English respondents are more evenly split. In each case, equal identities—those assigning equal strength to both state and sub state identities—outstrip other combinations, but in England this occurs to a far greater extent. These patterns are reflected in the summary statistics for the newly constructed variable, with average responses below 0 (towards British identity) in England and Wales and above 0 (towards sub-state identity) in Scotland and with smaller variation in England than in Scotland and Wales. In short, compared to Scotland and Wales the English are more likely to hold both identities equally.

We can use the same predictors employed earlier to determine if there is a pattern in the strength of sub-state identities relative to Britishness. This will help to clarify the effect of individual variables when the different relationships between state and sub-state identities across Britain are taken into account.

The results in Table 6.3 suggest that across Britain relative sub-state identities are weaker for those born elsewhere in the UK, born outside the UK, or resident in the region for less than 5 years. Unchangeable facts (place of birth) and time appear as possible limits to territorial identity strength. Race and religion matter, but not universally. Non-white respondents in England are less likely to feel strongly English (relative to British), and the same is true for non-Christians in Scotland, who are less likely to feel strongly Scottish

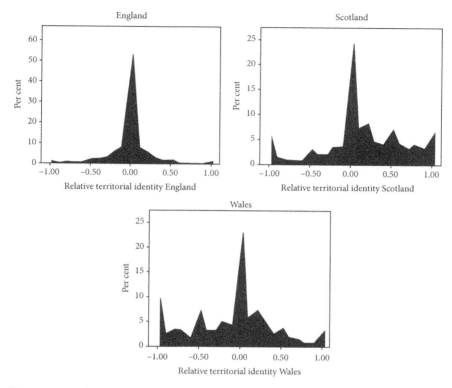

Figure 6.1 Relative identity strength in Scotland, Wales, and England
Source: FoES 2014. Results are distributions of relative territorial identity.

(relative to British). The behavioural embeddedness variables matter only in Wales, where those with greater rates of social capital are more likely to prioritize a Welsh identity. Older respondents are less likely to hold strong substate identities relative to Britishness in Scotland and Wales, as are wealthier respondents in Scotland and England. It is not immediately clear why those who are poorer would feel more strongly attached to a more proximate political community. In both Scotland and Wales, it could be associated with national myths about egalitarianism. In Wales, it might also reflect a traditional view that 'getting ahead' meant 'getting out', either physically or by leaving one's Welshness (including language) behind. In both countries we have evidence that those with middle-class incomes are more likely to describe themselves as working class. There is clearly more to unpack than is possible here. Viewed in terms of the crude if still widely used distinction between civic and ethnic dimensions, these findings offer something of a mixed bag. Place of birth matters, but length of residency, and, in Wales at

Table 6.3 Relative territorial identities in Scotland, Wales, and England

	Scottish—British	Welsh—British	English—British
Age	−0.18 (0.09) **	−0.24 (.09) ***	0.02 (0.03)
Female	0.10 (.04) **	−0.05 (0.04)	−0.01 (0.01)
Education	0.03 (.06)	0.10 (0.05) **	−0.04 (0.02) **
Social class ABC1	−0.16 (.05) ***	0.04 (0.04)	−0.04 (0.01) ***
Non-white	0.14 (0.11)	−0.02 (0.12)	−0.10 (0.03) ***
Non-Christian	−0.18 (0.08) **	0.04 (0.05)	0.02 (0.02)
Non-citizen	0.16 (0.16)	0.36 (0.20) *	0.10 (0.05) *
Born rUK	−0.61 (0.06) ***	−0.72 (0.05) ***	−0.53 (0.03) ***
Born outside UK	−0.10 (0.10)	−0.56 (0.11) ***	−0.16 (0.03) ***
In region <5 yrs	−0.45 (0.11) ***	−0.25 (0.10) ***	−0.17 (0.09) **
Political interest	0.16 (0.08)	−0.08 (0.07)	−0.02 (0.02)
Religiosity	0.00 (0.07)	−0.05 (0.07)	−0.03 (0.02)
Social capital	0.01 (0.16)	0.27 (0.16) *	0.01 (0.05)
Constant	0.26 (0.08) ***	0.28 (0.08) ***	0.08 (0.02) ***
Adj R²	0.36	0.47	0.20

Source: FoES 2014. Results are unstandardized coefficients from OLS regression with standard errors in parentheses. * = p < .1, ** = p < .05, *** = p < .01.

least, how engaged you are in the society around you, make you more likely to prioritize a sub-state identity relative to Britishness. Taking these results together, we can see that there are different patterns in identity strength and the relationships between state and sub-state identities across Britain. As we will see, these identities mean different things or are aligned with different views in different parts of the state.

Two Unions in Scotland and Wales?

We know from Chapter 4 that English devolution anxiety and hostility to the European Union are linked, and that both are aligned with Englishness: the more one prioritizes a sub-state identity in England, the more hostile to England's two unions one is. To assess how this compares with the situation in Wales and Scotland, Table 6.4 shows the relationship between attitudes to the European Union and attitudes to various elements of the domestic union in the three territories. We have included two types of devolution sentiment. First, we include attitudes to the distribution of resources within the UK, summarized typically as the level of territorial grievance. Second, we address attitudes to Scotland in particular, which we find highlights a considerable degree of devo-anxiety in England. We are not, it should be noted, implying

Table 6.4 Attitudes to Britain's two unions?

	Scotland		Wales		England	
	EU bad	EU good	EU bad	EU good	EU bad	EU good
'x' less than	43	37	61	59	42	28
Scotland more than fair share	16	18	30	25	48	37
Wales more than fair share	10	8	7	7	30	21
England more than fair share	51	43	49	48	5	13
NI more than fair share	13	17	17	12	26	22
Scottish MPs no vote(a)	71	68	63	54	75	62
Reduce Scottish spending (a)	33	21	61	43	68	54
n	274	436	333	354	1243	1253

Source: FoES 2014. Results are column percentages of those who selected that response option, with exception of (a) which provides total percentage agreeing with that statement.

that attitudes to one union cause attitudes to the other union. For the moment we are interested only in whether they covary.

Across many of the questions to the domestic union, we see significant differences between the two sides of the European debate. In general, those who are more supportive of the European Union are less anxious about devolution, and particularly less likely to judge that their own territory is getting less or other territories are getting more than their fair share. The exception to this is when regions are evaluating themselves. In Scotland and England, those who believe the EU is a good thing are more likely to believe that they are getting more than their fair share of resources. In Wales there is no difference between the two groups, with both sides apparently equally certain their country is unfairly treated.

In general, Table 6.4 suggests that we can distinguish between attitudes to the European Union—where attitudes in England and Wales are more similar—and attitudes to the domestic union—where attitudes in Scotland and Wales are more similar. Respondents in Scotland and Wales hold similar views on territorial grievance, with similar attitudes to the distribution of resources in Wales and Northern Ireland. Furthermore, while it is true that respondents across Britain believe that their own territory gets less than its fair share of resources, the gap across the views of different EU 'camps' is telling, particularly if we look at the rows indicating that England and Wales get more than their fair share of resources. For the response option showing Wales receives more than it should, Scottish and Welsh responses are in single digits, with next to no difference depending on one's evaluation of the EU. In England, however, figures across both Euro camps are not only markedly higher but differ depending on one's views of the EU. Respondents in Scotland

and Wales appear much more convinced that England gets more than its fair share, contrary to views in England. EU attitudes lead to sizable gaps in how one evaluates England in Scotland and England but not in Wales. Indeed, we can see too that Scotland and Wales are typically less polarized in their vision of the domestic union than is England. When we look at support for English votes for English laws (EVEL), for example, there is a two-point gap between the two Euro camps in Scotland, a nine-point gap in Wales, and a thirteen-point gap in England.

In short, while there is a general link between attitudes to the two unions, the relationships among variables differs across Britain. At the risk of over-simplifying things, Scotland and Wales have a more similar attitude to the domestic union, while Wales and England have a more similar attitude to Europe. We know from previous chapters, however, that attitudes to the domestic union and to Europe vary by national identity, with British identi-fiers in England less concerned about devolution and the EU. In the light of this, the following section explores (a) whether there is a relationship between nation identity and attitudes to the two unions in Scotland and Wales and, if so, (b) how they align.

The Diversity of Britishness

Table 6.5 summarizes the relationship across Moreno national-identity cat-egories for a series of questions related to both devo-anxiety and Euroscepticism, doing so for Wales, Scotland, and England. An initial, obvi-ous observation is simply to conclude that Britishness in Scotland and Wales looks a lot like Englishness in England. British identifiers outside England are more likely to think that the EU has produced too many regulations, while those most likely to hold this view in England are English identifiers. But, while there is truth in this generalization, the reality is a little more nuanced. Taking a more fine-grained approach we can detect four types of effects. First, we can see national effects across the territories. Here the attitudes of, for example, Scots are, regardless of identity, different from English attitudes, regardless of identity. Many of the questions on Europe display this pattern, with Scots markedly less likely to believe in a special relationship with the US or the benefits of being an island than those in England.

Second, we see examples of linear effects, where, as one moves across the identity categories, attitudes become more supportive or less supportive in a more-or-less direct relationship. It is worth noting that these patterns do not

Table 6.5 National identity and political attitudes (%)

	x not British	More x than British	Equally	More British than x	British not x
National grievance					
Scottish MPs prevented from voting					
Scotland	61	67	73	62	59
Wales	53	46	51	64	59
England	77	73	60	61	58
Reduce Scotland's public-spending levels					
Scotland	9	20	32	42	42
Wales	38	49	49	55	51
England	65	67	57	53	49
Possible reform (Scotland)					
Scotland should be independent					
Scotland	82	48	9	6	4
Wales	45	18	11	15	15
England	36	22	14	12	23
Scot Parl control over maj of taxes					
Scotland	87	81	53	48	52
Wales	61	44	36	37	38
England	45	41	41	54	48
Scot Parl control over welfare					
Scotland	87	76	51	46	47
Wales	59	50	38	40	37
England	43	40	40	47	45
British culture					
Good if migrants move to x (8,9,10/10)					
Scotland	33	35	27	23	27
Wales	11	10	15	23	23
England	8	10	14	29	30

Continued

Table 6.5 *Continued*

	x not British	More x than British	Equally	More British than x	British not x
EU					
Good thing					
Scotland	41	46	44	42	45
Wales	35	31	37	35	35
England	15	27	36	52	47
As an island…					
Scotland	32	21	35	31	34
Wales	38	40	38	43	38
England	55	48	38	31	32
Great deal in common					
Scotland	32	36	35	31	42
Wales	31	23	33	36	28
England	17	25	31	43	38
Special relationship with US					
Scotland	18	19	26	34	20
Wales	21	25	28	35	31
England	44	37	30	28	26
Benefit greatly					
Scotland	56	52	55	43	45
Wales	40	39	37	49	40
England	27	36	45	52	57
Too many regulations					
Scotland	57	56	70	60	
Wales	60	64	65	70	
England	80	77	69	60	

Promotes freedom and democracy					
Scotland	45	48	45	43	47
Wales	35	33	36	41	43
England	25	35	39	59	45
Migration too easy					
Scotland	57	54	68	61	67
Wales	66	71	67	74	71
England	79	79	69	62	56
Human rights guarantee freedom					
Scotland	46	47	33	36	43
Wales	33	35	35	33	35
England	23	31	38	54	45
Multi-level politics					
SG/WA has most influence					
Scotland	34	34	47	43	62
Wales	36	26	35	39	43
SG/WA/EP[a] should have most influence					
Scotland	90	81	55	41	49
Wales	77	73	52	48	41
England	49	42	29	20	18
Westminster has most influence					
Scotland	53	52	30	34	44
Wales	46	59	42	33	33
England	46	55	62	70	61

Continued

Table 6.5 *Continued*

	x not British	More *x* than British	Equally	More British than *x*	British not *x*
Westminster should have most influence					
Scotland	2	6	27	45	33
Wales	8	16	33	37	43
England	74	76	76	70	75
Europe has most influence					
Scotland	3	4	6	8	6
Wales	9	3	6	9	7
England	43	32	25	15	26
Europe should have most influence					
Scotland	0	0	0	0	0
Wales	1	0	1	0	0
England	1	1	1	2	5

Source: FoES 2014. Results are column percentages. (a) The English questions ask whether local, UK, or European levels have or should have most influence. A follow-up question asks, if there are new institutions in the future, which should have most influence: stronger local councils, elected regional assemblies throughout England, an English Parliament, the UK government, and EU. The English Parliament figures are from this follow-up question. We urge caution with the interpretation of these figures. The English option presents survey respondents with a range of possible future arrangements with little follow-up information on how they would function, while Scottish and Welsh respondents are comparing four existing institutions.

necessarily work in the same direction in Scotland, Wales, and England. We have examples where, as one moves towards the British end of the scale, agreement in Scotland, England, and Wales drops (such as the attitude to European regulations), but rather more frequent are situations where the movement is in opposite directions in Scotland and England, with Wales something of a midpoint. In addition, even if the identity groups are moving in opposite directions, they do not quite meet or cross. So, on public spending, the Scots keenest to cut Scottish spending (British not Scottish, 42 per cent) are still more generous than those most likely to cut services in England (British not English, 49 per cent). Here, Scottish and English identifiers are poles apart: as one moves to the British end of the identity scale in Scotland, respondents want lower levels of funding, whereas in England the opposite is true (but leaving British identifiers in both countries in roughly in the same location). In terms of attitudes to migrants, for example, British identifiers are more supportive in Wales and England but less so in Scotland, but the least supportive Scottish respondents are still more supportive than those in Wales and roughly the same as those most supportive in England.

Another variation of these linear patterns is when the identity groups appear to offer mirror responses of each other. Here, the British in England appear more like those prioritizing a sub-state identity in Scotland or Wales. Take, for example, attitudes to whether one benefits greatly from being able to live and work in other EU countries. Scottish not British identifiers agree with this (56 per cent) and a similar proportion (57 per cent) of British not English identifiers believe this, but the British in Scotland (45 per cent) and the English in England (27 per cent) hold less supportive views.

Third, we see issues where those at the poles, holding only one identity, have different views from those with shared identities. There appears to be no obvious pattern across the different questions that are likely to prompt this in Scotland, Wales, or England. It is true for attitudes to human rights in Scotland, where support is more tepid among those who hold both identities than those who prioritize a Scottish or a British identity, but support is uniformly low for this proposition in Wales, while in England support increases as one moves to the British end of the scale. A similar pattern can be observed about regulations—greater frustration among the Equally Scottish and British but not those at the poles, linear responses in Wales and England but in the opposite direction, with greater frustration at the British end in Wales and the English end in England.

Last, we see issues where the degree of polarization is higher or lower—in other words, where identity discriminates more or less across the territories.

On migration, for example, the English electorate is fairly polarized, with a twenty-two-point gap between those least supportive (8 per cent) and those most supportive (30 per cent). The equivalent gaps for Scotland and Wales are six and twelve points respectively. By contrast, on attitudes to the European Union, there is typically little difference across the identity groups in Scotland or in Wales (no more than five points difference in Scotland and six points difference in Wales). Across the identity groups in England, however, we go from 15 per cent of 'English not British' identifiers thinking that the EU is a good thing, to 47 per cent of British not English identifiers feeling the same way. In this case, identity helps us to discriminate responses in England better than in Scotland and Wales.

Notwithstanding these different types of trends and relationships, we can see that Scottish and Welsh identities are typically more pro-European than those prioritizing their English identity. It is also very obviously the case that, even as previous chapters have shown that attitudes to devolution vary across different identity groups in England, these differences are dwarfed by the differences in attitudes to devolution, in particular the future of devolution in Scotland, found across the different identity groups in Scotland itself. This may in part be an artefact of the questions we have used, asked in a period in which attitudes in Scotland were highly polarized. But they also clearly chime with what we know of the relationship between identity categories and constitutional preferences—namely, that those with a stronger sense of Scottish identity are more supportive of devolution but also more supportive of greater self-determination and independence.

In addition to illuminating the relationship between national identity and political attitudes, the responses in Table 6.5 help us to understand something of the desire for constitutional change in Britain. In particular, the questions about which levels of government have and should have the most influence help us to understand the wildly different visions of how Britain should best develop. If we examine perceptions of European influence, for example, English respondents are markedly more likely to believe that the EU exerts the most influence over the way that their territory is run. The figures for Scotland and Wales are, by contrast, in the single digits. Support for the EU having most influence is extremely low across the board, but it is worth noting, if only for curiosity value, that it is highest among British identifiers in England.

If we look at possibilities for domestic institutional reform, we see that voters in Scotland, Wales, and England have markedly different preferences for the role of Westminster vis-à-vis regional institutions. English respondents, regardless of their national identity, want an enhanced role for Westminster in the running of England. Voters in Scotland and Wales would like to see their existing devolved legislatures exercise greater power, a view especially prevalent among Scottish and Welsh identifiers. Note in this context, however, that in England we find that, when offered the option, almost half of those who describe themselves as English not British want an English parliament to have the most influence over the way England is run. In other words, even if support lags that found in Scotland and Wales, the identity pattern is similar: the more one identifies with the territory rather than with Britain, the more one wants a sub-state national legislature to exert greater influence.

Overall, we can distinguish two different effects for national identity and constitutional preferences. First, national identity acts in different ways in England depending on whether we are asking about other devolved nations (and particularly Scotland) or whether we are asking about England. English identifiers express more devo-anxiety about Scotland (and Wales), but English identifiers are also, as in Scotland and Wales, more likely to call for greater authority to be exercised by a sub-state legislature in their own territory. Second, national identity distinguishes between those areas where English respondents are more like Welsh respondents and those where English respondents stand apart. Nowhere is this clearer than with regards to the perceived influence of the European Union.

We can examine these differences in further detail in Table 6.6, where we report responses (by national identity) in the three countries to our Euroscepticism battery of question. This battery of Euroscepticism combines both institutional (regulations, migration control, human-rights regulation, freedom, and democracy) and cultural (common culture, island, great deal in common, special relationship) elements.[3] We should note that we accept that it is, of course, possible to debate whether migration is best understood in terms of regulation (or absence of regulation) or whether it is more

---

[3] Cultural dimensions: As an island, Britain has less reason to belong to the EU than other European countries; Britain has a great deal in common with the cultures and peoples of other EU countries (REVERSED); Britain's special relationship with the US makes EU membership less important for it; British people benefit greatly from being able to live and work in other EU countries (REVERSED). Cronbach's alphas for Scotland, Wales, and England are 0.79, 0.79, and 0.75 respectively. Institutional dimensions: The EU produces too many regulations interfering with the lives of ordinary people; The EU helps to promote freedom and democracy across Europe (REVERSED); The EU has made migration between European countries too easy; European human-rights law helps guarantee the basic freedoms of British citizens (REVERSED). Cronbach's alphas for Scotland, Wales, and England are 0.82, 0.81, and 0.80 respectively.

Table 6.6 National Identity and Attitudes to Europe

	Scotland		Wales		England	
	Culture	Institutional	Culture	Institutional	Culture	Institutional
x not British	.41 (.25)	.54 (.27)	.45 (.25)	.60 (.27)	.60 (.20)	.72 (.19)
x more than British	.40 (.22)	.51 (.24)	.51 (.22)	.62 (.22)	.54 (.19)	.67 (.20)
Equally x and British	.44 (.22)	.62 (.23)	.49 (.23)	.62 (.22)	.48 (.20)	.61 (.22)
More British than x	.49 (.19)	.59 (.22)	.48 (.23)	.65 (.23)	.40 (.22)	.52 (.24)
British not x	.42 (.23)	.58 (.27)	.50 (.23)	.63 (.22)	.42 (.24)	.54 (.27)
F	2.23***	4.73***	1.78	.82	51.06***	51.82***

Source: FoES 2014. Results are mean scores with standard deviations in parentheses. F is ANOVA.* = p <.1, ** = p <.05, *** = p <.01.

appropriately viewed in cultural terms, but here we treat it as a structural feature of European membership and therefore as an institutional matter.

If we focus on the two sides of this scale and then create scores for each, we can see whether it is cultural or institutional elements that are driving Euroscepticsm across Britain. As is clear, there are significant differences across both the cultural and the institutional dimensions of Euroscepticism in England, but this is only true at the same (0.001) level for institutional components in Scotland and for none of these in Wales. In other words, the differences in national identity matter more significantly in England than they do in Scotland and Wales. There are stronger Euroscepticism scores for British identifiers in Scotland and Wales (although the differences are small in Wales) and for English identifiers in England, but English Eurosceptics are the most opposed in Britain to Europe. For these voters, both cultural and institutional reasons matter, but the institutional objections appear to be stronger.

Our data suggest that Britishness is working in different ways in different parts of Britain. Not only do different types of people describe themselves as British depending on whether they live in England, Scotland, or Wales, but British identifiers across these three nations hold different views of the state, have different preferences for how its internal constitutional architecture should operate, as well as how it should relate to the wider world. In England, those who describe their national identity as 'British only' are less anxious about devolution and less Eurosceptic. This is not true in Scotland or in Wales. So, the first main finding is that Britishness operates in different ways across Britain.

Second, the relationship between state and sub-state identity groups and how these connect to wider political evaluations suggests that Scotland and England are approaching mirror images of each other. On a number of dimensions, Scottish identifiers behave as do British identifiers in England; English identifiers behave as do British identifiers in Scotland. Specifically, the 'British not Scottish' group behaves much like the 'English not British' group, both of whom hold more punitive views towards Scotland and more negative views towards the domestic union than respondents in Wales. So, it is not just that Britishness operates differently across Britain, but the nature of the variation that matters. England is not like Scotland. The English might well take a dim view of devolution for others, but they appear to want it for themselves. In this respect, they are very much like Scottish and Welsh identifiers in terms of what they want for themselves, but, unlike Scottish and Welsh identifiers, they are unhappy with the way devolution is working in the UK at the moment. Given that we know core values in Scotland and England are broadly similar (Curtice 1988, 1992; Henderson 2015), it is likely that some of this can be attributed to the political discourse as fostered by the governing parties in London and Edinburgh, which occupy different positions on the left–right spectrum, and hold different views of the European Union. Put another way, the political values might be similar, but the political cultures certainly are not (Berns-McGown 2005; Henderson 2015).

Wales is not like Scotland but neither—and this warrants shouting from the rooftops given how that country has typically come to be analysed—can it simply be lumped in with England. If English and Scottish attitudes to the two unions appear as mirrors of each other, the story in Wales is more nuanced and complex. There are two obvious reasons for this. On the one hand, levels of English migration to Wales make it much more like England than is Scotland. In the most recent census, just over one-fifth of the Welsh population was born in England (Office of National Statistics 2011). Obviously, the proportion of one's life spent away from England could condition attitudes, behaviours, and identity; nonetheless, it is clearly the case that English migration to Wales exerts a stronger influence on attitudes than is the case in Scotland, where the English-born population represents less than one-tenth of the Scottish population (National Records for Scotland 2011). On the other hand, linguistic diversity in Wales introduces a further level of heterogeneity. The same census shows that one-fifth of the Welsh population speaks Welsh (StatsWales 2012), far higher than the proportion of Gaelic speakers in Scotland. Furthermore, the geographic distribution of these two populations—English born and Welsh speaking—are not the same, with English residents clustered along the eastern border and greater numbers of Welsh speakers in the west and north. If English-born Welsh residents hold attitudes that make them more like English identifiers in England, our data show that Welsh-speaking Welsh identifiers (that is, those who prioritize a Welsh identity and who speak Welsh) are more similar to Scottish identifiers. We do not examine Wales in all its diversity here, largely because of issues of space, but plan to do so in future publications (in the interim, see Wyn Jones 2019).

Third, it is not just that particular national identities align with this or that view, but that, across the different identity groups, identity works differently in England, Scotland, and Wales. Put another way, it is not just that Britishness is aligned with different attitudes but that national identity as a variable discriminates more among people—in other words, it plays more of a role—in some places than others.

As we made clear in Chapter 5, by focusing on national identity we run the risk of ignoring other possible explanations for attitudes and behaviour. One obvious candidate for this is the political party to which one feels closest. In Table 6.7 we show the relationship between partisan idenfication in Wales, Scotland, and England, again distinguishing between cultural and institutional elements of Euroscepticism. We find significant variations across party supporters in the three countries. In Scotland and Wales, this means it is a better way to explain different attitudes to Europe. Arguably, though, national identity is more 'independent' of attitudes to Europe than is party identification. One could well imagine voters turning to political parties precisely because of their attitudes to Europe rather than feeling attached to a party and holding views that happen to chime perfectly with party policies.

The scores in Table 6.7 show that cultural sources of anti-Europeanism lag institutional concerns and that UKIP voters have the highest scores on both dimensions, followed by Conservative voters. UKIP voters also show the greatest gap between the cultural and institutional dimensions, so it is not just that UKIP voters object to Europe more, but that the nature of that objection is slightly different.

We discussed earlier how Britishness 'works' differently in different parts of Britain. Part of the benefit of exploring things in this way is that it allows us to determine whether party supporters hold similar views of the UK. Do Scottish Tories and English Tories hold similar attitudes to Europe? In 2014, two years before the Brexit referendum, Conservative and Labour voters in England were slightly less Eurosceptic than Conservative and Labour voters in Scotland. They might well have come to different conclusions when it came to casting a ballot, but, in terms of core objections to different dimensions of EU membership, supporters of the largest parties in Scotland were not poles apart from their English brethren. As with the Labour and Conservative voters, Scottish UKIP supporters have higher average scores on both dimensions. The most anti-European voters in Britain are not English UKIP voters but Scottish UKIP voters (although there are vanishingly few of the latter). Although the distance between them is not large, it is the same as that between the SNP and Plaid; the supporters of two different parties have as much in common as UKIP supporters in Scotland and England.

These scores suggest that the core values and beliefs of the constituent nations differ less than the evaluations they make about how to proceed, and the constitutional futures that they deem desirable. These are a product of the contexts in which they find themselves rather than prima facie beliefs. In general, territories with devolution for themselves are happier with the way it works for Britain as a whole. That level of subsidiarity enjoyed in Scotland

Table 6.7 Euroscepticism by vote intention (F=ANOVA by Euro vote intention)

	Scotland		Wales		England	
	Culture	Institutional	Culture	Institutional	Culture	Institutional
Conservatives	.50 (.19)	.69 (.19)	.54 (.19)	.67 (.17)	.50 (.18)	.65 (.18)
Labour	.42 (.20)	.53 (.20)	.43 (.24)	.54 (.22)	.41 (.20)	.50 (.21)
Lib. Dems	.29 (.21)	.40 (.22)	.28 (.19)	.41 (.22)	.31 (.20)	.41 (.22)
SNP/Plaid	.38 (.23)	.50 (.25)	.38 (.21)	.54 (.24)		
UKIP	.63 (.19)	.83 (.16)	.66 (.17)	.82 (.16)	.64 (.17)	.79 (.15)
F	15.22***	26.23***	26.98***	35.49***	140.70***	190.56***

Source: FoES 2014. Results are mean scores with standard deviations in parentheses. F is ANOVA. * = p <.1, ** = p <.05, *** = p <.01.

and Wales has no equivalent in England, and the desire for subsidiarity has no obvious domestic expression, or rather to date has had nothing but an administrative treatment through EVEL. If we recall that in campaigns for devolution in 1997 it was seen as desirable to put democratic flesh on the bones of administrative devolution, this level of English discontent with devolution for others, and with the EU, can perhaps be viewed as a reaction to a missing opportunity for democratic expression.

If we recall that party competition in Scotland and Wales has two axes—left–right and nationalist—then the attitudes of English voters (especially when clustered by party) suggest there are now two axes at work in England. As in Scotland and Wales, these axes are left–right and nationalist (status quo to change), but the nationalist expression in England is focused on independence from Europe rather than on independence from (or territorial differentiation within) the UK. The goal to date self-determination for Britain rather than for England alone.

The Union of Ignorance?

In any large state, particularly one that has clear internal boundaries—as in a federation or in a multi-level state like the UK—we might expect individuals to distinguish between their own unit and other parts of the state. One consequence of this is that individuals can develop a sense of social solidarity focused on their particular part of the state that does not necessarily extend to others (Henderson et al. 2012). They can also develop a sense that their part of the state is unfairly treated in comparison with others. In Chapter 3 we analysed evidence showing that the electorate in England tends to feel that it is unfairly treated in terms of the distribution of public spending, in particular in comparison with Scotland. But how do English attitudes compare to those in other parts of Britain? The statistics in Table 6.8 report the proportion of respondents in Scotland, Wales, and England who think that different parts of the UK get more than their fair share of resources, their fair share, or less than their fair share.

These statistics show that respondents in each part of Britain tend to think that their particular part is getting less than its fair share. Indeed, English respondents are the least likely to believe this, with the Welsh most convinced that they are being unfairly treated (31 per cent in England, 38 per cent in Scotland, 57 per cent Wales). If respondents believe that they are getting less than their fair share, they also have a clear sense of who they think is getting

Table 6.8 Territorial grievance in Scotland, Wales, and England

	Scotland thinks...	Wales thinks...	England thinks...
...Scotland gets			
More than its fair share	14	24	38
Its fair share	28	23	20
Less than its fair share	38	22	4
DK	21	32	38
...Wales gets			
More than its fair share	7	6	23
Its fair share	30	16	26
Less than its fair share	30	57	10
DK	33	21	41
...England gets			
More than its fair share	42	48	8
Its fair share	30	23	25
Less than its fair share	7	8	31
DK	22	22	36
...Northern Ireland gets			
More than its fair share	13	12	21
Its fair share	26	23	27
Less than its fair share	26	25	8
DK	35	40	45
n	*1,014*	*1,027*	*3,695*

Source: FoES 2014. Results are column percentages.

more than their fair share. Voters in Wales and Scotland are convinced that England is getting more than its fair share (42 per cent in Scotland, 48 per cent in Wales) and are much less likely to think that the same is true for Wales/Scotland (respectively) or Northern Ireland. By contrast, voters in England think it is Scotland that is getting more than its fair share (38 per cent). Taken together, these findings suggest that the English are not exceptional in their level of grievance, but that the general level of grievance across Britain is high—and typically higher in Wales than in Scotland and England. If grievance unites Britain, it is worth noting that the targets of grievance are different. Scotland and Wales think that England is the problem. England thinks the problem is Scotland. These data put into context our earlier findings about English attitudes to the union. This in itself is interesting but there are patterns worth exploring here beyond grievance.

When we ask questions in surveys, we tend to ask respondents to express a preference from among a number of predetermined options or statements. Sometimes this also includes an 'other' option, in which respondents can supply responses that we had not previous identified (as discussed earlier in the context of national-identity questions). For most of these closed-ended questions, we also allow individuals to indicate that they do not know how they feel or what they think. This ensures that we are capturing attitudes without forcing individuals to identify views or standpoints on the hoof, as it were. From our data, we know that certain types of questions are more likely to elicit higher proportions of 'don't know' responses. Subjective assessments, or questions about individuals themselves, such as national-identity questions, typically have low levels of 'don't knows', while knowledge questions, or those asking individuals to express preferences about little-heard-of administrative solutions to problems, tend to generate a higher proportion of 'don't knows'.

The patterns of 'don't knows' tell us interesting things about the state of the union. We find, for example, that the proportion of 'don't know' responses from Labour supporters on various constitutional questions tends to outstrip the levels of 'don't know' responses from the supporters of other parties, which could point to confusion about party cues on a range of domestic and European policies. The 'don't know' responses in Table 6.8 also seem to suggest something significant about views of the union, and specifically that in some important ways the United Kingdom might be considered a union of ignorance.

The levels of 'don't know' are high—never below 20 per cent—regardless of whether we are surveying respondents in Scotland, Wales, or England, and regardless of which part of the UK we are asking them to evaluate. That said, the 'don't know' responses are particularly high in some instances. Respondents in Wales and Scotland appear as willing to state an opinion on England as about their own nation, but 'don't know' figures rise when considering the other 'Celtic' nation. There is, therefore, both a level of grievance about England and a degree of certainty about making that determination that is absent in other contexts. The one region about which respondents in Scotland, Wales, and England all offer similar responses is Northern Ireland. When asked to evaluate whether Northern Ireland gets its fair share, the levels of 'don't' knows' range from 35 per cent (Scotland) to 45 per cent (England). Northern Ireland is something of a black box as far as many voters in Britain are concerned. This general pattern—greater confidence in responding when the question is about England or one's own territory—suggests that individuals across Britain have uneven understandings of the union. Indeed, it calls to mind James Mitchell's argument (2009) that the union is not a four-nation partnership so much as a series of bilateral unions with England.

This notion of a union of ignorance chimes well with what we know about levels of knowledge. Efforts to poll what people know about the constitutional status quo, about legislative competence, about how different electoral systems or the European Union work, have been relatively patchy. For the most part, surveys of voters in Wales ask about the legislatures in Cardiff and Westminster, while Scottish surveys focus on Holyrood and Westminster. GB-wide surveys designed to evaluate knowledge across the union are rare. Reviewing multiple sources such as the BSAS, the Welsh Election Study, and the Scottish Election Study, however, provides us with some contextual data about levels of knowledge—and ignorance—of the union.

Knowledge of legislative competence in devolved areas is generally high, with more than 50 per cent of Scots and Welsh voters able to identify what their legislature controls. In 2003, the Welsh Life and Times survey found that roughly 60 per cent knew the National Assembly could take spending decisions about education but could not (then) change income-tax levels. Over three-quarters knew that Westminster controlled defence, and two-thirds knew you could vote for two different parties in Welsh elections. Fewer than one in five knew the size of the Assembly. Second, when asked about other parts of the UK, knowledge is much lower. The 2001 BSAS shows that 37 per cent of English respondents knew Scottish MPs could vote on English laws, 18 per cent knew the number of Scottish MPs was falling, and 12 per cent knew that the Scottish Parliament could not (then) increase social benefits in Scotland. By comparison, one-third knew that London was England's only regional assembly. The knowledge questions asked of English respondents were not replicated in Scotland and Wales.

These findings echo what we have already documented with our own data: voters know their own territory better than that of others. Likewise, voters are less likely to say they have no opinion when asked about their own territory— or England—but are much more likely to say they don't know or have no opinion about other component parts of the union. Third, the direction of ignorance is consistent, if in opposite directions, depending on who one is asking. Asked about the Scottish Parliament, when Scots get it wrong they tend to underestimate Holyrood's level of policy control, whereas English voters, when they get it wrong, tend to overestimate the areas of policy in which Holyrood can legislate.

All of this chimes with what we also know, which is that general levels of reporting about the specifics of what is devolved and what is not are vague and poor. Announcements about policy innovations from Westminster frequently do not make clear whether the policy applies to the whole of the

UK or to Britain or to England and Wales or just to England.[4] In such a context, it would be churlish to chide English voters for their lack of knowledge given: (i) the widespread lack of clarity from government ministers and the media; and (ii) the imperfect levels of knowledge in those territories to which power has already been devolved. If there is a union of ignorance, it appears to have four dimensions: a general level of discontent with the status quo; lack of knowledge about the status quo; a lack of awareness when changes are introduced; and differential attention—in other words, paying attention to some parts of Britain more than others.

Conclusion

In this chapter we have compared patterns of national identity and related attitudes to the domestic union and the European Union in England, Wales, and Scotland. The picture that has emerged is a complex one that defies simple summary. We have pointed to patterns of difference as well as to commonalities—areas in which Scotland and Wales appear similar and England appears dissimilar, and others where England and Wales appear to have more in common with each other and Scotland would appear to be the outlier. We have discussed the ways in which Britishness works differently in different parts of Britain. With respect to EU attitudes, for example, British identifiers in Scotland and Wales have more in common with English identifiers in England. There is, moreover, much more work to be done in comparing attitudes across Britain, and adding Northern Ireland to the comparison would further enrich our understanding of differences as well as common ground across the UK. But, as we return our attention in the final chapters of this book to England, there is perhaps one key point from the preceding discussion to bear in mind.

In the context of attitudes to the domestic union, those in Wales and Scotland— namely, Britain's devolved nations—are happier with the way that devolution works for Britain as a whole than those in non-devolved England. People in Wales and Scotland, and, in particular, those who feel a strong sense of Scottish or Welsh identity, also feel a greater sense of political efficacy than those with a strong sense of English identity. Yet, despite this, and despite the

---

[4] The lack of clarity has prompted two recent twitter campaigns: Wales-based #thatsdevolved and from England #sayEngland.

evidence we have marshalled that shows there is indeed an appetite among England's population for some form of recognition of that nation within the governmental structures of the state, accommodating England and English sentiment in any meaningful way has—so far—proven to be an intractable challenge for the UK. This is the focus of our next chapter.

7
Accommodating England

In previous chapters we have argued that contemporary English nationalism is characterized by its unstable referent object: England within the state, but Britain without. This nationalism manifests itself through a valorization of an idealized past; a sense of grievance about England's allegedly unfair treatment within a post-devolution UK; and resentment at the perceived undermining of Britain's sovereignty and status as a result of EU membership. All of this underpins the demand that England be in some way recognized as a political unit in its own right (on this point, see also Wyn Jones et al. 2102, 2013) and that Britain regain past autonomy via Brexit. Even more fundamentally, these views and perceptions about the past, present, and potential future are associated with a 'theory of legitimate government'—a strong sense of how England/Britain should be governed—that is, uniformly under a sovereign parliament. Our discussion has further shown that many of the sentiments that attach to Englishness in England attach to British identity in Scotland and Wales.

The following chapter focuses on what this English nationalism means for the British state by tracing past attempts to accommodate it within the domestic political structures and evaluating prospects for future success. We focus on internal arrangements within the state, not because we regard the external implications of English and wider Anglo-British nationalism as somehow unimportant or irrelevant. Rather it is simply too soon to say what precisely will emerge from the UK government's current attempts to reconcile the tenets of English nationalism as manifested in the result of the 2016 referendum with geopolitical reality, let alone comment on the impact of those outcomes on English nationalist sentiment. Because of the less than fulsome and apparently conditional support for the union among exclusively English identifiers disclosed in Chapter 3, consideration of the impact of Brexit on the cross-territorial coalition that underpins the Leave vote must also be deferred for a future date. In the interim, however, it is possible to investigate and assess the ways in which the political institutions of the state have already responded—or failed to respond—to the domestic challenges posed by the rise of English nationalism.

As will become clear in our discussion, positive moves to recognize England qua England remain rare, and meaningful moves rarer still. This should perhaps not surprise us. Were this a simple situation to resolve, then perhaps we would have arrived at a stable constitutional architecture by now. That we have failed to do so is due not to a lack of proposals but rather to three chief constraints on action. These are, first, the institutional merger of England and Britain. This merger has deep roots in the state-formation process itself, which is, in essence, a story of the way in which the writ of English (or Anglo-Norman) state institutions was extended variously by conquest, assimilation, and agreement, to cover, at its high tide, all of these islands. It re-emerges as a key issue in the context of the devolution of power to the other three constituent units. As we illustrate in the first section of the chapter with reference to political parties, devolution has seen England re-emerge as a distinct administrative and legislative unit. Yet such is the degree of institutional merger between England and Britain that anything beyond the most token recognition of England as a distinct entity within it would entail the wholesale reorganization of the state as a whole.

This brings us to the second constraint limiting attempts to accommodate England—namely the set of attitudes associated with Englishness already explored in detail in Chapters 3 and 4. These attitudes would seem to render deeply problematic if not doomed both of the approaches to accommodating England that have been either proposed or enacted by the political parties (as discussed in the chapter's second section)—namely some kind of regional solution or English votes for English laws (EVEL).

On the one hand, low levels of public support for regionalization have contributed to an incoherence of constitutional design, such that, even in the unlikely event that England were ever to be successfully divided into meaningful regional units, this would still leave the sources of English grievance untouched. On the other hand, English grievance appears to centre *both* on the undue influence of other parts of the union—crystallized in the West Lothian question—*and* on an absence of English voice. Direct efforts to address this through the introduction of a form of EVEL in the House of Commons does indeed treat England as a unit within the UK polity and, as we have seen, clearly enjoys overwhelming public support. Yet this reform is, also deliberately, very tightly limited in scope and, to all but a handful of experts of parliamentary procedure, arcane to the point of unintelligibility. Moreover, it is designed to deal with only one dimension of what the McKay Commission sensibly—if not yet successfully—sought to reframe as the 'English Question' (The McKay Commission 2013). It seeks to exclude elected representatives from the other territories of the state from English legislative matters. But in doing so it makes no attempt to provide England qua England with a forum of its own—a national democratic locus from which distinctively English voice or voices can emerge. This, again, because creating such a forum would almost certainly entail the wholesale reorganization of the state as whole—a development for which there is scant evidence of strong public support. The weight of opinion in England may well have meant that the eventual introduction of EVEL was an inevitable corollary of devolution; but those same attitudes make it unlikely that EVEL can provide a long-term solution for the tensions and challenges to the union state that we have outlined.

There is a third structural factor shaping attempts to accommodate English nationalism within the structure of the state. Quite simply: England is massively, disproportionately larger in population size than the other three constituent units of the state separately or even in combination. It is home to 84 per cent of the UK's electorate. This overwhelming numerical dominance extends to Westminster. Even if Wales and Northern Ireland, in particular, but also to a lesser extent Scotland, have more MPs per head, England nonetheless provides 82 per cent of the members of the House of Commons. As the House of Lords is not organized territorially, it is more difficult to calculate how many of the members of the House of Lords can be considered to be English, but in this case too it would appear to amount to at least 82 per cent of the total (House of Lords Library 2014: 4–5).[1] International comparisons help underline the extent to which this level of dominance is unusual. The largest constituent unit in federal or decentralized states tends to represent a much smaller proportion of the population and typically no greater than 25 per cent. Of those states where the largest constituent unit is home to at least ten million people, exceptions include Pakistan (Punjab 56 per cent), Canada (Ontario 39 per cent), Argentina (Buenos Aires 35 per cent), Bangladesh (Dhaka 29 per cent), and Ethiopia (Oromia 26 per cent). Indeed, to find comparative population distributions to England/UK, we have to look to countries with overseas, often colonial, possessions. Netherlands is 98 per cent of the population of the wider Kingdom of the Netherlands, for example. Yet the status of Aruba, Curaçao, and Sint Maarten is clearly more akin to that of the crown dependencies of the Isle of Man, Jersey, and Guernsey than Scotland, Wales, and Northern Ireland. Perhaps more

---

[1] This estimate specifically excludes the twenty-six Lords Spiritual, all of whom are members of the Anglican Church in England.

germane, therefore, is the fact that the population of England's South-East region alone is greater than the combined populations of both Wales and Scotland. Northern Ireland is roughly the size of Essex.

This results in something of a paradox in the context of the structure of public attitudes associated with English national identity that has been the main focus of this book so far. In the aftermath of the 2016 referendum, it is the relatively small size of the UK compared to the world's largest trading blocks that serves as one of the main barriers to realizing that vision of the future currently animating Anglo-British nationalism. Yet, in the case of English nationalist grievances and aspirations focused on the internal union, it is England's overwhelming dominance over the rest of the UK that serves as one of the main barriers. The fusion of English and British functions built into the very architecture of the state means that to recognize England qua England in any serious way would necessitate a fundamental restructuring of the state itself: everything would have to change (our first constraint). Even if public acquiescence could be secured for such a venture (the second constraint), any systematic attempt to separate out English and British institutions would ultimately still require a choice between rendering English institutions subservient to those of the UK, even if the former would be very much larger than the latter in terms of budget and staffing levels, or recognizing the brute fact of English numerical dominance, with predictable consequences across the rest of the state (our third constraint).

The size of England relative to the state's other constituent units combines with the Anglo-British fusion that defines its core structure as well as the constitutional attitudes that attach to English identity, to set what would appear to be some very hard limits to accommodation. While devolution means that England exists ever more clearly as a *de facto* political unit, institutional history, public attitudes, and demographic weight all combine to hinder meaningful *de jure* recognition of this fact. In the following section we explore in greater detail how these constraints operate within the state and shape responses to English nationalism.

England and the Political Parties

The complex history of the expansion of the English—or Anglo-Norman— state to encompass (until 1921) all of these islands goes far beyond the scope of this book and has anyway been well told by others (e.g. Norman Davies 1999; R. R. Davies 2000). One of the consequences of this history, however, is that, even as the writ of Westminster expanded, civil society in the different constituent units of what became the United Kingdom of Great Britain and Northern Ireland remained distinct: it was never organized on an all-UK basis.

With some exceptions, Northern Ireland has always been a distinctive organizational unit (a continuation of the pre-secession period in which the island of Ireland as a whole tended to be treated separately). Even if the histories are very different, the same is generally true of Scotland. Wales was, by contrast, formally assimilated into England in the sixteenth century. But, since the high point of institutional assimilation in the early nineteenth century, Wales has gradually achieved recognition as a distinct administrative unit across both political and wider civil society in a process traced by the historian Kenneth O. Morgan (1987) in a book whose title remains resonant: *Rebirth of a Nation*. While the institutionalization of Wales may remain 'incomplete' in comparison to Scotland and Northern Ireland, there is now nonetheless a dense thicket of organizations that treat Wales as a distinct national–territorial unit deserving of at least some measure of distinctive treatment. All of this means that, for very many purposes, England, too, is a distinct organizational unit for wider civic life. Strikingly, however, this is rarely recognized as such. 'England' and 'English' are notable only by their absence from formal titles of institutions and organizations. Typically, de facto English organizations tend either to describe themselves as British or 'national' or completely to avoid any geographical denominator.

Political parties offer a specific example of this wider pattern of territorial organization in all its complexity and contradiction. None of the major 'British' parties has a serious, statewide organizational presence, as Northern Ireland has always had its own distinctive party system.[2] It is true that, in recent years, the Conservatives have been a (wan) organizational presence there. True also that, during its brief heyday, UKIP enjoyed the allegiance of a handful of elected representatives in Northern Ireland, all of whom had defected from the various parties under whose banner they had stood for election. But, even if the Conservative Party is currently registered in Northern Ireland, its presence there cannot be regarded as more than tokenistic. Meanwhile, neither Labour nor the Liberal Democrats are

---

[2] Although, as already mentioned in Chapter 1, during most of its extended period of electoral dominance, the Ulster Unionist Party was umbilically linked to the Conservative Party at Westminster. Moreover, since the establishment of the nationalist Social Democratic and Labour Party in 1970, its MPs have tended to work very closely with the Parliamentary Labour Party. For Northern Ireland politics, see, *inter alia*, Mitchell and Wilford (1998).

registered in Northern Ireland but rather have formal sister parties in the six counties—namely, the Social Democratic and Labour Party (SDLP) and the Alliance Party respectively. Indeed, until 2003, the Labour Party's rules prohibited Northern Ireland residents from joining the party (BBC News 2003).

Both of the main parties have long histories of treating Scotland as a distinct organizational unit. Labour has produced separate Scottish (and Welsh) general election manifestos since 1959, with the Conservatives following suit since 1964.[3] In both cases, devolution has been accompanied by further internal reforms aimed at enhancing policymaking capacity and, sometimes hesitantly, bolstering autonomy (Laffin and Shaw 2007; Covery 2016). In contrast to Labour and the Conservatives, the Liberal Democrats are formally a federal party. We shall return to how meaningful this appellation might be in the context of England, but, in the case of Scotland, the Scottish Liberal Democrats exist as a distinctive state-level organization within the wider party, enjoying extensive autonomy as well as formal channels through which to influence decision-making processes at the federal level. All three parties in Scotland are separate accounting units for the purposes of electoral law and registration.[4]

The situation in Wales is more complex and convoluted, reflecting the broader movement from assimilation to more autonomy. Nonetheless, the overall story is clear: since the advent of mass parties in the late nineteenth century, all the political parties operating in Wales (bar Plaid Cymru, of course) have undergone a process of gradual and uneven transformation, which has seen Wales recognized as a distinct administrative and organizational unit. The young Lloyd George cut his political teeth in campaigns to unite the north and south Wales Liberal Federations into a single, all-Wales national party (Morgan 1987: 90–122). Today's Welsh Liberal Democrat Party—the much-diminished inheritor of that tradition—has the same status and privileges as its Scottish sister. Accordingly, it registers in Wales for the purposes of electoral law and regulation. This is not the case for either the Welsh Conservatives or Welsh Labour, yet both parties (to different degrees) recognize Wales as a distinctive organizational unit (Hopkin 2001). Reversing

---

[3] For the 1959 election, the Conservatives appended different introductions to both the Scottish and Welsh versions of its British manifesto. (See Craig (1990: 519–21) for details of territorial manifestos between 1959 and 1987.)

[4] The Scottish Green Party (a constant presence in the Scottish Parliament since its inception) separated from the England and Wales Green Party in 1990 and has operated independently ever since. The Green Party in Northern Ireland operates as a regional subdivision of the Irish Greens.

the traditional situation in Scotland, in Wales Labour has tended to be more 'advanced' in doing so and now enjoys substantial autonomy. By contrast, the Welsh Conservatives have far less autonomy compared to either Welsh Labour or their own Scottish sister party (Convery 2016: 89 and *passim*), remaining closely tied to the 'English' party. Yet the pressure to grant the Welsh party greater autonomy remains significant, and the direction of travel seems certain (Masters 2018).

This brief digression into the complexities of political party organization across the UK underlines two key points. First, there are no serious statewide political parties in the UK. Notwithstanding the marginal presence of the Conservatives and UKIP, Northern Ireland is home to a wholly distinctive party system. Secondly, in both Scotland and Wales, even if the journeys travelled have been different, the main all-Britain parties operate in ways that (to a greater or lesser extent) recognize their national difference and allow for differentiation from the 'central' party.

But what of England?

Organizationally, the very fact that Scotland and Wales are recognized for at least some purposes as distinctive organizational and policymaking spaces means that, for the all-Britain parties, England too acts as a distinctive space for these same purposes. Significantly, however, neither the Conservative Party nor the Labour Party chooses to name this space as 'England' or 'English'. There is no English equivalent of Welsh Labour or the Scottish Conservatives. Rather, England is the de facto space in which the British parties operate for particular purposes. The Anglo-British fusion that characterizes the territorial constitution of the UK state is replicated in the structures of that state's two largest parties, with the Liberal Democrats serving as the exception that proves the rule. While formally speaking there is indeed an English Liberal Democrat 'state party', in practice the operation of the English-level and federal parties have been almost completely fused. Even a self-proclaimed federalist party seemingly cannot escape the gravity well of Anglo-British fusion (Evans 2014).

By extension, the same pattern holds for party manifestos. We have already noted that there is now a long history of producing distinctive manifestos for Wales and Scotland. While we should certainly not exaggerate the extent of distinctiveness in the pre-devolution period, since devolution all the 'British' parties have substantially ramped up their policymaking capacity in both nations. But even if—post-devolution—much of the contents of the 'main' party general manifestos now applies only to England, there are no 'English manifestos', and those policies that are, in effect, England only are only very rarely labelled as such. Again, the example of the Liberal Democrats serves to illustrate the wider point. Even if there exists—formally—an English state party, there is no English manifesto separate or distinct from the federal-level manifesto. The only exception to this general pattern of (unacknowledged) Anglo-British fusion—and, as of this writing, it remains a singular exception—is the English manifesto produced by the Conservative Party for the 2015 UK general election, an election in which that party specifically— and successfully—sought to mobilize English grievance. Time will tell how long that document retains its current, unique status.

The pattern of political party organization reflects the wider pattern of civil society organization and indeed the organization of the UK state itself. There is very little explicit recognition of England as a distinctive unit. Rather, England is the (usually un-named) space 'left over', as it were, once the devolved territories are 'subtracted'.[5] In the context of Anglo-British fusion, England is, paradoxically, both utterly dominant and almost completely sub-merged, in party politics as well as in wider social and political life.

Proposals for England

All this said, it would be wrong to give the impression that there has been no thought given to the governance of England. Rather various schemes have been put forward reflecting different interpretations of the 'problem' posed by England to the UK territorial constitution (Table 7.1). We may differentiate between two main types:

- Proposals for regional government within England; and
- Proposals aimed at recognizing England as a distinct unit within the operation of the UK parliament.

These schemes for accommodating England attempt to deal with the three constraints that we have identified in very different ways. Proposals for regional government seek to divide England into smaller units, an outcome that, if achieved, might appear very significantly to reduce the challenges

---

[5] Which is perhaps one of only a few ways England could be compared to the Northwest Territories in Canada—rumps that remain once other parts were granted self-determination.

Table 7.1 The governance of England in party manifestos, 1997–2019

Continued

	General	Regionalising Regionalizing England	Recognising Recognizing England
1997	**Con.:** Regional government (in England) 'dangerously centralising measure' Oppose devolution in Scotland and Wales (which, *inter alia*, 'would raise serious questions about whether the representation of Scottish and Welsh MPs at Westminster—and their role in matters affecting English affairs—could remain unchanged.') **Lab.:** Devolution to Scotland and Wales but, NB, 'Our proposal is for devolution not federation. A sovereign Westminster Parliament will devolve power to Scotland and Wales.' **Lib. Dems:** 'Home Rule' for Scotland and Wales with PR and tax powers.	**Lab.:** Establish regional chambers based on existing structures for regional government. 'Directly elected regional government' if: (1) if approved by referendum; (2) if 'predominantly unitary system of local government' is in place; and, (3) subject to confirmation by independent auditors that no additional public expenditure overall would be involved. **Lib. Dems:** 'make existing regional decision-making in England democratically accountable', and enable the establishment of elected regional assemblies, where there is demonstrated public demand.	
2001	**Con.:** Abolish regional development agencies (RDAs) and scrap Labour's plans for new regional assemblies. **Lab.our:** Oppose EVEL ('the Conservatives… threaten the stability of the UK with their proposals for two classes of MP'; 'no case for threatening the unity of the UK with an English Parliament or the denial of voting rights to Scottish, Welsh and Northern Ireland's MPs at Westminster'). **Lib. Dems:** Replace separate UK ministers for the devolved nations with one Secretary of State for the Nations and Regions.	**Lab.:** 'Enhance the scrutiny functions of regional chambers' over RDAs with possibility of referendums on directly elected regional government 'where predominantly unitary local government is established.' **Lib. Dems:** Support referendums on elected regional assemblies—normally based RDA boundaries, but scope for smaller areas if appropriate.	**Con.:** EVEL and EWVEWL.

Table 7.1 *Continued*

	General	Regionalising Regionalizing England	Recognising Recognizing England
2005	**Con.**: People do not identify with arbitrary "regions". Abolish regional assemblies. **Lab.**: 'In our first term we devolved power to Scotland and Wales and restored city-wide government in London. Britain is stronger as a result. In the next Parliament, we will decentralise power further.'	**Lab.**: 'devolve further responsibility to existing regional bodies in relation to planning, housing, economic development and transport.' **Lib. Dems**: "The powers of many unelected regional and national quangos and administrators will be given to cities and counties' & and '[S]treamline remaining regional functions into a single agency … [with] executive comprising councillors elected from the cities and counties.'	**Con.**: EVEL.
2010	**Con.**: 'Abolish the entire bureaucratic and undemocratic tier of regional planning.' **Lib. Dems**: Scrap the Government Offices for the Regions regions and regional ministers and 'Address address the status of England within a federal Britain, through … Constitutional Convention'.	**Lab.**: Regional growth fund will be established by the RDAs & and enhanced role for regional ministers. Core cities and city regions to become power houses of innovation and growth, with a devolution of local transport powers. Where new city–region authorities created, opportunity to trigger a referendum for directly elected major.	**Con.**: EVEL to 'to address the so-called "West Lothian Question"'.
2015	**Con.**: No to imposition of 'artificial regions'. **Lab.**: Replace Lords with elected Senate of the Nations and Regions & and Constitutional Convention process to consider, *inter alia*, McKay proposals for EVEL. **Lib. Dems**: Constitutional Convention to address, *inter alia*, the West Lothian Question. **UKIP**: St George's Day bank holiday in England.	**Con.**: Devolve economic development, transport and social care powers to large cities 'which choose to have elected mayors.' **Lab.**: 'English Devolution Act' devolving powers to city and country regions & and 'English Regional Cabinet Committee', chaired by PM including Ministers and city and county region leaders. **Lib. Dems**: 'Devolution on Demand … to Councils or groups of Councils working together—for example to a Cornish Assembly.'	**Con.**: EVEL ('Give English MPs a veto over English-only matters, including on Income Tax—answering the West Lothian Question'). **Lab.**: 'Time to consider EVEL. **Lib. Dems**: EVEL to be 'considered', but if English legislative committee constituted should reflect % percentage of votes not seats. **UKIP**: EVEL.

2017	Lib. Dems: Constitutional Convention to address, *inter alia*, the West Lothian Question. Lab: St George's Day bank holiday across UK (as part of a package of 4 four new national patron saints' bank holidays) & Constitutional Convention to consider 'the option of a more federalised country'.	Con.: 'With devolution now established…we will consolidate our approach, providing clarity across England…so all authorities operate in a common framework' & Support the adoption of elected mayors for combined authorities in cities (but not rural counties). Lab: Restore 'regional offices' & and 'be guided by public opinion' whether future 'devolution deals' should require directly elected mayors. Lib. Dems: 'Devolution on demand' to councils or groups of councils working together—'for example to a Cornish Assembly or a Yorkshire Parliament'.	Lib. Dems: Support EVEL but with English legislative committee constituted to reflect % percentage of votes not seats. Lab: Create a Minster for England 'who will sit under the Secretary of State for Communities and Local Government, and will work with the Secretaries of State for Scotland, Wales and Northern Ireland.'
2019	Lab: Replace Lords with elected Senate of the Nations and Regions & Constitutional Convention to consider 'how nations and regions can best relate to each other' & and 'four new bank holidays celebrating our four patron saints' days.' Con.: Committed to 'devolving power to people and places [cf. nations?] across the UK'. Lib. Dems: Support 'home rule for each of the nations of a strong, federal and united United Kingdom.'	Lab: 'Re-establish regional Governmental Offices' & make directly elected mayors more accountable to local government. Con.: 'Full devolution across England, building on the successful devolution of powers to city region mayors, Police and Crime Commissioners and others.' Lib. Dems: 'Enact permissive legislation to empower groups of authorities to come together to establish devolved governance—for example to a Cornish Assembly or a Yorkshire Parliament.'	Lib. Dems: Support EVEL but with English legislative committee constituted to reflect % percentage of votes not seats.

caused by the overwhelming numerical dominance of England. By effectively ignoring England as a unit of government, regionalism also seems to sidestep the challenge of demerging England from Britain at an institutional level. Efforts to treat England as a distinct unit through EVEL offer a deliberate if extremely limited attempt at the demerger of the Anglo-British institutional architecture. Recognizing that the state's legislature is also, increasingly, acting in an England-only capacity, EVEL seeks a means to provide safeguards (*sic*) for England within a legislature that remains otherwise unchanged. Ultimately, however, neither approach can escape the pull of those limiting conditions. Public attitudes appear to form a particular intractable barrier. Regional solutions in whatever form appear deeply unpopular. This same is not the case for EVEL, support for which would appear to be overwhelmingly strong. The problem here is rather that, while EVEL may have given England safeguards, it would appear that what the nation actually wants is a voice, something that EVEL simply cannot facilitate.

Recent proposals for England have deep historical roots, not least because, in the decades before Irish secession, the territorial constitution was a key preoccupation in UK politics in debates and controversies that, occasionally, extended to the place of England in any putative arrangements (Hazell 2006). In what follows we confine our analysis to the ideas put forward by the political parties since the 1997 general election that led to the advent of Scottish and Welsh devolution and acted as a precursor to the re-establishment of devolved institutions in Northern Ireland. Table 7.1 summarizes the different party positions on English governance since then, as set out in their respective general-election manifestos. It notes not only their different positions (organized according to the two main types of scheme outlined above) but also attempts to explain the diagnosis of the 'problem' that these proposed solutions were designed to address. Before we explore these various proposals in more detail, it is worth drawing attention to a number of general points that emerge when the whole period is viewed in comparative perspective. We shall note four, in particular.

First, there has been clear and persistent difference between the Conservatives, on the one hand, and Labour, in particular, on the other. For most of the period, the former concentrated on changes to legislative procedures at Westminster as a means of addressing the apparent iniquities summarized by the West Lothian question—that is, through EVEL. At the same time, the party deplored and/or promised to reverse moves towards regional devolution within England. This position was premised on the perceived need to rebalance the constitution following devolution in order to ensure that

England was not subject to iniquitous treatment, a belief that 'artificial regions' within England are wasteful and unnecessary, as well as support (in principle if seldom in practice) for stronger local government. Similar arguments were heard from UKIP during the 2015 general election—which was the only general election in which it was a genuinely significant political force.

For Labour and, at least up until the 2010 general election, for the Liberal Democrats, the alleged imbalances that required correction related largely if not wholly to the position of England's regions rather than to England qua England. Moreover, these imbalances were regarded as being at least as much economic as constitutional in character. Hence, support for the establishment of elected regional assemblies in England and, following the failure of the referendum for an Elected Assembly for North-East England in 2004, for a strengthening of regional-level institutions of other kinds.

Secondly, while this broad pattern of inter-party differentiation has persisted throughout the period covered in this analysis, with, in particular, Labour retaining a tenacious commitment to the utility of England's nine standard regions as units of governance, more recent elections have suggested an at least partial breakdown of the England versus English regions binary. By 2015, the Conservatives were supporting regional 'growth deals', the development of city and county regions, and the 'devolution' of some health and justice responsibilities to city region mayors, all while continuing to champion EVEL. They have continued to promote 'devolution' within England ever since, even if at a bewildering variety of different regional scales. Meanwhile, if only by implication, the party seems to believe that, with the introduction of EVEL, all that needed to be done to ensure equitable treatment for England has been achieved. The 2015 general election also suggested that Labour and the Liberal Democrats were at least willing to consider the possibility of establishing England-only procedures at Westminster, even as they continued to support the 'devolution' of power within England itself. Since then the Liberal Democrats have apparently reconciled themselves with the principle if not the exact form of EVEL. However, Labour's view appears less settled. It would seem that the party has decided simply to ignore the introduction of EVEL, while its 2017 pledge to establish a 'Minister for England' was not repeated in 2019.

The third point to make is that there appears to be very little appetite among any of the parties for any changes to the structure and organization of Whitehall in order to accommodate England. This is a further illustration of one of the most striking features of the story of UK-devolution-so-far—namely the deep reluctance to consider reforms to the structure of the central state as part of that wider devolution process. There could scarcely be a better illustration of this than the continued survival of the Scotland and Wales Offices—with their related cabinet positions—even after the overwhelming majority of both their staffs and functions have been transferred to the respective devolved administrations. The vagueness and constitutional incoherence of Labour's 2017 proposal for a Minister for England can also be called in evidence in support of this more general point.

Finally, it is striking that, with the sole exceptions of UKIP's 2015 plan for a St George's Day bank holiday for England and Labour's 2017 and 2019 pledges to introduce a St George's Day bank holiday as part of a package of four new patron saint bank holidays, the political parties have either not sought or have struggled to find other, more symbolic means of recognizing England and Englishness. This, in turn, may well be regarded as an inevitable consequence of the Anglo-British fusion that is one of the defining features of the state. After all, while recognizing or otherwise supporting distinctive institutions and/or languages/cultures is an option for assuaging national sentiment around the state's periphery, it is far from clear what the equivalent might be in the case of England. Again, England's dominance of the Anglo-British state serves almost totally to occlude England itself.

Regionalizing England

The case for delineating and empowering some form of regional level of government (however defined) within England exists independently of the case for or the reality of Scottish and Welsh devolution. By any comparative standard, England's governmental structures are among the most centralized in any modern democratic society. The corollary of this is that English local government is particularly weak and lacking in autonomous authority (Corpus et al. 2017). This weakness is long-standing but has been exacerbated in recent decades as a result of reforms pursued by both Labour and Conservative governments that have served—*inter alia*—to reduce or even remove altogether some of the key traditional functions of local government, as well as the severe budgetary challenges arising from post-financial-crisis austerity.

This centralization of power is accompanied by strikingly wide regional disparities in terms of economic performance and prospects. Notwithstanding the existence of pockets of deprivation in the capital, especially, prosperity is heavily skewed towards the south-east in general, and to London in particular.

As such, it is hardly surprising that there have been for many decades recurring arguments in favour of establishing intermediate-level institutions that would aim to 'rebalance' economic and wider social development (see, e.g.. Hogwood and Keating 1982). Logically speaking, these arguments do not lose their force whether Wales, for example, is governed via a pre-devolution Secretary of State or by the devolved National Assembly for Wales and Welsh Government.

It is also worth pointing out that there is no necessary contradiction between arguing in favour of some form of all-England layer of government and simultaneously arguing in favour of enhanced structures of regional governance within England. All-England structures of governance do not necessarily provide for an effective means of challenging regional disparities within England. Neither, conversely, does the development of regional governance structures within England necessarily address English grievances around England's place within the post-devolution UK (a point to which we return). It is possible to believe in both delineating England as a unit within the UK and an enhanced regional layer within England itself.

All that said, whatever the dictates of logic, it is nonetheless the case that, for most of the past few decades, the case for English regionalism has in practice been strongly linked to the arguments for and then the reality of Scottish and Welsh devolution. Until recently at least, the case for an enhanced regional tier of government (in whatever precise constitutional form) has been presented by both opponents and proponents as an alternative to the more explicit delineation of England qua England within the structures of the UK state.

There are several reasons why this might have been the case. Without aiming or claiming to be exhaustive, we might cite the following factors. First, the political momentum in favour of devolution generated in Scotland after the 1987 general election, in particular, created a 'political opportunity structure' of which campaigners in other parts of the state sought to take advantage. This was equally as true of campaigners for Welsh devolution as it was for supporters of English regional assemblies (see Mawson 1997; Wyn Jones and Scully 2012). They all sought to enter the political slipstream of the apparently unstoppable drive towards a Scottish parliament.

Secondly, in this period at least, there were striking similarities in terms of the arguments advanced in favour of Scottish and Welsh devolution, on the one hand, and arguments in favour of regional government in England, on the other. Indeed, before the results of the 2004 referendum crushed the hopes of campaigners for a North-East elected assembly, the arguments were more or less identical. In the early to mid-1990s, what we might term small 'n' nationalist arguments in favour of recognizing national identity were not the most significant element in the rhetorical armoury of supporters of Welsh and Scottish devolution (for Scotland, see Edwards 1989; Paterson 1998; for Wales, see Morgan and Roberts 1993; Wyn Jones 2001). Rather, campaigners focused on the need to democratize an existing layer of government so as to make it more legitimate and accountable to those whom that layer of government was meant to serve. This was also very much the case being advanced by enthusiasts for English regional government, including, at that point, the Labour Party itself (Labour Party 1995).

It is true, of course, that the existing structures of regional government in England were far weaker and much younger than those existing in Wales let alone Scotland. It is also true that, even if un- or understated, national identity played an important role in underpinning support in the latter two countries for some form of home rule. Nonetheless, the arguments deployed to make the case for English regions were essentially analogous: it was all about 'devolution'. Even if the case for regional governance now focuses on 'city and county regions' rather than government standard regions, and if democratic control or even legitimacy are of little contemporary concern, the language of 'devolution' lives on as a legacy of this different time. It lives on in part because it was regarded as political useful, which brings us to a third point.

Even if the policy justifications for English regionalism (in whatever form) have never relied on Scottish and Welsh devolution for their intellectual force, it has nonetheless suited the Labour Party, in particular, to give the impression that the development of an enhanced regional layer of government was the equivalent in England of the devolution processes for Scotland and Wales. In this regard, we should not underestimate the interest or the influence of Scottish and Welsh Labour MPs—or indeed, as already noted in Chapter 1, of their Scottish Liberal Democrat colleagues. In truth, English regionalism has had few more passionate advocates over the past two decades than unionist centre-left MPs representing non-English constituencies. For them, enhanced regional structures within England have been regarded as a means of heading off a reduction in their own status at Westminster, a development that they have equated with a threat to the long-term stability of the UK state itself (for a recent restatement, see Hain 2016).

Taking a diametrically opposed position, some of the staunchest opposition to English regionalism emanated from the Eurosceptic right, whose proponents regularly branded efforts to establish elected regional assemblies within England as part of a 'European plot' designed to divide and therefore neuter Britain.[6] Their argument provides a striking mirror image of the arguments deployed by 'Celtic' centre-left unionists. As we have already seen, for this latter group English regionalism was necessary to preserve Westminster, an institution whose very essence would allegedly be undermined if pressure to create 'two classes of MP' was not successfully resisted. But, for many on the Eurosceptic right, it was regional government itself that was the threat to Westminster. This venerable institution had already been gravely weakened by European integration. On this reading, the creation of elected regions within England would effectively deliver the *coup de grâce*. As already indicated, there was a distinctly conspiratorial dimension to this argument. The European Union, it was claimed, had demanded regionalization in order to 'abolish England'; proponents were merely willing dupes (see Sandford 2009a: 45).

Eurosceptic objections to English regions went beyond the merely theoretical. UKIP supporters, as well as, on occasion, supporters of the Campaign for an English Parliament, actively engaged in the constitutional conventions that had been intended to presage the establishment of regional assemblies for the South-West and the West Midlands. There is no doubt that their 'extremely vocal' presence stymied the work of the conventions (see Sandford 2009a: 45). In truth, however, the failure to achieve the establishment of elected regional assemblies, either there or in any other part of England, was overdetermined.[7]

There is no need here to rehearse the full story of the rise and fall of the elected regional assemblies project, and its replacement with the current, extraordinarily complex patchwork of meso-level governance arrangements that now exists in England. A brief chronology will suffice in order to provide a broad-brush outline of the process (see, *inter alia*, Mawsom 1997; Jeffery 2009; Sandford 2009a, b, 2016, 2017).

Even this much simplified overview in Table 7.2 serves to underline a fundamental truth about the English devolution experience. It is a story of complexity and instability; a story of almost constant churn and serial ad hoc-ery. Bodies have been established only to be abolished and replaced by new bodies, which often look quite similar to their predecessors but operate on the

---

[6] Dominic Cummings can be seen as embodying the close ties between Euroscepticism and opposition to English regionalism. The Director of Vote Leave first rose to political prominence as a leading figure in the (successful) campaign to oppose the Labour government's plans for a regional assembly for the North-East of England in 2004.

[7] In this context the establishment of the London Assembly is best understood as part of a process of re-establishing city-wide government for the capital city rather than as a species of regional government as envisaged by proponents of English regionalism.

Table 7.2 Regional-level governance in England since 1997—Timeline

1998	UK Government establishes regional development agencies (RDAs) for each English region
1998/9	UK Government establishes 'voluntary' regional chambers to oversee the RDAs
2002	UK Government government publishes its 'Your Region, Your Choice' white paper
2003	The Regional Assemblies (Preparations) Act becomes law, creating the opportunity for referendums on the establishment of elected regional assemblies
2004	(July) Draft Regional Assemblies Bill published, at the same time as referendums in the North- West and Yorkshire & Humber are postponed. (November) Referendum held in North- East in which proposals for an elected assembly are rejected by 77.9% per cent to Yes at 22.1% per cent (on a turnout of 47.1 per cent%)
2007	Following John Prescott's departure from Governmentgovernment, the already limited role of regional chambers reduced still further, with phasing- out to follow in 2010. HM Treasury publishes its review of sub-national economic development and regeneration, stating its aim of working together with local government to establish a statutory framework for city regional activity
2010	UK Government government announces the abolition of the regional development agencies (RDAs)—which takes place in 2012. Also announce the intention to establish Local Enterprise Partnerships (LEPs)—voluntary partnerships between local government and business—that will carry out some of the function of the RDAs
2011	First LEPs established
2012	Publication of 'No Stone Unturned: In Pursuit of Growth' (the 'Heseltine report') advocating the merging of various UK Government funding streams and their transfer to LEPs to allow greater local responsibility for economic development
2014	(September) In the aftermath of the Scottish independence referendum, alongside EVEL David Cameron speaks of the need to 'empower our great cities' (November) The first 'devolution deal' between the UK Government government and the Greater Manchester Combined Authority is announced ('the Northern Powerhouse')
2016	Cities and Local Government Devolution Act becomes law, allowing the creation of directly elected mayors for combined authorities and the 'devolution' of various powers, including housing, transport, planning, and police

basis of different boundaries and on the basis of different governance arrangements. Powers have also varied, not only over time but even—as is the case with the UK government's current 'devolution deals'—from area to area at the same time (see Sandford 2016: 267). This, it must be said, with little obvious rationale. One constant, however, is that, however configured, the powers of regional bodies always remain weak. There is certainly nothing in this story to suggest that there has been a decisive break from a highly centralized model of government that has characterized England for centuries past. Thus, even if we were to assume that the current model of city and county region-based 'devolution' has a long-term future—a heroically optimistic assumption given the history of the past two decades—it is very hard to envisage how it could ever become a stable model of governance covering the whole of England.

Why do schemes for English regional government have such an air of impermanence? Whatever other factors may be at play—Whitehall's deeply engrained centralist mindset, the personalities and predilections of various political leaders, and so on—most fundamental of all, we suggest, is the structural constraint imposed by the lack of public support. However packaged, empowered, and territorially delineated, regional schemes of government simply lack public legitimacy among the English electorate. Complexity and instability are a symptom of this absence of public support. In its absence, ad hoc-ery, secrecy, and convolution abound.

The key point, however, is that, even if the move to develop a regional tier of governance in England had begat a system that was more coherent and enjoyed wide public legitimacy, it could never provide a means of dealing with English grievance, let alone a means for positive recognition of English identity. Even in an administrative sense, England cannot be regionalized out of existence. For, unless there were to be regional legislatures in England endowed with full legislative powers along the lines of the devolved 'Celtic' parliaments, Westminster would remain England's de facto parliament for most legislative purposes. This has always been the fundamental weakness of the argument on the liberal left that regionalizing England was a means of 'balancing' the constitutional impact of devolving power to Scotland and Wales. Anything short of full constitutional parity leaves space for the West Lothian question to be asked and reasked. The Conservatives, by contrast, have correctly identified that assuaging English opinion requires explicitly recognizing England as a unit within the constitutional architecture of the state. As we shall see, their difficulty is rather that recognizing England in a manner that does not fundamentally challenge the Anglo-British fusion on which that state rests leads to a degree of change that is so minimal that it would appear to be barely recognizable to the general public.

Recognizing England

The warning was clear. The Conservatives' 1997 general-election manifesto stated that devolution to Scotland and Wales, a development to which the party was implacably opposed, 'would raise serious questions about whether the representation of Scottish and Welsh MPs at Westminster—and their role in matters affecting English affairs—could remain unchanged' (Table 6.1). In the event, the Scottish and Welsh electorates chose emphatically to reject John Major's party and its dire warnings about the way that Labour's devolution plans 'could well pull apart the Union'. Not a single constituency in either country would return a Conservative Member of Parliament at that election (nor in Wales, at least, at the subsequent one.) The Tories were also on the losing side in the referendums held in both countries on Labour's devolution proposals. Unsurprisingly, perhaps, the party would soon have to accept the reality of Scottish and Welsh devolution: indeed, the semi-proportional elect-oral systems used for the devolved legislatures (also, incidentally, opposed by the Conservatives) would offer the party a way back to relevance after their twin electoral wipeouts. Nonetheless, the party held fast to its belief that devo-lution to Scotland and Wales required some form of response for England.

As we have seen, however, the manifesto's wording was vague. It could be read as opening the door to either one (or even both) of the main options that have been canvassed as providing a means of assuaging English sensibilities since the time of the debates about Irish home rule in the late nineteenth and early twentieth centuries. These are, on the one hand, measures aimed at altering the composition of the House of Commons, and, on the other hand, proposals to change the way that Westminster operates internally (the classic discussion in Bogdanor 1999: 29–35).

The 'Stormont discount' approach, as it has become known, suggests that the appropriate way of responding to devolution outside England is to reduce the number of non-English MPs to the point that the devolved territories are under-represented (per head of population) in the House of Commons as compared to England.[8] The effect of this is to make it even less likely that non-English MPs would ever be in a position to overturn the views of the English majority. This was not only the 'solution' posited in some of the (abortive) attempts to legislate for Irish home rule but was the situation that actually pertained with respect to Northern Irish representation during the period in

---

[8] Scottish devolution was accompanied by a move to (largely) end previous Scottish over-representation at Westminster, which occurred at the time of the 2005 UK general election. By con-trast, Welsh over-representation never attracted the same degree of political attention, presumably because of the National Assembly's gradual evolution to its current status as a law-making Parliament. The consequence, however, is that, in comparative terms, Wales is now the most over-represented part of the state. The 2019 attempts to equalize constituency sizes across the UK were no more successful than the previous attempt by the Conservative-Liberal Democrat coalition in 2011, with the order paper never laid for the new recommendations of the four boundary commissions. As of this writing new legislation appears set to press forward with more equal constituencies but on the basis of retain-ing a 650-seat House of Commons.

which that territory was governed by the Stormont parliament—a period in which Northern Ireland had around a third fewer members of the Westminster parliament than was its 'due' (this approach has more recent champions—for example, Mclean 2013).

The alternative 'in-and-out' approach, as it was dubbed by Gladstone, suggests changing the internal procedures of Westminster, and in particular of the House of Commons, to ensure that an English majority cannot simply be ignored or carelessly overridden when legislating on domestic English matters. The basic idea is simple: deceptively so, perhaps. Non-English MPs would be included in some deliberations/procedures and excluded in others, all depending—of course—on the territorial reach of the matters under discussion. In truth, however, there are a host of potential versions of 'in-and-out' procedures. Furthermore, there is also plenty of room for disagreement over the extent to which those procedures that exclude non-English MPs should be binding over parliament as a whole. It should be apparent that these disagreements raise fundamental and unavoidable questions about the composition of the executive (for example, could a UK government function if it did not have a majority in England?) and, relatedly, about the doctrine of parliamentary sovereignty.

Whatever their differences, both the 'Stormont discount' and 'in-and-out' approaches share at least two common assumptions. The first and most obvious is that the policy challenge to be addressed is framed in terms of the danger that the views of a majority of English MPs could be overridden in a context in which Westminster continues to act at the sole legislature for England, while Scotland, Wales, and Northern Ireland enjoy devolved control over their own domestic affairs. In other words, the problem is the West Lothian question, and the goal is essentially defensive or negative: it is to avoid a situation in which the weight of English opinion could be overwhelmed by representatives from the state's periphery. But implicit in all of this is a second more fundamental assumption—an assumption so commonsensical that it appears to require no thought let alone exposition: the English require no other legislature than Westminster, for Westminster is England's parliament. Here stands revealed the central conundrum from the combination of devolution and the Anglo-British institutional fusion at the heart of the United Kingdom state. How can Westminster be simultaneously Britain's and England's parliament in a context in which non-English parts of the UK also have their own parliaments too?

Given New Labour's overwhelming parliamentary majorities (among English MPs too), the West Lothian question remained largely in abeyance during the early years of devolution. Nonetheless the very few examples of policies 'foisted' upon England by non-English MPs were, obviously, controversial enough to have generated a split in Labour ranks sufficient to allow Scottish and Welsh MPs voting with the government line to make the crucial difference.[9] Hence they were high enough in profile to ensure that the anomaly highlighted by the question did not entirely disappear from sight. The Conservatives maintained their general commitment to EVEL—or, less pithily, 'English and Welsh Votes for English and Welsh Laws' (EWVEWL!)—in both their 2001 and 2005 manifestos, while also maintaining their opposition to Labour's 'arbitrary regions' (Gay 2006).

The party's thinking about what EVEL might mean in practice remained rather rudimentary—more slogan than substance, as it were—until the publication of the report of the Conservative Democracy Task Force in 2008 (Conservative Democracy Task Force 2008). It remains an illuminating document, not least because of its influence on subsequent events. Chaired by Kenneth Clarke, the task force framed the problem to be addressed in essentially defensive terms. Asymmetric devolution had created the possibility—and occasional example—of England being unfairly treated. The aim was, therefore, to allow England a means of self-defence against such depredations. Or, in the words of the report, it sought to 'protect England from having measures that a majority of English MPs found unacceptable being passed by non-English votes'.

As for how to achieve this goal, the task force recommended a limited version of EVEL (which it contrasted with what it termed the 'full strength version') that would not challenge the 'tight linkages between executive and legislature that characterises the British system'. Under its proposals, only English MPs would be allowed to vote on England-only clauses at the committee and subsequent report stages of the legislative process (or English and Welsh MPs if they were England and Wales clauses[10]). The key point of the scheme is that English MPs would be handed an absolute veto. If a majority chose to reject a particular clause, that clause would fall. In order, however, to preserve parliamentary sovereignty—and ensure that a UK government could continue to govern even if its majority relied on non-English

---

[9] In 2003, the government relied on the votes of non-English MPs to override the wishes of a majority of English MPs in order to introduce foundation hospitals in England—a pattern repeated the following year for the introduction of university top-up fees in England (Russell and Lodge 2006: 70–5).

[10] Recall that it was only in 2007 that the National Assembly for Wales was granted the power to pass primary legislation, and then only under very tightly circumscribed conditions. These restrictions were very substantially eased in 2011.

members—the task force emphasized that at the final, Third Reading stage, the whole of the House would have the last word. It could at this point itself veto any amendments that had been previously put forward by English MPs for England-only legislation. The task force's preferred version of EVEL would operate, therefore, as a 'double-veto' or 'double-lock' system. If a UK government attempted to govern without an English majority, then both sides would have a strong incentive to compromise—or so the task force believed.

It was without doubt an ingenuous solution. But, without seeking to downplay the significance of parliamentary procedure, it can hardly be denied that theirs was a highly technical scheme proposing changes to procedures that few who were not intimately involved in them would claim to understand. Given that the task force's declared aim was to provide a backstop—a defence in extremis, so to speak—then, in its own terms, this was not an issue. But, in a context in which EVEL was being framed by some of its most vocal proponents as a necessary response to a very serious threat to English interests, and indeed as the equivalent of the creation of a de facto English parliament, Clarke and his colleagues might equally well be regarded as having summoned up a mouse.

The tension between the often-expansive rhetoric that has tended to accompany calls for EVEL, on the one hand, and carefully and deliberately constrained institutional solutions, on the other, was even more apparent in the report of the McKay Commission (The McKay Commission 2013). Chaired by a former Clerk of the House of Commons, Sir William McKay, the Commission was established as a result of the coalition agreement between the Conservatives and the Liberal Democrats after the 2010 general election. It sought to bridge the divide between the Conservatives' support for EVEL and the Liberal Democrats' opposition—which was in fact much more marked than the party's manifesto commitment to consider the position of England might imply. The political sensitivity of the subject highlighted the Commission's very tightly constrained terms of reference, with, for example, the 'Stormont discount' option explicitly disbarred.[11]

Its eventual report sought to advance two, almost certainly incommensurable, aims. On the one hand, it sought an institutional solution that could gain consensus support across the main political parties, which in turn put a premium on solutions that minimized change to prevailing practices. Thus, the

---

[11] The terms of reference are outlined on p. 5 of the Commission's report. Note, however, that the Commissioners nonetheless made clear their view that the 'Stormont discount' approach 'would be—and would be seen to be—unfair and inimical' to the electorates of the devolved territories' (The McKay Commission 2013: 25).

idea of an English veto was rejected in favour of a 'double-counting' approach. When the Commons voted on England-only clauses, two results would be published: the first would include all Members; the second only those MPs representing English constituencies. While the former would be binding, in those cases where the latter result was different, it was expected 'the UK majority' would, 'eventually', recall the need to defend its seats in England at the next General Election' (The McKay Commission 2013: 49). This was EVEL *de minimis*.

Yet, at the same time and apparently persuaded by evidence from, *inter alia*, the Future of England Survey (FoES), the Commissioners also sought to recast the 'Welsh Lothian Question' as a broader 'English Question' (The McKay Commission 2013: 14–21). They argued that the English were not only resentful about the anomalies crystallized by the West Lothian question, but that they also craved wider recognition of England itself within the United Kingdom. Accordingly, the Commission's recommended response was that the polity as a whole do more to recognize England as a unit in its own right. Political parties should publish 'sections on policies for England in the manifestos', while 'some time in the debate on the Queen's Speech each session should be specifically allocated to the Government's proposals for England' (The McKay Commission 2013: 53). In other words, it was not simply a matter of constructing a mechanism to defend English interests: England needed and deserved a voice of its own, even if, in the House of Commons at least, it was to be a deliberately muted one.

Given the deep antipathy among Scottish Liberal Democrat MPs, in particular, to any form of EVEL, the McKay recommendations did not even gain the support of the government that had commissioned them. Labour also remained implacably hostile, with the Commission's carefully crafted attempt to find a solution acceptable to it falling on the stoniest of grounds. Indeed, when David Cameron announced in the wake of the Scottish independence referendum that there was an 'English question' (*sic*) to be answered, in contrast to the all-party post-referendum deliberations in both Scotland and Wales (the Smith Commission and the so-called St David's Day process, respectively), the process established to address the position of England was in effect boycotted by both the Conservatives' coalition partners and the official opposition alike. Unsurprisingly, perhaps, the recommendations of the Conservative-dominated committee tasked with answering the West Lothian question, chaired by William Hague, were closer to the Democracy Task Force proposals than to those of the McKay Commission (BBC Politics 2014). Crucially, they supported the establishment of a 'double-veto' system, with the English veto to be wielded via newly created 'legislative grand committees' to be inserted in the legislative process after the report stage. It was, in essence, this proposal that would be introduced following the Conservatives' 2015 general-election victory (see Glover and Kenny 2018).

Unlike Scottish, Welsh, and Northern Irish devolution, statute-based constitutional reforms introduced following popular referendums, EVEL is nothing more (or less) than a revision of the procedures of the House of Commons—procedures that can be changed on the basis of a simple majority vote among its members. Despite the vocal opposition of Labour and Scottish National Party (SNP) MPs (not a single opposition MP supported its introduction), by October 2015 EVEL was a reality.[12] Since then the system has operated with remarkably little fuss or, indeed, attention (see Glover and Kenny 2018). There can be little doubt that some of the dire warnings made by opponents of the system have proven to be unfounded. Parliamentary draftswomen and men do not appear to have found the task of drafting legislation in ways that make clear which particular clauses apply to which particular parts of the United Kingdom particularly difficult or onerous. Nor does the Speaker's role appear to have become unduly politicized as a result of the process of territorial designation. Even so, it must also be admitted that the system has been operating in particularly benign circumstances. The Conservative governments in power from 2015 to 2017, from 2017 to 2019, and then subsequently have all held a majority of English seats. Not only that, but consumed by the ramifications of the 2016 referendum, both have had thin domestic policy agendas. In such a context, the EVEL arrangements were never likely to do more than operate quietly in the background as an unused failsafe device. The test will come if and when English and UK House of Commons majorities ever diverge.

Herein lies the rub. The overwhelming numerical dominance of England within the UK state and the partisan preferences of the four UK electorates mean that, when envisaged in purely defensive terms, EVEL is unlikely ever to act as a serious constraint on a Conservative government but might well be a source of considerable irritation to a Labour or Labour-led administration. As a result, it is not hard to envisage that one of the first acts of any such government would be to sweep away the current arrangements. All it would require would be a simple vote in the House of Commons. With the current arrangements unobtrusive to the point of invisibility and un-noticed by all

---

[12] For the key debate and vote, see HC Debate, 22 October 2015.

but a very few constitutional aficionados, they can hardly be described as entrenched. Indeed, recent FoES data suggest that the majority of voters in England are completely unaware of them, and, to the extent that some individuals are aware, they believe the proposals do not go far enough.[13] The introduction of EVEL does not appear to have stemmed demand for EVEL. Even after implementing by far the most popular option for English governance, public opinion in England remains unassuaged.

As a thought experiment it is worth considering how different things might have been had EVEL somehow been envisaged and enacted as a means of creating an institutional forum through which a distinctively English political debate could emerge. Could this have helped entrench and legitimate the new order? It would certainly have been an outcome consistent with the admittedly still inchoate public attitudes explored in Chapter 3. But, as we have seen, the architects of EVEL always had a much more limited aim in mind—namely, providing England with a defence mechanism against the possibility of an English majority being overridden by the votes of non-English MPs. This because doing more would immediately run up against the structural constraint that is the institutional fusion of English and UK-wide governmental institutions. Indeed, to create a forum that provides England with a voice—not de facto, by dint of omission, but deliberately, by dint of positive recognition—would surely mean a decisive rupture of this fusion. Even if this were achieved, this would inevitably bring into play a further structural constraint—namely, the overwhelming size of England. If England were to be demerged from the statewide apparatus in some meaningful way, what kind of statewide constitutional order could accommodate and manage the resulting, heavily imbalanced polity? EVEL avoids raising these issues precisely by being so deliberately limited in scope and ambition.

Conclusion: The Limits of Accommodation

This chapter has explored the way in which three key constraints—the pattern of public attitudes in England we have outlined in earlier chapters, the institutional fusion of English and all-UK governmental institutions, and the overwhelming size of England relative to the other constituent territories of the union—have served to shape, limit, or undermine attempts to accommodate England within the post-devolution United Kingdom. The verdict

[13] See Henderson (2018b); Henderson and Wyn Jones (2018).

has been a harsh one, but unavoidably so. One might be forgiven for concluding that each successive scheme for regional government has been even less coherent than its predecessor. Nothing has challenged—or so far seems likely to challenge—the highly centralized Whitehall way. And, to the extent that English regionalism is meant to assuage English grievance, it seems entirely to miss the point. EVEL has operated since 2015 as a highly technical failsafe defence against an eventuality that is likely to occur only very, very occasionally, given the demographic realities of the state. Unsurprisingly, very few seem to have noticed its existence. Meanwhile the English, it would appear, continue to feel aggrieved and continue to feel that they are being denied the voice they erroneously seemed to believe that they would be given by EVEL.

What, then, are the alternatives? Schemes for an English parliament certainly exist, with two different constitutional models having been identified (Russell and Sheldon 2018). The first might be described as EVEL-max. Westminster would continue to operate as both an English and a UK parliament, but non-English MPs would be completely removed from the legislative process for England, and, indeed, most sittings would be wholly devoted to English business. Only on those days dedicated to statewide issues would both English and non-English MPs sit together. Most proponents of this 'dual-mandate' approach envisage that the UK government would also retain its current English and all-UK roles. This, of course, means that the government would be accountable to two different chambers (one English only and the other all state) with (almost certainly) a different political balance in each and even (though far less likely) different political majorities—prospects that raise the spectre of some pretty obvious practical difficulties for the operation of parliament as well as real doubts as to how such a system would be viewed in the three other constituent territories.

The second proposed model envisages the creation of an English parliament and government operating alongside similarly constituted parliaments and governments in the currently devolved territories, all nested below a separate UK parliament and government that would control all-state functions, all of which would clearly constitute a degree of constitutional change that has no parallel in the history of the modern state. We have argued in a previous chapter that the English, in particular, seemed supportive of radical constitutional change. But, crucially, this is constitutional change in the service of continuity and tradition. It is hard to envisage how significant support could be mustered for a massive programme of constitutional change that would, in essence, throw over the key institutions of the current Anglo-UK state. But, even if it could, it is surely likely that an English parliament and government representing 84 per cent of the state's population would soon begin to chafe at the restrictions inherent in operating under UK-level institutions with responsibility for foreign and macro-economic policy.

Whatever the model, schemes for an English parliament also remain trapped by the constraints we have identified—constraints which, at least until now, seem to describe some very real limits to the possibilities for accommodating England and English sentiment. Which of course does not necessarily mean that one or other—or even yet another—scheme should not be attempted. The UK has a long history of coping with arrangements that constitutional theorists regard as anomalous or problematic: an English parliament may one day join their number. Our point has not been to advocate any particular approach to the governance of England within the UK but rather to illuminate how the British state has sought to accommodate English nationalism, and the extent to which such efforts are constrained by certain seemingly immutable facts. Finally, it is worth underlining that England is not the only player in this particular drama. We noted at the outset of this chapter that it remains unclear how the experience of Brexit will impact on attitudes in England. But the same is equally true of attitudes in the rest of the UK, as well. It is often suggested that Brexit is making a united Ireland and independent Scotland more likely. If so, then we also need to acknowledge that either eventuality (and certainly both in combination) would significantly impact on the nature of the challenge that is accommodating England.

8

Analysing England

In this book we have explored political and, in particular, constitutional preferences in England through the prism of national sentiment. English political attitudes are not as they once were. English identity has strengthened, and, to the extent that Englishness was ever truly apolitical, then this is clearly no longer the case. Instead, Englishness has become associated with devo-anxiety—that is, a sense of grievance about the way that England is treated within the UK and associated support for the recognition in some form of England as a political community in its own right. Beyond the borders of the state, Englishness is strongly associated with deep Euroscepticism as well as pride in Britain's imperial past and a continued commitment to aspects of its legacy. The other side of this story is that Britishness works differently in different parts of Britain, with elements of what we have termed an English world view shared by those who identify as British in Scotland and Wales.

During the course of our discussion we have sought to identify possible explanations for the emergence of this world view. Exasperation at the consequences for England of devolution to other parts of the UK and the perceived unfairness of differential levels of public spending, as well as deep resentment against the influence of external others, are clearly part of that story. Another theme running through the work is that, for many in England, change appears necessary, not for its own sake, but rather to ensure that everything can 'remain the same'. But incremental change to facilitate a broader status quo has had unintended consequences. What we have termed serial ad hocery—namely, a series of constitutional tweaks and reforms that appear detached from concern with first principles—seems only to have further undermined faith in the status quo while strengthening preferences for an English model of governance.

Chapter 7 examined the profound challenges posed to the state by some of the domestic dimensions of this English world view. In this final chapter, we shift our attention from the political realm to the analytical. We set ourselves three tasks. First, we explore how various academic literatures help us to explain more fully why we are seeing what we are seeing in England. Second, we identify how our findings settle debates—or at least lend more support for some views than others—about the relationship between Englishness and Britishness as well as contribute to the wider academic literature. Third and finally, we outline how our findings suggest necessary adaptations to the way that British politics is studied. The methodological and, for want of a better term, infrastructural implications of our findings are far-reaching, calling into question some of the most deep-seated and taken-for-granted assumptions about how, for example, we collect data as well as the lenses through which we analyse them.

On English Nationalism

When we established the Future of England Survey (FoES) in 2011 we did so on the basis that it seemed likely to us that the increasingly obvious manifestations of English national identity might well have political–constitutional implications. Here was something worth exploring. At that point we did not envisage that we would end up preparing a monograph-length study of an English nationalism that has subsequently transformed UK politics.

Despite the evidence of the past few years, any mention of nationalism in the context of England and English remains incongruous to many. As Michael Ignatieff (1994: 166) once said: 'Living on an island, having exercised imperial sovereignty over more excitable peoples, priding themselves on possessing the oldest continuous nation state in existence, the English have a sense of a unique dispensation from nationalist fervour.' Nonetheless, the literature on nationalism has much to offer those seeking further to investigate the emergence, adaptation, and reproduction of the world view that we have sought to capture and analyse in these pages (our own previous work on nationalism includes Henderson 2007; Wyn Jones 2007). Specifically we believe that it can help us to understand several features in our data: the elision between Englishness and Britishness; the fact that Britishness does not mean the same things in different parts of the state and that it operates as something of an empty vessel; and the way that Englishness is characterized by devo-anxiety and Euroscepticism as part of a wider world view that contains an at-least implicit set of assumptions about the nature of legitimate government.

Much of the literature on nationalism has famously been constructed around a series of binaries that contain within them a strong (if sometimes implicit) normative ranking: civic nationalism (positive) versus ethnic

nationalism (negative); political nationalism (positive) versus cultural nationalism (negative); western nationalism (positive) versus eastern nationalism
(negative); anti-imperialist nationalism (positive) versus great state nationalism
(negative), and so on. Even more ubiquitous is the juxtaposition of 'our' patriotism (positive) to 'their' nationalism (negative). Some of these categorizations
make explicit use of the English case. So, for example, Hans Kohn's hugely
influential 1944 book *The Idea of Nationalism*, which famously juxtaposes
western-civic with eastern-ethnic nationalism, is based in part on his 1940
essay 'The Genesis and Character of English Nationalism' (Kohn 1940, 1944).
But, however derived, these various binaries now tend to be regarded by most
scholars of nationalism as being of little use analytically speaking—occluding
more than they illuminate. Real-world nationalisms cannot be so neatly
corralled—or, it should be said, so easily tamed. There is little to be gained,
therefore, from attempting to shoehorn the English nationalism explored in
the previous chapters into one or other of these categorizations.

But there are nonetheless insights from the nationalism literature that—at
the very minimum—point to areas worthy of further exploration if we wish
to make sense of the 'why' and 'how' of English nationalism. In the first
instance we discuss four: Miroslav Hroch's insights concerning nationalist
mobilization (which we have already briefly alluded to in Chapter 3);
arguments by Tom Nairn, supplemented by Matthew Levinger and Paula
Franklin Lytle, about the contemporary and future-oriented relevance of
nationalist historiography; Michael Billig's arguments on 'banal nationalism';
and John Breuilly's on political nationalism.

Czech historian Miroslav Hroch's path-breaking comparative study (1985)
of nationalist movements among the (then) stateless nations of nineteenth-
century Europe is regarded as one of the bona fide classics of nationalism
studies. In it Hroch seeks both to identify the common elements in these
otherwise very different stories as well as to develop an explanation for why
some of those movements enjoyed success while others did not. Given his
focus on smaller nations, it is not surprising that England and English
nationalism feature hardly at all. Yet, despite this, Hroch's analysis may well be
relevant to the subject matter of this book. In order to understand why, it is
necessary (briefly and brutally) to summarize some of his key arguments.

Hroch argues that there are three stages to nationalist agitation. Step A is
what we might term the antiquarian stage. Here a national past is forged
through a focus on tradition, linguistic codification, and so forth, some of
which may consist of historical recovery, but 'the invention of tradition' is a
rather typical feature (Hobsbawm and Ranger 1984). Step B occurs when

conscious efforts are made to persuade or otherwise inculcate within the target population the belief that they are indeed part of a nation and inheritors to the national patrimony identified or developed at Step A—it is worth recalling here that one of the central if controversial insights of the nationalist literature is that nationalists create nations.[1] Step C occurs when the national consciousness so-formed ('reborn' is the classic nationalist formulation) becomes a mass social phenomenon.

There is a great deal that could be said about how Hroch's schema could potentially throw light on developments even in twenty-first-century England. Particularly germane are Hroch's arguments about the determinants for nationalist 'success' in moving from Step B to Step C. According to his analysis, a necessary condition for success is that nationalists link their national cause to the material interests of their target, national audience. So, on this reading, the fear that 'undue' Scottish influence over a UK Labour government would lead to Scotland being given even more favourable (and therefore unfair) treatment in terms of public spending, and so on, made concrete more abstract concerns about the role of non-English Members of Parliament in legislative votes for England, creating the conditions for successfully nationalist mobilization by the Conservatives. Similarly, a precondition for nationalist success in 2016 was a belief—justified or not—that leaving the European Union would release additional funding for and capacity in public services by stopping the transfer of 'billions of pounds' to Brussels and putting an end to 'uncontrolled' immigration. In other words, contra much of the current debate among political scientists about the Brexit referendum result, it is not a matter of choosing between 'cultural' or economic concerns as the key determinant of the Leave campaign's victory. The issue is rather the success (or otherwise) of campaigners in persuading voters that they are linked to each other in ways that demand a nationalist response.

Another key argument from the nationalism literature portrays how nationalism simultaneously looks back into history and forward into the future. Tom Nairn's essay (1981b) 'The Modern Janus' is one of the most famous exemplars of this argument. Far from living in the past, as their critics are wont to claim, nationalists utilize particular understandings of the nation's past for wholly contemporary purposes, in order to promote both particular views of the here and now as well as present visions of a potential future. Matthew

---

[1] The view associated with Ernest Gellner, in particular. For a brilliant critical overview, see O'Leary (1998).

Levinger and Paula Franklin Lytle (2001) suggest that nationalist rhetoric has a triadic structure: the 'golden age' of the past juxtaposed with a 'fallen present' with the promise of a 'new dawn' should the nation return to the values and habits that propelled it to its past glories. All very biblical, of course, but all deeply resonant of the rhetorical structure of the arguments put forward by proponents of Brexit in the run-up to and aftermath of the 2016 referendum. For the Brexiteers, an arguably idealized version of Britain's Second World War history has acted as a promissory note for a better future—and of a solution to all practical difficulties—once the nation has 'freed' itself from the shackles of Europe. After all, if we could 'stand alone' in 1940, then nothing except an absence of the requisite grit and determination can stop 'the nation' almost eighty years later (for an illustrative example, see Littlejohn 2019; cf. d'Ancona 2018).

Here again is a key area of study for those who would seek to understand better the politics of Brexit. While this apparent fixation with the Second World War clearly strikes many Remain-inclined observers as gauche or embarrassing, the literature on nationalism would suggest that it has been a vital tool for securing English nationalist success. As already argued in Chapter 4, a key part of the difficulty for those seeking to counter its rhetorical powers is that this version of the Anglo-British past would appear to be hegemonic—shared by 'reluctant Europeans' such as David Cameron and ardent Eurosceptics alike. It need hardly be said that this is the version of the Anglo-British past that is endlessly reproduced through everyday processes both banal and more deliberate. What is less clear from this particular perspective is why English nationalism would seek to draw on an explicitly British past. For this we turn to a third approach to nationalism.

Michael Billig's much cited *Banal Nationalism* (1995) focuses on the ways in which a certain ordering of territory and identity are made to appear natural and 'commonsensical' by uncounted numbers of everyday, unnoticed (hence banal) signs and social interactions. The central motif of the book is the 'Stars and Stripes' banner flying largely unbidden on post-office buildings in the US. But other examples abound, from the delineation of state boundaries on television weather maps to the routine use of dozens of small national flags to decorate Christmas trees in Norway. In this way the basic claims of particular nationalisms about the ordering of identity, territory, and governance are constantly reproduced in the everyday without most of us ever being fully conscious of this. Moreover, flags on buildings, lines on maps, and faces or symbols on stamps are merely the tip of the proverbial iceberg. School and university curriculums, public rhetoric, the names of state institutions, and so on all play the same role, all serving to naturalize a certain ordering of identity and political–territorial organization. At the risk of stating the obvious, then, it is important to underline that this is true of England too. Nationalist assumptions are being constantly reproduced.

What our research makes clear is that England is different or at least highly unusual as the referent object of this nationalist reproduction—that is, the identity of the nation that is being referred to and hence reproduced is opaque and unstable. It is seldom straightforwardly England. Yet England is also always present. This apparent paradox becomes more readily understandable when we recall our discussion of the Anglo-British fusion that is so central to the state's institutional architecture – a fusion that has as one of its characteristic consequences a deep reluctance on the part of the UK government, public and civil-society bodies, political parties, and indeed journalists, to name 'England'. And yet it is England that politicians and commentators are referring to when they cite, as they routinely do, 'a thousand years of British history'. Post-devolution it is England and not Britain (and certainly not the UK) that is the real referent when mention is made of 'British' health policy or education policy or housing or local government, and so on. Some sports provide the only real exception to this general rule. The overall result is that the banal nationalism that reproduces nationalism in England tends to reproduce simultaneously the 'English' and 'British' dimensions of English nationalism that were the focus of Chapters 3 and 4 in particular, thus reinforcing the tendency to elide between Englishness and Britishness. This contrasts sharply with the Scottish and Welsh manifestations of banal nationalism, which demarcate Scottish and Welsh identities that are distinct from Britishness—a characteristic that long predated devolution but has arguably become ever marked since then, as devolved instititions have sought to stress distinctive Scottish and Welsh values and policy preferences.

But, relatedly, even as the elision between Englishness and Britishness continues to be reproduced among the English populace, the very fact of devolution, the Scottish independence referendum, and so on all serve to render this elision less stable. Recognizing this helps to clarify, in turn, what might otherwise appear to be a contradiction at the heart of the structure of attitudes associated with English nationalism that has been explored in previous chapters—namely, that first, as the English component of the English–British elision has assumed greater importance, the political salience of Britishness in England has shifted, resulting in a depoliticized Britishness in England and a fractured Britishness across Britain. Second, the elision, references to an explicitly British past, and the triadic structure of nationalist rhetoric all help to explain how English nationalism can appear to be simultaneously a form of imperialism nationalism and, for want of a better description, a form of anti- or post-colonial nationalism. In its imperial nationalist guise, English nationalism manifests a sense of state destiny—a civilizing mission as yet unfilled (Kumar 2000). This mission is a British one rather than restricted to England, but it is the English who are portrayed as its creators and its custodians. It was they who forged an internal union ('the first English empire') across these islands and then expanded its power across the globe. Self-determination for former colonies brought the external empire to an end, and now devolution seems to be bringing to an end, or at least fundamentally transforming, the first, internal empire, thus severely constraining the English mission. At the same time, anti- or postcolonial English nationalism—here focused on England not Britain—views England as being maligned and mistreated by the internally imperial British state, largely erased from public life by a reluctance to mention England explicitly, abandoned by former partners through devolution, and hemmed in by outsiders exerting influence where they should not. The two are bound together, superiority lost and abandonment by others—Holmes and Moriarty over the Reichenbach Falls.

Not only can we draw on the nationalism studies literature to make sense of the politicized English national identity that has been the focus of this book, but our study also raises far-reaching questions for some of the most revered contributions to that literature. Briefly to illustrate this point, let us focus on John Breuilly's celebrated book *Nationalism and the Nation State*. As the title suggests, Breuilly's key argument (1993: 14) is that nationalism—which (cf. Michael Billig) he views almost exclusively in terms of oppositional politics to the prevailing status quo—can be understood only in the context of 'the character of the modern state'. It is this (reciprocal) relationship between particular nationalism and the particular modern state that, in his view, explains why English nationalism, for example, focuses on parliamentary institutions rather than cultural or other markers. Noting the 'crystallisation of an English national idea around parliament', he goes on to observe that this had 'implicit implications of subordination for those who were not defined or did not wish to define themselves as English within the British Isles' (Breuilly 1993: 85, 87). Other nationalisms reflect their own particular contexts, and specifically different types of relationships with different types of states.

Classifying across a very wide range of cases, Breuilly (1993: 2–14) distinguishes between three types of nationalism: separation nationalism, reform nationalism, and unification nationalism, all three of which exist in opposition either to states that make no claims to being nation states (for example, Austro-Hungary or the Ottoman Empire), or, alternatively, to those that do. In Breuilly's terms, the Anglo-British nationalism that we have explored in the preceding chapters is an example of 'reform nationalism' within a state that evidently understands itself as fully-fledged nation state. It would be labelled as reform nationalism in part by default, because it makes no sense to classify English or Anglo-British nationalism as an example either of unification nationalism or, despite hyperbolic talk about a 'European super-state', of separation nationalism, but also, as has been amply demonstrated in previous pages, because English nationalism seeks to reform the state in fundamental ways.

But this classification in turn raises two fundamental challenges for Breuilly's arguments. First, he has almost nothing to say about what he terms 'reform nationalism in old nation-states' beyond a discussion of fascism during the interwar years in Germany, Italy, and Romania (Breuilly 1993: 288–318). The only other form of reform nationalism he considers, what he terms 'reactionary nationalism', 'rarely becomes very powerful' (Breuilly 1993: 251). Secondly, Breuilly seems to suggest that nationalism is certain to lose— if it has not already lost—much of its salience in developed states. Towards the end of his best-known work, Breuilly (1993: 401) argues that, 'especially in the developed world where those states are increasingly concerned with the effective management of more or less free market economies, the conditions for the emergence of...nationalist movements largely cease to exist'.

Given, however, that it would be politically ill-advised and analytically nonsensical to seek to understand English nationalism as a species of fascism, and given also the importance of its impact on the UK's geopolitical posture, it seems clear that there is much more that could be said about 'reform nationalism' than is allowed for in Breuilly's treatment. Not only that, but the efflorescence and subsequent reverberations of English and Anglo-British nationalism suggest very strongly that any suggestion that nationalism has lost its potency even in developed societies is wide of the mark. All of which suggests in turn the need to think again about the claims central to some of the classics of nationalism studies.

Having highlighted briefly how key works in nationalism might help us to understand what is and what is not happening in England (and vice versa), we turn now to how our findings relate to some of those debates that relate more specifically to England and Englishness.

Taking Englishness Seriously

Unsurprisingly, one key issue in the extant literature on Englishness is precisely the relationship between Englishness and Britishness and, by extension, English and British nationalism. It is a relationship that has been conceived in multiple different ways. It is possible, however, to differentiate between three general approaches. The first regards Britishness as constraining and containing what would otherwise be a dangerous Englishness. In direct contrast, the second regards Britishness as a hard, geopolitical carapace that, depending on perspective, alternatively facilitates or stifles an Englishness that is conceived as being softer and gentler in character. A third view regards Britishness as an extension of Englishness. Here we consider the extent to which our findings provide support for one or other of these understandings.

There is a long-standing tendency, most obvious among Scottish unionists but certainly not limited to them, to regard Britishness as a transnational identity that transcends (while remaining complementary with) the different national identities of these islands (Kidd 2008). A more recent strand of thought, perhaps most obviously linked to the movement for racial equality but also to New Labour's post-devolution attempts actively to promote Britishness, posits that Britishness provides the basis for an inclusive, multi-ethnic national identity—with British nationalism (or, invariably, 'patriotism') supplying an important social glue (Brown and Alexander 1999—cf. Wyn Jones 2001; Nairn 2006).

All of this is based on two (largely unstated) assumptions. The first is the notion that Britishness is separate or at least separable from Englishness and can therefore become the carrier for a different set of values and attitudes from those associated with the latter. The second is that, unconstrained by the ameliorating effects of Britishness, Englishness is dangerous, either because—for unionists—left as the legitimating narrative for the state's institutions, it will lead to tensions with other national groups within the state, who will be left with an intolerable choice between assimilation and separation; or, alternatively, because—for those concerned with integrating the ethnic minorities that have settled in England since the Second World War—Englishness is regarded as irredeemably tainted in ways that make it unsuitable as a vehicle for promoting a genuinely inclusive society. At times Englishness itself is the target—as being apparently more insular and xenophobic than its more civic counterparts in Scotland and Wales. At other times, however, we see all sub-state identities being viewed as inherently more tribal and atavistic than those statewide identities that are the bedrock of flourishing democratic societies. But, whatever the reasoning, the conclusion is clear: English nationalism must be vigorously resisted.

The second approach posits the existence of a softer, gentler, even bucolic English core sheltering within the hard, polished shell of Britishness. Michael Kenny's study *The Politics of English Nationhood* (2014) is particularly enlightening on the ways in which so much of the traditional discussion of Englishness has been premised on this high-political British versus apolitical Englishness binary. Normatively speaking, both the British and English dimensions of this binary have been viewed in positive terms—the security of British protection allowing George Orwell's famed 'crowds in big towns, with their mild knobby faces, their bad teeth and gentle manners' and 'old maids biking to Holy Communion through the mists of the autumn morning' to continue with their lives unmolested (Orwell 1941: 10–11). But this understanding of England and Englishness also allows for a very different sense of the possibilities of England if, for whatever reason, the future of Britain is called into question.

For some commentators on the right, the combination of devolution to the state's periphery and the hollowing-out of Englishness at home (symbolized by the continuing decay of the Anglican Church) means that it is time for England to slough off the increasingly tattered shell of Britishness. Not only could England survive such a development; it may well be the only way of saving it (Heffer 1999; Scruton 2000). In a rather different vein, some English progressives believe that, by more clearly differentiating Englishness from the remains of imperial Britishness, a different sense of national identity can be forged—a sense of identity that could undergird a more inclusive and equal society as well as facilitating a different kind of relationship with the other peoples of these islands (see, e.g., Bragg 2006; Kingsnorth 2009). Relatedly, some associated with the Labour Party in England have argued that, not only can their party ill afford to abandon Englishness to the right and centre-right, but that Englishness contains within it the resources for a revived centre-left (for one example among many, see Denham 2018). There are clearly fundamental differences between these views. It is nonetheless noteworthy that both assume that England and Englishness are (potentially) seperable from Britain and Britishness and treat England as a so-far unrealized political community.

A third approach views British nationalism as an extension of English nationalism. There are several variants of this argument. For Linda Colley

(2009), British nationalism served to engender loyalty for the institutions of the expanded English state among the Scots, in particular, after the Treaty of Union of 1707. The belief that modern Britishness is an effort to engender loyalty to a substantively English state explains why some Celtic nationalists have viewed British nationalism as a form of false consciousness (Evans 1981). In equally pungent vein, academic John Loughlin (2011: 131, 133) argues that British nationalism 'is essentially the imperialist form of English nationalism'; 'an English nationalism that imposed itself on the other three nations of the kingdom'. More benignly, others have viewed post-Second World War 'welfare state nationalism' as inculcating a common sense of British identity based on and bound by common endeavour (Béland and Lecours 2008).

Others see British nationalism as an extension of English nationalism—according to Liah Greenfeld (1993), the first nationalism of all—in the sense that it has served as a legimating narrative for the governing institutions of the (originally English) state whose territorial reach was expanded to encompass—at its high-water mark—all of these islands (see also Kumar 2006). This would also appear to be an implication of Wellings's seminal exploration of the relationship between Euroscepticism and English nationalism. For him, English nationalism is 'a defence of Westminster sovereignty': thus 'resistance to Europe became England's nationalism, even as it sought to defend British sovereignty' (Wellings 2012: 11, 223).

Our findings offer cold comfort to adherents of two of the three understandings of the relationship between Englishness and Britishness that we have just outlined. The idea that Britishness is somehow 'untainted' by the claims of English nationalism is clearly called into question. Rather, English identifiers are strongly attached to a version of Britishness that is freighted with nationalist 'content'. While this is a sense of Britishness that is shared by many/most of those who feel British in Scotland and Wales, it is—paradoxically enough—a view that does not tend to be shared by those in England who feel exclusively or predominantly British. Given this, it is far from obvious how Britishness can act as a multinational unifing force embracing everyone in the state or how it might be repurposed to undergird an inclusive, multi-ethnic society.

Similarly, the desire to recover or reinvent a version of political Englishness that might sit more easily alongside the political identities of the rest of the post-devolution UK may well be laudable (although for a recent dissenting opinion, see Niven 2019). Moreover, we would certainly not wish to claim that the emergence of different understandings of Englishness is neither possible nor of normative benefit: there are many potential narratives of

Englishness that have been and might yet been woven from the available raw materials (an argument we have made repeatedly—see Wyn Jones et al. 2012: 31–4; 2013: 37–9; Jeffery et al. 2014: 33–4). Nonetheless, it is also very clear from our analysis that a political and politicized Englishness not only already exists but is also widely felt. This Englishness is associated with a sense of grievance towards Scotland, in particular, as well as a still inchoate sense that England should be governed differently—a feeling that we believe is ultimately unlikely to be satisfied with the English votes for English laws (EVEL) reforms introduced in 2015. It is also strongly associated with a set of assumptions about Britain and the country's rightful place in the world. For progressives and traditionalists alike, this makes the task of reinvention all the more challenging.

Our findings suggest that it is more appropriate to view British nationalism as an extension of rather than a negation of English nationalism. Metaphorically speaking, England and Englishness would seem to stand as the high-walled keep at the centre of concentric circles of belonging. Britain forms the inner curtain wall. The 'kith and kin' of old White Dominions and the US make up an outer wall. Beyond that lies a moat separating those who belong from those who do not. While moats can, of course, be crossed, walls scaled, and buildings repurposed, it would be a mistake to underestimate the solidity of this mental construct or underplay the magnitude of the task facing those who might wish to challenge the ways that those who feel English understand England, Britain, and their place in the world.

In addition to throwing light on the ways in which the relationship between Englishness and Britishness tends to be framed, our findings have wider implications for the study of multinational states and contemporary nationalism, more generally.

Given the dominant position of England within the UK, one might assume that the study of English nationalism would draw heavily on the 'majority nationalism' literature (Lecours and Nootens 2009a; Gagnon et al. 2011). After all, it is ostensibly a literature that focuses on the ways in which 'state nationalism'—that is, the nationalism that forms a central part of the legitimating narrative for the institutions of the central state—'is often penetrated by the culture and traditions of a dominant group' within that state (Lecours and Nootens 2009b). Thus, even if the formal rhetoric of state nationalism might well seek to portray the political community of the state in plurinational or multinational terms, the reality (at least according to critics) is that this portrayal has at its core 'representations of the state's national identity as that [dominant or majority] group sees it' (Gagnon et al. 2011: 10). All of which might suggest that this literature is particularly relevant to the England/Britain case. In reality, however, this is not the case.

The majority nationalism literature draws heavily on the Canadian and Spanish examples—cases characterized by nested national identities (see Loughlin 2011 for an exception). Its focus is on the competing nationalisms of the state and sub-state units and, in particular, on the way that sub-state units (most obviously, Quebec and Catalonia) exert influence over the dominant understandings of the state at the core. As such, the concept translates unevenly into the UK context. Majority nationalism may indeed provide a useful framing for examining the interaction of Scottish and British nationalisms, both of which are not only distinct from each other but are embodied in different, nested, levels of government. But, as the preceding analysis makes clear, English identity and English nationalism also need to be taken seriously if we aim to understand the national and nationalist dynamics at work within the state, and it is far from clear how the majority nationalism framework facilitates that task. Rather, what is required is a recognition of the ways that rival understandings of the state and state identity that can exist across different sub-state units, with one or some exerting greater influence than others over dominant understandings of the state. Relatedly, appreciation is also required of the ways in which demographic dominace—which is, of course, particularly pronounced in the UK context—might well further an elision between the nationalisms of the state and that of one particular sub-state unit within it. In other words, greater attention to the (horizontal) interplay between rival understandings of the state across and within levels, as well as the different relationships that sub-state units have with the state, would allow for a more rounded understanding of nationalist dynamics within multinational states and—in our case—help to shed light on the relationship between Englishness and Britishness.

Another literature one might expect to have featured prominently in the preceeding chapters is that focused on populism. Certainly, as far as the 2016 Brexit referendum is concerned, both academic and non-academic work appears to be converging on viewing the result through this prism. Indeed, according to one of its most influential interpreters, populism now 'defines our age' (Mudde 2018). As we explore the relationships between wider academic literature and our findings, it would be remiss not to touch on this now increasingly ubiquitous framing.

The disparate and rapidly expanding nature of the populism literature makes it difficult to generalize; nonetheless, it is obvious that nations and nationalisms are at the heart of the populist phenomenon. Take, for example, three of the most high-profile contributions to the current debate. Cas Mudde and Cristóbal Rovira Kaltwasser (2017: 6) define populism as an 'ideology that considers society to be ultimately separated into two homogenous and antagonistic camps, "the pure people" versus "the corrupt elite", and which argues that politics should be an expression of the volonté générale (general will) of the people'. They stress the centrality of what they term 'nativism'— elsewhere described by Mudde as 'a xenophobic form of nationalism'—in most populist attempts to delineate this 'people' Mudde and Kaltwasser 2017; Mudde 2018). For Jan-Werner Müller (2017: 3, 57), populism is 'an exclusionary form of identity politics' that posits the existence of 'the single, homogeneous authentic people'—a view that he seems to regard as a form of 'cultural nationalism'. In an effort that seeks to bridge the nationalist–populist divide, Roger Eatwell and Matthew Goodwin (2018: p. ix) report that 'national populists prioritize the culture and interests of the nation, and promise to give voice to a people who feel that they have been neglected, even held in contempt, by distant and often corrupt elites'. One of the key social trends around which this 'national populism' revolves is the fear of 'destruction' of the national group's historical identity as a result of immigration and what the authors term 'hyper ethnic change' (Eatwell and Goodwin 2018: 129–222).

Yet, even if nations and nationalism are regarded as central to the populist phenomenon, it is fair to say that they are nonetheless not a key preoccupation of the literature on populism, which rather tends to focus on the sources of the populist upsurge, its implications for (liberal) democracy, and so forth. These are hugely significant questions, to be sure: pursuing them certainly requires no apology. Indeed, it should also be pointed out that, despite the ubiquity of the Brexit referendum result as a frame of analysis among the wider commentariat, it is unclear to what extent populism specialists themselves regard it as a manifestation of the phenomenon that is the object of their studies.[2] But whether or not we view these developments partly or wholly through the frame of populism, if we want to understand Englishness and it political impact then a serious engagement with nation and nationalism are essential.

---

[2] Mudde and Kaltwasser mention UKIP and the British National Party (BNP) but not Brexit, while Müller ignores the UK context altogether. Eatwell and Goodwin make regular reference to the Brexit result throughout their analysis, and indeed—alongside Donald Trump's election victory—it forms one of the key framing moments for the book as a whole. Yet a distinct note of ambiguity is nonetheless apparent when they claim that, 'while the shock vote to pull Britain out of the EU was presented as part of the populist wave, there were some unique factors at play' (Eatwell and Goodwin 2018: 17).

This is most obviously so because the specificities of the dominant national myths matter. The Conservative campaign in 2015 was appealing to specific beliefs about post-devolution Scotland (and not simply the Scottish National Party (SNP)). These beliefs were certainly not confined to potential-UKIP voters, but, as our data show, were widely held among those with a strong sense of English national identity. Similarly, in order to understand the appeal of Brexit to particular segments of the electorate—and why the key arguments of the Remain campaign seem to have had so little purchase among them— we need to understand the core beliefs of English nationalism about Britain and its place in the world. In the aftermath of the 2016 referendum, much has been made by critics of the inability of Remainers to construct a 'positive case' for the European Union. It should be obvious from our analysis that even more fundamental is the fact that the Remain campaign's 'counter-narrative' about Britain's place in the world was rooted in the soil already being tended by Leavers.

Analytically speaking, the danger of focusing through the frame of populism rather than nationalism is that we focus on the fringes rather than main event. Even if we accept that UKIP is an expression of a wider populist upsurge, neither our general findings, the 2015 general election result, nor the 2016 referendum can be reduced to a story about that party or its leader.[3] While populism may or may not be on the march, nationalisms remain the key legitimating narrative for contemporary states. Nationalist assumptions frame attitudes and political choices and are all the more powerful precisely because they tend to be unexamined and even unconscious. Understanding the particularities and peculiarities of English nationalism is a prerequisite if we are to understand the contemporary politics of this state and of these islands.

By focusing on the interplay between 'the people' and an 'elite', there is a danger that populism ignores the importance of boundaries around the people. Even if Brexit is widely portrayed as the revolt of the people against elite experts, it was, at heart, an expression of English nationalism; a call for self-determination from a population that felt its future hemmed in by external others both within and outside the state that failed to respect their English judicial traditions, their venerated Anglo-British political institutions, and their history of a proud and independent Britain. Leaving aside the fact

---

[3] Indeed, it is clear from Tim Shipman's account (2016) that, in the run-up to the 2015 election, a determined attempt to 'capture' UKIP was made by parts of the Eurosceptic wing of the Conservative Party—a move intended both to pressure their own party leadership into redeeming the pledge to hold a referendum on EU membership and also to ensure that some of the wilder populist impulses within UKIP did not taint the wider Eurosceptic cause.

that campaigns led by a series of individuals who, to outside eyes, would appear to exemplify a privileged elite make for a peculiar form of anti-elite politics, the objections of English voters—that the Scottish Parliament gets too much money, that Scottish MPs exert too much influence, that Europe thwarts an independent line on trade or social policy—were tied not to anti-elite sentiment but to resentment at the perceived undue influence of others.

Uncovering England and Englishness

This book is an extended exploration of the role played by Englishness in the current transformation of British politics. But, even if it would appear that increasing numbers of political commentators are willing to recognize the centrality of Englishness to the decision to Leave the European Union in the 2016 referendum, in particular (e.g. O'Toole 2018), it remains the case that relatively few academic analyses place any great weight on its wider salience and significance. Here we want to consider why this might be the case. Our key contention is that the methodological approach adopted for major polls and surveys conducted in 'Britain' precludes consideration of the impact of English identity and the sentiments that attach to it. To be clear, we do not ascribe this to some kind of grand conspiracy to ignore England and the English. It is rather the result of a series of unquestioned and almost certainly unconscious assumptions about the nature of British society and the wider state. To illustrate our point, let us focus initially on one of the first book-length studies to explore the 2016 vote—namely, Harold Clarke, Matthew Goodwin, and Paul Whiteley's *Brexit: Why Britain Voted to Leave the European Union* (2017a; see also Clarke et al 2017b).

The authors seek to identify possible factors that distinguish Leave and Remain voters based on surveys conducted as part of the Essex Continuous Monitoring project. This survey, with a sample size of around 2,000, is intended to be representative of the British electorate, meaning, inevitably, that it is dominated by England-domiciled respondents.[4] The survey measures the national identity of respondents by asking them to choose a single identity. The result is a sample in which 48 per cent identify as British, 33 per cent as English, 6 per cent as Scottish, 3 per cent as Welsh, 3.5 per cent as European, and the remaining 6 per cent as either some other national identity or don't

---

[4] The pre-referendum wave had a sample size of 2,218 and the post-referendum wave 1,993 (Clarke et al. 2017a: 153).

know (Clarke et al. 2017a: 159). In their analysis. they argue that Scottish identity was significantly correlated with Remain voting. Beyond Scotland, national identity is seen as playing a less decisive role, lying 'further back in the causal chain' than more directly influential factors such as attitudes to risk, attitudes to the EU, and evaluations of leaders' (Clarke et al. 2017b: 460). Nonetheless, they suggest that English and Welsh identifiers are more likely to vote Leave, with Scottish and European identifiers more likely to vote Remain, because

> the former identities (English, Welsh) are narrower than a more inclusive identity of being 'British' or, a fortiori, 'European'. However, in the case of Scotland, the recent upsurge of nationalism suggests that many of those espousing a Scottish identity see EU membership as an attractive alternative to staying in the UK.   (Clarke et al. 2017b: 451)

Here, it would seem, is another addition to the list of binaries cited at the start of this chapter: insular versus inclusive nationalism.

In the light of the analysis of Englishness offered up in the preceeding pages, there are multiple problems with this approach. The limitations of a forced-choice measure of national identity, in a society where dual identities are both so prevalent and relevant, will be obvious. We also know that strength of identity matters, as well as the precise relationship between Englishness and Britishness. Britishness is used as the reference category in the modelling, even if it is clear that feeling predominantly or exclusively British in England is associated with very different attitudes from feeling strongly British in either Wales or Scotland. Furthermore, given what we know of identity in Scotland, a single choice identity variable for Scotland would find a considerable majority of Scots labelling themselves as Scottish. As a result, a Scottish identity variable used in this way becomes, essentially, a proxy for living in Scotland. The model shows that Scots, included here as Scottish identifiers, voted to Remain, which we already knew from the referendum result itself. The analysis therefore offers limited insight into the operation of identities within England.

The point of this brief discussion is not to chastise these authors in particular. They are important scholars, whose work offers valuable insights into broader trends in public debate. Indeed, to some extent they are atypical, because they at least try to engage with the national–territorial diversity of the state. More usually, even when scholars are relying on samples that are England dominated, very little if any consideration at all is given to the relationship between English identity and attitudes and behaviours. As we have seen, even in those cases where national identity is mentioned as a potential factor, the treatment lacks finesse, at least in comparison with the treatment of other potential influencing factors.

All this has analytical consequences (explored in more depth in Henderson et al. 2020). Returning to the now almost ubiquitous framing of the 2016 referendum result, what are we to make, methodologically speaking, of arguments to the effect that the Leave result represented the revolt of the 'left-behinds'—those who are culturally alienated and/or economically dis-advantaged (the exact range of factors at work as well as the ways (if any) in which they combine varies from analysis to analysis)—if scholars producing these analyses systematically exclude or otherwise overlook respondents in other parts of the state who appear to suffer similar levels of alienation and/or disadvantage but nonetheless voted differently in June 2016? To put matters no more strongly than this: is this not all rather problematic?

In recent years, in particular, political and other social scientists have criticized and sought to overturn what has been termed the 'methodological nationalism' of their disciplines. That is the tendency unthinkingly to assume that the statewide level is the 'natural' unit of analysis, and to ignore or otherwise assume away the potential significance of sub-state regional and/or national differences (Jeffery and Wincott 2010; Henderson et al. 2013). The United Kingdom has its own particular—and perhaps typically idiosyncratic version—of methodological nationalism. It can be characterized as having three elements—or, as we have argued elsewhere, as consisting of three 'effacements' (Henderson et al. 2017: 632). First, Northern Ireland is completely ignored. In the UK there is very little truly statewide political science analysis. The flagship British Election Survey (BES), for example, has never collected data on the Northern Irish electorate at the time of UK general elections, on the basis that Northern Ireland has its own party system. Secondly, analysis of Scotland and Wales is, in the main, left to the country specialists, who tend to utilize their own survey vehicles to conduct fieldwork. Thirdly—and more importantly for present purposes—analysts conduct their analyses of 'British politics' based on what are overwhelmingly English data without taking England and Englishness seriously as analytical categories—indeed, more often than not without ever mentioning 'England'. In these three very different ways, the four constitutive territories of the union tend to be written out of the story of 'British politics'. Scottish and Welsh frustration with this is well documented, but this also has implications for how we understand England.

There are, to be sure, some practical reasons that help explain this state of affairs. As we have seen, the party system in Northern Ireland *is* different. Moreover, such is England's numerical domination within the state that, when British samples of, say, 1,000 voters are created, only around 50–60 respondents are likely to be based in Wales and some more 70–80 in Scotland. Serious consideration of Wales or Scotland therefore demands specialist survey vehicles or all-Britain surveys that are large (and therefore well funded) enough to allow for serious Welsh and Scottish subsamples. That said, in particular with regards to the effacement of England in the treatment of what is, paradoxically enough, an overwhelmingly England-dominated sample, the dominant approach is also based on what appears to be a largely unconscious set of assumptions by British political scientists about the nature of the state. These are:

- that sub-state national sentiment is likely to be politically salient only around the Celtic periphery of the state;
- that there are no politically meaningful differences between Englishness and Britishness, which means that we can safely ignore the former; and
- that 'Britishness' means the same thing across the state.

This book has demonstrated that none of these assumptions survives contact with the empirical evidence.

What, therefore, is the appropriate response? Following on from the analysis presented in the preceding chapters, researchers clearly need to be alert to the possible structuring effects of Englishness and Britishness while exploring data that are derived from or dominated by respondents from England. Simultaneously, they also need to remain open to the possibility that Britishness may well have different effects across the union or that larger narratives about the way things work might only work in England. Doing so requires the inclusion of survey questions that seek to tap into the national identity or identities of survey respondents. It also requires 'aggregating up'.

If we are to speak authoritatively about differences and similarities both within and across the four constitutive territories of the state, then the traditional approach—the 'effacements' we have outlined—will not suffice. Rather, research design must seek to take seriously the (possible) specificities of the four territories. Only on this basis is it possible to 'aggregate up' and determine in which dimensions beyond the constitutional the complex pattern of (often intersecting) national identities found across the UK actually do matter for contemporary politics.

None of this is difficult in itself. Even if national identity has never been a central consideration for scholars and analysts of 'British politics', scholars and analysts interested in the so-called territorial politics of the UK—and, of course, scholars of many other polities—have plenty of experience that can be exploited (even if, as illustrated in Chapter 2, they will seldom offer simple answers). There is also, relatedly, plenty of experience to draw on in constructing survey vehicles that would allow analysts to 'aggregate up' in the way suggested. True, cost is an issue. Sample sizes are smaller—and hence surveys cheaper—if we are content to generalize about 'British politics' on the basis of samples that are dominated by England-based respondents. That said, the development of internet-based survey methodologies have served dramatically to lower the cost of surveys. Indeed, the main barriers to change are likely to be attitudinal rather than financial. What we have termed the Anglo-British fusion is so fundamental to the structure of the state—and the elision of Englishness and Britishness so engrained in its political culture—that the mental shift required in order to take England qua England seriously remains profound. It is far from certain that even the political earthquakes of recent years will be enough to force a change in mindset and behaviour.

Conclusion

It is over four decades since Tom Nairn published a collection of essays under the title *The Break-up of Britain*. Despite devolution, despite the near-death experience of 2014, that clearly has not happened. Even so, to the extent that it ever existed, it may well be that a unified understanding of Britain and Britishness has disintegrated. In our analysis we have explored the striking differences in attitudes that exist between those in England who feel predominantly or exclusively British and those who feel predominantly or exclusively English. The events of 2015 and 2016 have underlined that the latter's views about England, Britain, and the world remain dominant—a mainstream view underpinned by all the hegemonic power of nationalism both banal and more self-conscious. Yet, even if this remains the view of the majority, it is not shared by significant pockets of the state's population. In their admittedly different ways, those within England who feel exclusively or predominantly British and those outside England who do not feel British at all have very different senses of nation and nationhood from those who feel English. Indeed, they would appear to be incompatible with the English world view examined in these pages.

Looking to the future raises an uncertain and concerning prospect. For those in England who cleave to the traditional and still-dominant view of their own national identity and national destiny, there is a danger that by their actions they could end up undermining the very basis of their own world view, not only because their efforts to leave the external (European) Union may well result in their cherished view of Britain's place in the world being exposed as a conceit, but, in the process, because they may also undermine the UK itself. And, while it is true that a perhaps surprising number seem not to be overly concerned about the latter, it is hard to imagine that any break-up would not be the source of regret and recrimination.

Bibliography

Abell, Jackie, Susan Condor, and Clifford Stevenson (2006). '"We are an Island": Geographical Imagery in Accounts of Citizenship, Civil Society and National Identity in Scotland and in England', *Political Psychology*, 27/2: 207–26.

Abell, Jackie, Susan Condor, Robert D. Lowe, Stephen Gibson, and Clifford Stevenson (2007). 'Who Ate All the Pride? Patriotic Sentiment and English National Football Support', *Nations and Nationalism*, 13/1: 97–116.

Almond, Garbriel, and Sydney Verba (1963). *The Civic Culture: Political Attitudes and Democracy in Five Nations*. Princeton: Princeton University Press.

Anderson, Perry (1992). *English Questions*. London: Verso.

Arnold, Matthew (1867). *On the Study of Celtic Literature*. London: Smith, Elder and Co.

Aughey, Arthur (2012). 'Englishness as Class: A Re-examination', *Ethnicities*, 12/4: 394–408.

Baldwin, Stanley (1926). *On England, and Other Addresses*. London: Philip Allan.

Bale, John (1986). 'Sport and National Identity: A Geographical View', *International Journal of History of Sport*, 3/1: 18–41.

Banks, Arron (2016). *The Bad Boys of Brexit: Tales of Mischief, Mayhem and Guerrilla Warfare in the EU Referendum Campaign*. London: Biteback.

Bar-Tal, Daniel (1990). *Group Beliefs: A Conception for Analyzing Group Structure, Processes and Behavior*. New York: Springer-Verlag.

Barker, Ernest (1947) (ed.). *The Character of England*. Oxford: Clarendon Press.

Barnett, Anthony (2017). *The Lure of Greatness: England's Brexit and America's Trump*. London: Unbound.

Barton, Allen H., and R. Wayne Parsons (1977). 'Measuring Belief System Structure', *Public Opinion Quarterly*, 41: 159–80.

BBC News (2003). 'Labour NI Ban Overturned', 1 October, http://news.bbc.co.uk/1/hi/ northern_ireland/3154222.stm.

BBC Politics (2014). '"English Votes for English Votes" Plans Revealed', 16 December, https://www.bbc.co.uk/news/uk-politics-30484453.

Bechhofer, Frank, and David McCrone (2013). 'Imagining the Nation: Symbols of National Culture in England and Scotland', *Ethnicities*, 13/5: 544–64.

Bechhofer, Frank, and David McCrone (2014a). 'Changing Claims in Context: National Identity Revisited', *Ethnic and Racial Studies*, 37/8: 1350–70.

Bechhofer, Frank, and David McCrone (2014b). 'What Makes a Gael? Identity, Language and Ancestry in the Scottish Gàidhealtachd', *Identities: Global Studies in Culture and Power*, 21/2: 113–33.

Béland, Daniel, and André Lecours (2008). *Nationalism and Social Policy: The Politics of Territorial Solidarity*. Oxford: Oxford University Press.

Bell, Duncan (2017). 'The Anglosphere: New Enthusiasm for an Old Dream', *Prospect*, 19 January.

Bennett, Owen (2015). *Following Farage: The Ultimate Political Road Trip*. London: Biteback.

Bennett, Owen (2016). *The Brexit Club: The Inside Story of the Leave Campaigns* (London: Biteback, 2016).

Berns-McGown, Rima (2005). 'Political Culture, not Values', *International Journal: Canada's Journal of Global Policy Analysis*, 60/2: 341–9.

Bew, Paul (2016). *Churchill and Ireland*. Oxford: Oxford University Press.

Billig, Michael (1995). *Banal Nationalism*. London: Sage.

Blair, Tony (2007). Resignation speech, Trimdon Labour Club, Sedgefield, 10 May, https://www.theguardian.com/politics/2007/may/10/labourleadership.labour2.

Bogdanor, Vernon (1999). *Devolution in the United Kingdom*. Oxford: Oxford University Press.

Bond, Ross (2015). 'National Identities and the 2014 Independence Referendum in Scotland', *Sociological Research Online*, 20/4.

Bond, Ross (2017). 'Sub-State National Identities among Minority Groups in Britain: A Comparative Analysis of 2011 Census Data', *Nations and Nationalism*, 23/3: 524–46.

Bradbury, Jonathan, and Rhys Andrews (2010). 'State Devolution and National Identity: Continuity and Change in the Politics of Welshness and Britishness in Wales', *Parliamentary Affairs*, 63/2: 229–49.

Bragg, Billy (2006). *The Progressive Patriot: A Search for Belonging*. London: Bantam Press.

Breuilly, John (1993). *Nationalism and the State*. 2nd edn. Manchester: Manchester University Press.

Breuilly, John (1996). 'Approaches to Nationalism', in Gopal Balakrishnan (ed.), *Mapping the Nation*. London: Verso, 146–74.

Brogan, D. W. (1943). *The English People: Impressions and Observations*. London: Hamish Hamilton.

Brown, Gordon (2004). 'The Golden Thread that Runs through our History', *Guardian*, 8 July, https://www.theguardian.com/politics/2004/jul/08/britishidentity.economy.

Brown, Gordon (2014). *My Scotland, Our Britain: A Future Worth Sharing*. London: Simon & Schuster.

Brown, Gordon (2015). *My Scotland, Our Britain: A Future Worth Sharing* (revised). London: Simon & Schuster.

Brown, Gordon (2016a). 'Leading not Leaving', *New Statesman*, 9 June, https://www.newstatesman.com/politics/uk/2016/06/leading-not-leaving-gordon-brown-makes-positive-case-europe.

Brown, Gordon (2016b). *Britain: Leading, not Leaving: The Patriotic Case for Remaining in Europe*. Selkirk: Deerpark Press.

Brown, Gordon, and Douglas Alexander (1999). *New Britain, New Scotland*. John Smith Institute, http://www.smith-institute.org.uk/wp-content/uploads/2015/10/NewScotlandNewBritain.pdf.

Bryant, Christopher G. A. (2003). 'These Englands, or where does Devolution Leave the English?' *Nations and Nationalism*, 9/3: 393–412.

Butler, David and Donald Stokes (1971). *Political Change in Britain: Forces Shaping Electoral Choice*. London: Penguin.

Cameron, David (2013). 'EU Speech at Bloomberg', 23 January, https://www.gov.uk/government/speeches/eu-speech-at-bloomberg.

Cameron, David (2015). 'Prime Ministers Speech on Europe', 10 November, https://www.gov.uk/government/speeches/prime-ministers-speech-on-europe.

Cameron, David (2016). Speech on the result of the Scottish independence referendum, London, 19 September, https://www.bbc.co.uk/news/uk-politics-29271765.

Cameron, David (2019). *For the Record* (London: William Collins).

Campanella, Edoardo, and Marta Dassù (2017). 'A Future of the English-Speaking Peoples', *Foreign Affairs*, 1 July.

Carmines, Edward G., and James A. Stimson (1982). 'Racial Issues and the Structure of Mass Belief Systems', *Journal of Politics*, 44/1: 2–20.

Carrington, Ben (1998). 'Football's Coming Home' but whose Home? And do we Want it? Nation, Football and the Politics of Exclusion', in Adam Brown (ed.), *Fanatics: Power, Identity and Fandom in Football*. London: Routledge, 101–23.

Charalambous, Giorgos (2011). 'All the Shades of Red: Examining the Radical Left's Euroscepticism', *Journal of Contemporary Politics*, 17/3: 299–320.

Chesterton, G. K. (1907). 'The Secret People', *Neolith* (November), 1–2.

Churchill, Winston S. (1940). 'Be Ye Men of Valour', BBC Broadcast, 13 May, http://www. churchill-society-london.org.uk/BeYeMofV.html.

Churchill, Winston S. (1946). 'The Sinews of Peace', Fulton, Missouri, 5 March, http:// www.churchill-society-london.org.uk/Fulton.html.

Churchill, Winston (1974). 'Is Patriotism Played out?', in Sir Winston Churchill, *If I Lived My Life Again*, compiled and ed. Jack Fishman. London: W. H. Allen.

Clarke, Harold D., Matthew Goodwin, and Paul Whiteley (2017a). *Brexit: Why Britain Voted to Leave the European Union*. Cambridge: Cambridge University Press.

Clarke, Harold, Matthew Goodwin, and Paul Whiteley (2017b). 'Why Britain Voted for Brexit: An Individual-Level Analysis of the 2016 Referendum Vote', *Parliamentary Affairs*, 70/3: 439–64.

Clegg, Nick (2016). *Politics: Between the Extremes*. London: Bodley Head.

Clegg, Nick (2017). *How to Stop Brexit (and Make Britain Great Again)*. London: Bodley Head.

Cohen, Anthony (1986). 'Personal Nationalism: A Scottish View of Some Rites, Rights and Wrongs', *American Ethnologist*, 23: 802–15.

Cohen, Anthony (1996). 'Owning the Nation, and the Personal Nature of Nationalism: Locality and the Rhetoric of Nationhood in Scotland', in Vered Amit-Talia and Caroline Knowles (eds), *Resituating Identities: The Politics of Race, Culture and Ethnicity*, Peterborough: Broadview Press, 267–87.

Cohen, Robin (1995). 'Fuzzy Frontiers of Identity', *Social Identities*, 1/1: 35–62.

Colley, Linda (1986). 'Whose Nation? Class and National Conscious in Britain 1750–1830', *Past and Present*, 113: 97–117.

Colley, Linda (2009). *Britons: Forging the Nation 1707–1837*. Rev. edn. New Haven: Yale University Press.

Colls, Robert (2002). *Identity of England*. Oxford: Oxford University Press.

Condor, Susan (2010). 'Devolution and National Identity: The Rules of English (Dis) engagement', *Nations and Nationalism*, 16/3: 525–43.

Condor, Susan, Stephen Gibson, and Jackie Abell (2006). 'English Identity and Ethnic Diversity in the Context of UK Constitutional Change', *Ethnicities*, 6/2: 123–58.

Conservative Democracy Task Force (2008). *Answering the Question: Devolution, The West Lothian and the Future of the Union*. London: Conservative Party.

Conservative Party (2015a). *The Conservative Party English Manifesto 2015*, London: Conservative Party.

Conservative Party (2015b). 'Final Party General Election Broadcast 2015', https://www. youtube.com/watch?v=xrqG6CbmZjw.

Conservative Party (2015c). *The Conservative Party Election Manifesto 2015*, London: Conservative Party, http://ucrel.lancs.ac.uk/wmatrix/ukmanifestos2015/ localpdf/ Conservatives.pdf.

Convery, Alan (2016). *The Territorial Conservative Party: Devolution and Party Change in Scotland and Wales*. Manchester: Manchester University Press.

Cooper, Andrew (2017). 'The Conservative Campaign', in Dominic Wring, Roger Mortimoreand Simon Atkinson (eds), *Political Communication in Britain: Polling, Campaigning and Media in the 2015 General Election*. London: Palgrave Macmillan, 123–32.

Corpus, Colin, Mark Roberts, and Rachel Wall (2017). *Local Government in England: Centralisation, Autonomy and Control*. London: Palgrave Macmillan.

Cowley, Philip and Dennis Kavanagh (2016). *The British General Election of 2015*. Basingstoke: Palgrave Macmillan.

Craig, F. W. S. (1990). *British General Election Manifestos, 1959–87*. Aldershot: Parliamentary Research Services.

Curtice, John (1988). 'One Nation', in Roger Jowell, Sharon Witherspoon, and Lindsay Brook (eds), *British Social Attitudes: The 5th Report*. Aldershot: Gower, 127–54.

Curtice, John (1992). 'The North South Divide', in Roger Jowell, Lindsay Brook, Gillian Prior, and Bridget Taylor (eds), British Social Attitudes Survey: The 9th Report. Aldershot: Gower, 71–88.

Curtice, John (2009). 'Is there an English Backlash? Reactions to Devolution', in Alison Park, John Curtice, Katarina Thomson, Miranda Philips, and Elizabeth Clery (eds), *British Social Attitudes: 25th Report*. London: Sage/NatCen, 1–23.

Curtice, John, and Anthony Heath (2001). 'Is the English Lion about to Roar? National Identity after Devolution', in Roger Jowell, John Curtice, Alison Park, Katarina Thomson, Lindsey Jarvis, Catherine Bromley, and Nina Stratford (eds), *British Social Attitudes: Focusing on Diversity—The 17th Report*. London: Sage, 155–74.

Curtice, John and Mark Sandford (2004). 'Does England Want Devolution too?' in Alison Park, John Curtice, Katarina Thomson, Catherine Bromley, and Miranda Phillips (eds), *British Social Attitudes: The 21st Report*. London: Sage, 201–19.

d'Ancona, Matthew (2018). 'Brexit will Bring a New 'Blitz Spirit'? This Is Nostalgia at its Most Toxic', *Guardian*, 30 December, https://www.theguardian.com/commentisfree/2018/dec/30/brexit-blitz-spirit-nostalgia-toxic-world-war-two.

Davidson, Neil, Minna Liinpaa, Maureen McBride, and Satnam Virdee (2018) (eds). *No Problem Here: Racism in Scotland*. Edinburgh: Luath Press.

Davies, Geraint Talfan (2018). *Unfinished Business: Journal of an Embattled* European. Cardigan: Parthian.

Davies, Norman (1999). *The Isles: A History*. London: Macmillan.

Davies, R. R. (2000). *The First English Empire: Power and Identities in the British Isles 1093–1343*. Oxford: Oxford University Press.

Dawson, Paul A. (1979). 'The Formation and Structure of Political Belief Systems', *Political Behavior*, 1/2: 99–102.

Deacon, David, John Downey, James Stanyer, and Dominic Wring (2017). 'The Media Campaign: The Issues and Personalities who Defined the Election', in Dominic Wring, Roger Mortimore, and Simon Atkinson (eds), *Political Communication in Britain: Polling, Campaigning and Media in the 2015 General Election*. London: Palgrave Macmillan, 183–96.

Degerman, Dan (2019). 'Brexit Anxiety: A Case Study in the Medicalization of Dissent', *Critical Review of International Social and Political Philosophy*, 22/7: 823–40.

Denham, John (2018). 'Labour Cannot Win if it Ignores the Future of England', *Labour List*, 8 June, https://labourlist.org/2018/06/john-denham-labour-cannot-win-if-it-ignores-the-future-of-england/.

Diffley, Mark (2017). 'The Election in Scotland', in Dominic Wring, Roger Mortimore, and Simon Atkinson (eds), *Political Communication in Britain: Polling, Campaigning and Media in the 2015 General Election*. London: Palgrave Macmillan, 49–62.

Donald, Adam (2014). 'Emily Thornberry: How One Tweet Led to her Resignation', BBC news website, 21 November, http://www.bbc.com/news/uk-politics-30142579.

Eatwell, Roger, and Matthew Goodwin (2018). *National Populism*. London: Pelican.

Edgerton, David (2018). *The Rise and Fall of the British Nation: A Twentieth-Century History*. London: Penguin.

Edwards, Owen Dudley (1989) (ed.). *A Claim of Right for Scotland*. Edinburgh: Polygon.

Eliot, T. S. ([1942] 1971). 'Little Gidding', *Four Quartets*. London: Faber & Faber.

Emes, Claire, and Josh Keith (2017). 'The Election Debates in 2015: The View from the Living Room', in Dominic Wring, Roger Mortimore, and Simon Atkinson (eds), *Political Communication in Britain: Polling, Campaigning and Media in the 2015 General Election*. London: Palgrave Macmillan, 235–46.

Evans, Adam B. (2014). 'Federalists in Name Only? Reassessing the Federalist Credentials of the Liberal Democrats: An English Case Study', *British Politics*, 9/3: 346–58.

Evans, Geoffrey, and Jonathan Mellon (2019). 'Immigration, Euroscepticism and the Rise and Fall of UKIP', *Party Politics*, 15 January (online).

Evans, Gwynfor (1981). *The End of Britishness*. Cardiff: Plaid Cymru.

Eurobarometer (2018). *Integration of Immigrants in the European Union: Special Eurobarometer*, 469. Brussels: European Commission.

Farage, Nigel (2015). *The Purple Revolution: The Year that Changed Everything*. London: Biteback.

Featherstone, Simon (2009). *Englishness; Twentieth-Century Popular Culture and the Forming of English Identity*. Edinburgh: Edinburgh University Press.

Fenton, Steve (2007). 'Indifference towards National Identity: What Young Adults Think about Being English in Britain', *Nations and Nationalism*, 13/2: 321–39.

Fielding, Steven (2015). 'The Correct Diagnosis but the Wrong Doctor', in Andrew Geddes and Jonathan Tonge (eds), *Britain Votes 2015*. Oxford: Oxford University Press, 54–69.

Fleishman, John A. (1988). 'Attitude Organization in the General Public: Evidence for a Bidimensional Structure', *Social Forces*, 67/1: 159–84.

Foos, Florian, and Daniel Bischof (2018). 'Can the Tabloid Media Create Eurosceptic Attitudes? A Quasi-Experiment on Media Influence in England', unpublished paper, www.florianfoos.net/resources/Foos_Bischof_Hillsborough.pdf.

Ford, Robert, and Matthew Goodwin (2014). *Revolt on the Right: Explaining Support for the Radical Right in Britain*. London: Routledge.

Gaitskill, Hugh (1962). Speech against UK membership of the Common Market, Labour Party Annual Conference, 3 October, https://www.cvce.eu/content/publication/1999/1/1/05f2996b-000b-4576-8b42-8069033a16f9/publishable_en.pdf.

Gamble, Andrew (2015). 'The Economy', in Andrew Geddes and Jonathan Tonge (eds), *Britain Votes 2015*. Oxford: Oxford University Press, 154–67.

Gagnon, Alain-G., André Lecours, and Geneviève Nootens (2011) (eds). *Contemporary Majority Nationalism*. Montreal: McGill—Queens University Press.

Gärdenfors, Peter (1990). 'The Dynamics of Belief Systems: Foundations vs Coherence Theories', *Revue internationale de philosophie*, 44/172(1): 24–46.

Gavin, Neil T. (2018). 'Media Definitely Do Matter: Brexit, Immigration, Climate Change and Beyond', *British Journal of Politics and International Relations*, 20/4: 827–45.

Gay, Oonagh (2006). 'The West Lothian Question', House of Commons Library SN/PC/2586, 26 June.

Gibbons, Tom (2011). 'English National Identity and the National Football Team: The View of Contemporary English Fans', *Soccer and Society*, 12/6: 865–79.

Gibbons, Tom (2014). *English National Identity and Football Fan Culture: Who Are Ya?* London: Routledge.

Gibbons, Tom (2017). 'Is St George Enough? The Relationship between English National Identity and Football', in Tom Gibbons and Dominic Malcolm (eds), *Sport and English National Identity in a Disunited Kingdom*. London: Routledge, 34–48.

Gilroy, Paul (2002). *'There Ain't No Black in the Union Jack': The Cultural Politics of Race and Nation*. Abingdon: Routledge.

Glover, Daniel, and Michael Kenny (2018). 'Answering the West Lothian Question? A Critical Assessment of "English Votes for English Laws" in the UK Parliament', *Parliamentary Affairs*, 71/4: 760–82.

Goodwin, Matthew, and Caitlin Milazzo (2017). *UKIP: Inside the Campaign to Redraw the Map of British Politics*. Oxford: Oxford University Press.

Greenfeld, Leah (1993). *Nationalism: Five Roads to Modernity*. Cambridge, MA: Harvard University Press.

Grender, Olly (2017). 'Chill Wind: The Liberal Democrat Campaign', in Dominic Wring, Roger Mortimore, and Simon Atkinson (eds), *Political Communication in Britain: Polling, Campaigning and Media in the 2015 General Election*. London: Palgrave Macmillan, 151–60.

Hain, Peter (2016). *England in a Federal UK*, Fabian Society, 12 May, https://fabians.org.uk/england-in-a-federal-uk/.

Hannan, Daniel (2013). 'The World of English Freedoms', *Wall Street Journal*, 15 November.

Hannan, Daniel (2015). *How We Invented Freedom & Why It Matters*. London: Head of Zeus.

Hannan, Daniel (2016a). *Why Vote Leave?* London: Head of Zeus.

Hannan, Daniel (2016b). Contribution to Pre-Referendum Oxford Union Debate, June, https://www.youtube.com/watch?time_continue=1&v=rJcuKfcxo9w.

Hazell, Robert (2006) (ed.). *The English Question*. Manchester: Manchester University Press.

Heffer, Simon (1999). *Nor Shall my Sword: The Reinvention of England*. London: Weidenfeld & Nicolson.

Henderson, Ailsa (2008). *Hierarchies of Belonging: National Identity and Political Culture in Scotland and Quebec*. Montreal: McGill-Queens University Press.

Henderson, Ailsa (2018a). 'Brexit, the Union and the Future of England', *Political Insight*, 6 November, https://journals.sagepub.com/doi/full/10.1177/2041905818815196.

Henderson, Ailsa (2018b). Oral Evidence to the House of Commons Public Administration and Constitutional Affairs Committee, Edinburgh.

Henderson, Ailsa (2019). 'Attitudes to Constitutional Change in Scotland', in Gerry Hassan (ed.), *The Story of the Scottish Parliament: The First Two Decades Explained*. Edinburgh: Edinburgh University Press, 45–51.

Henderson, Ailsa, and Richard Wyn Jones (2018). Written Evidence to the House of Commons Public Administration and Constitutional Affairs Committee.

Henderson, Ailsa, Charlie Jeffery, and Dan Wincott (2013) (eds). *Citizenship after the Nation State: Regionalism, Nationalism and Public Attitudes in Europe*. Basingstoke: Palgrave Macmillan.

Henderson, Ailsa, Ed Gareth Poole, Richard Wyn Jones, Daniel Wincott, Jac Larner, and Charlie Jeffery (2020). 'Analysing Vote-choice in a Multinational State: National Identity and Territorial Differentiation in the 2016 Brexit Vote', *Regional Studies*. DOI: 10.1080/00343404.2020.1813883.

Henderson, Ailsa, Charlie Jeffery, Robert Liñeira, Roger Scully, Dan Wincott, and Richard Wyn Jones (2016). 'England, Englishness and BREXIT', *Political Quarterly*, 87/2: 187–99.

Henderson, Ailsa, Charlie Jeffery, Dan Wincott, and Richard Wyn Jones (2017). 'How Brexit was Made in England', *British Journal of Politics and International Relations*, 17/4: 1–16.

Hewstone, Miles (1986). *Understanding Attitudes to the European Community: A Social Psychological Study in Four Member States*. Cambridge: Cambridge University Press.

Hobolt, Sara Binzer (2007). 'Taking Cues on Europe? Voter Competence and Party Endorsements in Referendums on European Integration', *European Journal of Political Research*, 46/2: 151–82.

Hobolt, Sara B., and James Tilley (2016), 'Fleeing the Centre: The Rise of Challenger Parties in the Aftermath of the Euro Crisis', *West European Politics*, 39/5: 971–91.

Hobsbawm, Eric, and Terence Ranger (1983) (eds). *The Invention of Tradition*. Cambridge: Cambridge University Press.

Hogwood, Brian W., and Michael Keating (1982) (eds). *Regional Government in England*. Oxford: Clarendon Press.

Hong, Y. Y., Michael W. Morris, Chi Yue Chiu, and Veronica Benet (2000). *American Psychologist*, 55/7: 709–20.

Hopkin, Deian, Duncan Tanner, and Chris Williams (2001) (eds). *The Labour Party in Wales 1900–2000*. Cardiff: University of Wales Press.

Houlihan, Barrie (1997). 'Sport, National Identity and Public Policy', *Nations and Nationalism*, 3/1: 113–37.

House of Lords Library (2014). *Regional Representation in the House of Lords*, 10 February (LLN 2014/005).

Hroch, Miroslav (1985). *Social Preconditions of National Revival in Europe: A Comparative Analysis of the Social Composition of Patriotic Groups among the Smaller European Nations*, trans. Ben Fowkes. Cambridge: Cambridge University Press.

Hunt, Tristram (2016a). 'Introduction', in Tristram Hunt (ed.), *Labour's Identity Crisis: England and the Politics of Patriotism*. Winchester: Centre for English Identity and Politics/Winchester University Press, 1–8.

Hunt, Tristram (2016b) (ed.). *Labour's Identity Crisis: England and the Politics of Patriotism*. Winchester: Centre for English Identity and Politics/Winchester University Press.

Hunter, Alistair, and Nasar Meer (2018). 'Is Scotland Different on Race and Migration', *Scottish Affairs*, 27/3: 382–7.

Ignatieff, Michael (1994). *Blood and Belonging: Journeys into the New Nationalism*. London: Vintage.

Ignazi, Piero (2003). *Extreme Right Parties in Western Europe*. Oxford: Oxford University Press.

Ipsos-MORI (2016). 'The Perils of Perception and the EU', 9 June, https://www.ipsos.com/ipsos-mori/en-uk/perils-perception-and-eu.

Jacoby, William G. (1995). 'The Structure of Ideological Thinking in the American Electorate', *American Journal of Political Science*, 39/2: 314–35.

James, Lawrence (2014). *Churchill and Empire: Portrait of an Imperialist*. London: Phoenix.

Jeffery, Charlie (2009). 'Elected Regional Assemblies in England: An Anatomy of Policy Failure', in Mark Sandford (ed), *The Northern Veto*. Manchester: Manchester University Press, 8–25.

Jeffery, Charlie, and Daniel Wincott (2010). 'The Challenge of Territorial Politics beyond Methodological Nationalism', in Colin Hay (ed), *New Directions in Political Science: Responding to the Challenges of an Interdependent World*. Basingstoke: Palgrave Macmillan, 167–88.

Jeffery, Charlie, Richard Wyn Jones, Ailsa Henderson, Roger Scully, and Guy Lodge (2014). *Taking England Seriously: The New English Politics*. Edinburgh: ESRC Future of the UK and Scotland.

Jeffery, Charlie, Ailsa Henderson, Roger Scully, and Richard Wyn Jones (2016). 'The Conservative Party and the New English Nationalism', *Political Studies Review*, 14/3: 335–48.

Johns, Rob, and James Mitchell (2016). *Takeover: The Extraordinary Rise of the SNP*. London: Biteback.

Johnson, Boris (2014). *The Churchill Factor: How One Man Made History*. London: Hodder and Stoughton.

Johnson, Boris (2018). 'Full Text: Boris Johnson's Brexit Speech', 16 February, https://blogs.spectator.co.uk/2018/02/full-text-boris-johnsons-brexit-speech/.

Kaufman, Eric (2004) (ed.). *Rethinking Ethnicity: Majority Groups and Dominant Minorities*. London: Routledge.

Kellas, James (1973). *The Scottish Political System*. Cambridge: Cambridge University Press.

Kenny, Michael (2014). *The Politics of English Nationhood*. Oxford: Oxford University Press.

Kenny, Michael, and Nick Pearce (2015). 'The Rise of the Anglosphere: How the Right Dreamed up a New Conservative World Order', *New Statesman*, 10 February.

Kenny, Michael, and Nick Pearce (2018). *Shadows of Empire: The Anglosphere in British Politics*. Cambridge: Polity.

Khan, Naushabah (2016). 'Rochester and Strood', in Tristram Hunt (ed.), *Labour's Identity Crisis: England and the Politics of Patriotism*. Winchester: Centre for English Identity and Politics/Winchester University Press, 61–6.

Kidd, Colin (2008). *Union and Unionisms: Political Thought in Scotland 1500–2000*. Cambridge: Cambridge University Press.

Kinder, Andrew (2019). 'One Third of Aults say Brexit has Affected their Mental Health, BACP Research Finds', British Association of Counselling and Psychotherapy, 11 April, https://www.bacp.co.uk/news/news-from-bacp/2019/11-april-one-third-of-adults-say-brexit-has-affected-their-mental-health-bacp-research-finds/.

King, Anthony (2000). 'Football Fandom and Post-National Identity in the New Europe', *British Journal of Sociology*, 51/3: 419–42.

Kingsnorth, Paul (2009). *Real England: The Battle against the Bland*. London: Portobello Books.

Knight, Jonathan, Robin Niblett, and Thomas Raines (2012). *Hard Choices: The Chatham House-YouGov Survey 2012*. London: Royal Institute for International Affairs.

Kohn, Hans (1940). 'The Genesis and Character of English Nationalism', *Journal of the History of Ideas*, 1/1: 69–94.

Kohn, Hans (1944). *The Idea of Nationalism: A Study in its Origins and Background*. New York: Macmillan.

Kriesi, Hanspeter (2014). 'The Populist Challenge', *West European Politics*, 37/2: 361–78.

Kumar, Krishan (2000). 'Nation and Empire: English and British National Identity in Comparative Perspective', *Theory and Society*, 29/5: 575–608.

Kumar, Krishan (2003). *The Making of English National Identity*. Cambridge: Cambridge University Press.

Kumar, Krishan (2006). 'Empire and English Nationalism', *Nations and Nationalism*, 12/1: 1–13.

Kumar, Krishan (2010). 'Negotiating English Identity: Englishness, Britishness and the Future of the United Kingdom', *Nations and Nationalism*, 16/3: 469–87.

Labour Party (1995). *A Choice for England: A Consultation Paper on Labour's Plans for English Regional Government*. London: Labour Party.

Laffin, Martin, and Eric Shaw (2007). 'British Devolution and the Labour Party: How a National Party Adapts to Devolution', *British Journal of Politics and International Relations*, 9/1: 55–72.

Lampedusa, Guiseppe di (1961), *The Leopard*, trans. Archibald Colquhoun. London: Reprint Society.

Langford, Paul (2000). *Englishness Identified: Manners and Character 1650–1850*. Oxford: Oxford University Press.

Law, Richard (1947). 'The Individual and the Community', in Ernest Barker (ed.), *The Character of England*. Oxford: Clarendon Press, 29–55.

Laws, David (2017). *Coalition: The Inside Story of the Conservative–Liberal Democrat Coalition Government*. London: Biteback.

Lecours, André, and Geneviève Nootens (2009a) (eds). *Dominant Nationalism, Dominant Ethnicity: Identity, Federalism and Democracy*. Brussels: PIE Peter Lang.

Lecours, André, and Geneviève Nootens (2009b). 'Nationalism and Identity in Contemporary Politics: Issues of Democratic Shared and Self-Rule', in André Lecours and Geneviève Nootens (eds), *Dominant Nationalism, Dominant Ethnicity: Identity, Federalism and Democracy*. Brussels: PIE Peter Lang, 11–31.

Levinger, Matthew, and Paula Franklin Lytle (2001). 'Myth and Mobilisation: The Triadic Structure of Nationalist Rhetoric', *Nations and Nationalism*, 7/2: 175–94.

Liberal Democrats (2015). *2015 Election Review*. London: Liberal Democrats, http://www.libdems.org.uk/2015_election_review.

Littlejohn, Richard (2019). 'Let's Revive the Bulldog Spirit of World War Two, Defy the Brexit Jeremiahs and Dig for Victory as we Prepare to Leave the EU', *Daily Mail*, 14 January, https://www.dailymail.co.uk/debate/article-6591937/RICHARD-LITTLEJOHN-Lets-revive-Bulldog-spirit-World-War-Two-dig-victory.html.

Lockett, John (2016). 'Driven to Despair: Psychiatrists Reveal Alarming Rise in Number of Patients Seeking Help for "Brexit Anxiety"', *Sun*, 11 July, https://www.thesun.co.uk/news/1426878/psychiatrists-reveal-alarming-rise-in-number-of-patients-seeking-help-for-brexit-anxiety/.

Loughlin, John (2011). 'British and French Nationalisms Facing the Challenges of European Integration and Globalization', in Alain-G Gagnon, André Lecours, and Geneviève Nootens (eds), *Contemporary Majority Nationalism*. Montreal: McGill—Queens University Press, 127–43.

McGrattan, Cillian, and Sophie Williams (2017). 'Devolution and Identity: Multidirectionality in "Welshness" and "Northern Irishness"', *Regional and Federal Studies*, 27/4: 465–82.

Mclean, Iain (2013). 'Report of the Commission on the Consequences of Devolution for House of Commons (the McKay Commission)', *Political Quarterly*, 84/3: 395–8.

McTague, Tom (2016). 'David Cameron Interview: Prime Minister Urges People to Vote in EU Referendum "Or You'll Find We're Out"', *Independent*, 19 March, https://www.independent.co.uk/news/uk/politics/david-cameron-interview-prime-minister-urges-people-to-vote-in-eu-referendum-or-youll-find-were-out-a6941436.html.

Macwhirter, Iain (2014). *Disunited Kingdom: How Westminster Won a Referendum but Lost Scotland*. Glasgow: Cargo Publishing.

Madood, Tariq, Richard Berthoud, Jane Laskey, James Nazroo, Patten Smith, Satnam Virdee, and Sharon Beishon (1997). *Ethnic Minorities in Britain: Diversity and Disadvantage—the Fourth National Survey of Ethnic Minorities*. London: Policy Studies Institute.

Mandler, Peter (2006). *The English National Character: The History of an Idea from Edmund Burke to Tony Blair*. New Haven: Yale University Press.

Major, John (1993). 'Speech to the Conservative Group for Europe', 22 April, *Guardian*, 23 April.

Mann, Robin (2011). 'It Just Feels English Rather than Multicultural: Local Interpretations of Englishness and Non-Englishness', *Sociological Review*, 59/1: 109–28.

March, Luke, and Charlotte Rommerskirchen (2015). 'Out of Left Field? Explaining the Variable Electoral Success of European Radical Left Parties', *Party Politics*, 21/1: 40–53.

Marr, Andrew (2000). *The Day Britain Died*. London: Profile Books.

Masters, Adrian (2018). 'Paul Davies Discussed Tory Leadership Status Question with Theresa May', 30 September, https://www.itv.com/news/wales/2018-09-30/conservative-conference-birmingham-wales/.

Mawson, John (1997). 'The English Regional Debate', in Jonathan Bradbury and John Mawsom (eds), *British Regionalism and Devolution: The Challenges of State Reform and European Integration*. London: Jessica Kingsley Publishers, 180–213.

Mead, Walter Russell (2007). *God and Gold: Britain, America and the Making of the Modern World*. London: Atlantic Books.

Miller, Warren E. (1986). 'Party Identification and Political Belief Systems: Changes in Partisanship in the United States, 1980–1984', *Electoral Studies*, 5/2: 101–21.

Miller, William L., Annis May Timpson, and Michael Lessnoff (1996). *Political Culture in Contemporary Britain: People and Politicians, Principles and Practice*. Oxford: Clarendon Press.

Mitchell, James (2009). *Devolution in the UK*. Manchester: Manchester University Press.

Mitchell, Paul, and Rick Wilford (1998) (eds). *Politics in Northern Ireland*. New York: Perseus.

Moreno, Luis (2006). 'Scotland, Catalonia, Europeanization and the "Moreno Question"', *Scottish Affairs*, 24: 1–21.

Morgan, Kenneth O. (1987). *Rebirth of a Nation: A History of Modern Wales 1880–1980*. Oxford: Oxford University Press.

Morgan, Kevin, and Ellis Roberts (1993). *The Democratic Deficit: A Guide to Quangoland*. Cardiff: UWCC Dept of City and Regional Planning.

Morton, H. V. (1927). *In Search of England*. London: Methuen.

Mudde, Cas (2018). 'How Populism Became a Concept that Defines our Age', *Guardian*, 22 November, https://www.theguardian.com/commentisfree/2018/nov/22/populism-concept-defines-our-age.

Mudde, Cas, and Cristóbal Rovira Kaltwasser (2017). *Populism: A Very Short Introduction*. Oxford: Oxford University Press.

Müller, Jan-Werner (2017). *What is Populism?* London: Penguin.

Mycock, Andrew, and Richard Hayton (2014). 'The Party Politics of Englishness', *British Journal of Politics and International Relations*, 16/2: 251–72.

Nairn, Tom (1981a). 'The English Enigma', in *The Break-up of Britain: Crisis and Neo-Nationalism*. 2nd expanded edn. London: Verso, 291–305.

Nairn, Tom (1981b). 'The Modern Janus', in *The Break-up of Britain: Crisis and Neo-Nationalism*. 2nd expanded edn. London: Verso, 329–63.

Nairn, Tom (1981c). 'English Nationalism: The Case of Enoch Powell', in *The Break-up of Britain: Crisis and Neo-Nationalism*. 2nd expanded edn. London: Verso, 256–90.

Nairn, Tom, et al. (2006). *Gordon Brown 'Bard of Britishness'*. Cardiff: Institute of Welsh Affairs.

National Records for Scotland (2011). *Scotland's Census 2011* Table DC2103SC Country of birth by age [FULL???]

Niven, Alex (2019). *New Model Island: How to Build a Radical Culture beyond the Idea of England*. London: Repeater.

Norris, Pippa, and Ronald Inglehart (2019). *Cultural Backlash and the Rise of Populism: Trump, Brexit and Authoritarian Populism*. Cambridge: Cambridge University Press.

O'Leary, Brendan (1988). 'Ernest Gellner's Diagnoses of Nationalism: A Critical Overview, or, what is Living and what is Dead in Ernest Gellner's Philosophy of Nationalism?', in

John Hall (ed.), *The State and the Nation: Ernest Gellner and the Theory of Nationalism*. Cambridge: Cambridge University Press, 23–88.

O'Toole, Fintan (2018). *Heroic Failure: Brexit and the Politics of Pain*. London: Head of Zeus.

Office of National Statistics (2011). *2011 Census: Key Statistics for Wales, March 2011*, https://www.ons.gov.uk/peoplepopulationandcommunity/populationandmigration/populationestimates/bulletins/2011censuskeystatisticsforwales/2012-12-11.

Office of National Statistics (2012). *Ethnicity and Nation Identity in England and Wales*, https://www.ons.gov.uk/peoplepopulationandcommunity/culturalidentity/ethnicity/articles/ethnicityandnationalidentityinenglandandwales/2012-12-11.

Oliver, Craig (2016). *Unleashing Demons: The Inside Story of Brexit*. London: Hodder & Stoughton.

Orwell, George (1941). 'England your England', in *The Lion and the Unicorn: Socialism and the English Genius*. London: Secker & Warburg.

Orwell, George (1947). *The English People*. London: Collins.

Paterson, Lindsay (1998). *A Diverse Assembly: The Debate on a Scottish Parliament*. Edinburgh: Edinburgh University Press.

Paxman, Jeremy (1999). *The English: Portrait of a People*. London: Penguin.

Pike, Joe (2015). *Project Fear: How an Unlikely Alliance Left a Kingdom United but a Country Divided*. London: Biteback.

Pounds, N. J. G. (1994). *The Culture of the English People: Iron Age to the Industrial Revolution*. Cambridge: Cambridge University Press.

Pryce, Huw (2001). 'British or Welsh? National Identity in Twelfth Century Wales', *English Historical Review*, 116/468: 775–801.

Rodriguez, Nathaniel, Johan Bollen and Yong-Yeol Ahn (2016). 'Collective Dynamics of Belief Evolution under Cognitive Coherence and Social Conformity', *PLoS ONE*, 11/11: e0165910, https://journals.plos.org/plosone/article?id=10.1371/journal.pone.0165910.

Rogers, David, and John McLeod (2004). *The Revision of Englishness*. Manchester: Manchester University Press.

Rose, Richard (1964). *Politics in England, and Interpretation*. London: Little, Brown.

Rose, Richard, and Mark Shepard (2016). 'The Long and the Short of the SNP Breakthrough', in Philip Cowley and Dennis Kavanagh, *The British General Election of 2015*. Basingstoke: Palgrave Macmillan, 126–39.

Ross, Tim (2015). *Why the Tories Won: The Inside Story of the 2015 Election*. London: Biteback.

Rowling, J. K. (2014). 'Let's Safeguard the Future by Staying in the Union, Able to Dictate Terms', *Independent*, 11 June, http://www.independent.co.uk/voices/jk-rowling-on-scottish-independence-let-s-safeguard-the-future-by-staying-in-the-union-able-to-9530520.html.

Russell, Meg, and Guy Lodge (2006). 'The Government of England by Westminster', in Robert Hazell (ed.), *The English Question*. Manchester: Manchester University Press, 64–95.

Russell, Meg, and Jack Sheldon (2018). *Options for an English Parliament*. London: The Constitution Unit, UCL.

Saeed, Amir, Neil Blain, and Douglas Forbes (1999). 'New Ethnic and National Questions in Scotland: Post-British Identities among Glasgow Pakistani Teenagers', *Ethnic and Racial Studies*, 22/5: 821–44.

Sandford, Mark (2009). 'The Grassroots and and the Elites: Campaigns for Promoting Regionalism in England', in Mark Sandford (ed.), *The Northern Veto*. Manchester: Manchester University Press, 26–52.

Sandford, Mark (2016). 'Devolution to Local Government in England', House of Commons Library Briefing Paper, No. 07029, 23 November.

Sandford, Mark (2017). 'Directly-Elected Mayors', House of Commons Library Briefing Paper, No. 05000, 12 June.

Schopflin, George (2000). Nations, Identity, Power, London: Hurst.

Scottish Government (2013). Scotland's Future: Your Guide to an Independent Scotland. Edinburgh: Scottish Government.

Scruton, Roger (2000). England: An Elegy. London: Chatto.

Shipman, Tim (2016). All Out War: The Full Story of how Brexit Sank Britain's Political Class. London: William Collins.

Simon, Bernd, and Bert Klandermans (2001). 'Politicized Collective Identity: A Social Psychological Analysis', American Psychologist, 56/4: 319–31.

Simpson, Ludi, Stephen Jivraj, and James Warren (2016). 'The Stability of Ethnic Identity in England and Wales 2001–2011', Journal of the Royal Statistical Society Series: A Statistics in Society, 179/4: 1025–49.

Sinclair, Jeremy, and Simon Atkinson (2017). 'An Interview with Jeremy Sinclair', in Dominic Wring, Roger Mortimore, and Simon Atkinson (eds), Political Communication in Britain: Polling, Campaigning and Media in the 2015 General Election. London: Palgrave Macmillan, 115–22.

Skey, Michael (2011). ' "Sod them, I'm English": The Changing Status of the "Majority" English in Post-Devolution Britain', Ethnicities, 12/1: 106–25.

StatsWales (2012). Welsh Language Skills by Local Authority, Gender and Detailed Age Groups, 2011 Census, https://statswales.gov.wales/Catalogue/Welsh-Language/ Census-Welsh-Language/welshlanguageskills-by-localauthority-gender-detailedagegroups-2011census.

Stimson, James A. (1975). 'Belief Systems: Constraint, Complexity and the 1972 Election', American Journal of Political Science, 19/3: 393–417.

Stride, Suzy, and Jacob Quagliozzi (2016). 'Harlow', in Tristram Hunt (ed.), Labour's Identity Crisis: England and the Politics of Patriotism. Winchester: Centre for English Identity and Politics/Winchester University Press, 52–60.

Stubager, Rune (2008). 'Education Effects on Authoritarian–Libertarian Values: A Question of Socialization', British Journal of Sociology, 59/2: 329–50.

Tetlock, Philip E. (1983). 'Cognitive Style and Political Belief Systems in the British House of Commons', Journal of Personality and Social Psychology, 46/2: 365–75.

Tetlock, Philip E. (1989). 'Structure and Function in Political Belief Systems', in Anthony R. Pratkanis, Steven J. Breckler, and Anthony G. Greenwald (eds), Attitude, Structure and Function. New York: Psychology Press, 129–51.

The McKay Commission (2013). Report of the Commission on the Consequences of Devolution for the House of Commons (The McKay Commission), https://webarchive. nationalarchives.gov.uk/20130403030728/http://tmc.independent.gov.uk/wp-content/ uploads/2013/03/The-McKay-Commission_Main-Report_25-March-20131.pdf.

Thompson, E. P. (1965). 'The Peculiarities of the English', Socialist Register, 2: 311–62.

Tilley, James R. (2005). 'Libertarian–Authoritarian Value Change in Britain, 1974–2001', Political Studies, 53/2: 442–53.

Towler, Gawain (2017). 'A Polite Insurgency: The UKIP Campaign', in Dominic Wring, Roger Mortimore, and Simon Atkinson (eds), Political Communication in Britain: Polling, Campaigning and Media in the 2015 General Election. London: Palgrave Macmillan, 161–8.

Vucetic, Srdjan (2011). The Anglosphere: A Genealogy of a Racialized Identity in International Relations. Stanford: Stanford University Press.

Walden, George (2004). 'Anthropologist, Study Thyself', *New Statesman*, 10 May.

Walker, Graham, and Gareth Mulvenna (2015). 'Northern Ireland Representation at Westminster: Constitutional Conundrums and Political Manoeuvre', *Parliamentary History*, 34/2: 237–55.

Watson, Iain (2015). *Five Million Conversations: How Labour Lost an Election and Rediscovered its Roots*. Edinburgh: Luath Press.

Watts, Jay (2016). 'The EU Referendum has Caused a Mental Health Crisis', *Guardian*, 29 July, https://www.theguardian.com/commentisfree/2016/jun/29/eu-referendum-mental-health-vote.

Weight, Richard (1999). 'Raise St George's Standard High', *New Statesman*, 8 January.

Wellings, Ben (2012). *English Nationalism and Euroscepticism: Losing the Peace,*. Bern: Peter Lang.

Wellings, Ben (2019). *English Nationalism, Brexit and the Anglosphere: Wider Still and Wider*. Manchester: Manchester University Press.

Wellings, Ben, and Helen Baxendale (2015). 'Euroscepticism and the Anglosphere: Traditions and Dilemmas in Contemporary English Nationalism', *JCMS* 51/1: 123–9.

Whipple, Amy (2009). 'Revisiting the "Rivers of Blood" Controversy: Letters to Enoch Powell', *Journal of British Studies*, 48/3: 731–3.

Wiley, Basil (1947). 'Thought', in Ernest Barker (ed.), *The Character of England*. Oxford: Clarendon Press, 321–39.

Wilker, Harry R., and Lester W. Milbrath (1970). 'Political Belief Systems and Political Behavior', *Political Attitudes*, 51/3: 477–93.

Wilson, Kathleen (2002). *The Island Race: Englishness, Empire and Gender in the Eighteenth Century*. London: Routledge.

Worsthorne, Peregrine (1998). 'England Don't Arise!'" *Spectator*, 19 September.

Wyn Jones, Richard (2001). 'On Process, Events and Unintended Consequences: National Identity and the Politics of Welsh Devolution', *Scottish Affairs*, 37: 34–57.

Wyn Jones, Richard (2007). *Rhoi Cymru'n Gyntaf: Syniadaeth Wleidyddol Plaid Cymru, Cyf. 1*. Cardiff: University of Wales Press.

Wyn Jones, Richard (2017). 'England's Idea of Unionism Is not Shared in the Rest of the UK', *Irish Times*, 21 March, https://www.irishtimes.com/opinion/england-s-idea-of-unionism-is-not-shared-in-the-rest-of-uk-1.3017660#sst.

Wyn Jones, Richard (2019). 'Divided Wales', Cardif University Politics and Governance Blog, 23 September, https://blogs.cardiff.ac.uk/brexit/2019/09/23/divided-wales/.

Wyn Jones, Richard, and Roger Scully (2012). *Wales Says Yes: Devolution and the 2011 Welsh Referendum*. Cardiff: University of Wales Press.

Wyn Jones, Richard, and Roger Scully (2015). 'Ydi Cymru'n cael ei chymhathu i wleidyddiaeth Lloegr?', *Barn* (July–August).

Wyn Jones, Richard, Roger Scully, and Dafydd Trystan (2002). 'Why Do the Conservatives Always Do (Even) Worse in Wales?', in Lynn Bennie, Colin Rallings, Jonathan Tonge, and Paul Webb (eds), *British Elections and Parties Review*, xii. *The 2011 General Election*. London: Frank Cass, 229–45.

Wyn Jones, Richard, Guy Lodge, Ailsa Henderson, and Daniel Wincott (2012). *The Dog that Finally Barked: England as an Emerging Political Community*. London: IPPR.

Wyn Jones, Richard, Guy Lodge, Charlie Jeffery, Glenn Gottfried, Roger Scully, Ailsa Henderson, and Daniel Wincott (2013). *England and its Two Unions: The Anatomy of a Nation and its Discontents*. London: IPPR.

Young, G. M. (1947). 'Government', in Ernest Barker (ed.), *The Character of England*. Oxford: Clarendon Press, 85–111.

Index

Note: Tables and figures, are indicated by an italic *t*, and *f* following the page number. Footnotes are indicated by the letter n after the page number.

For the benefit of digital users, indexed terms that span two pages (e.g., 52–53) may, on occasion, appear on only one of those pages.

Africa 92*t*
Alexander, Douglas 23–4, 23n.21
Alliance Party 171–2
Almond, Gabriel 132
Alsace 84*t*
Amery, Leo 31
Andrews, Rhys 139
Anglo-Saxon(s) 87, 94
Anglosphere 13–14, 87, 97–101, 127
Argentina 169–70
Aruba 169–70
Attlee, Clement 99
Australia 91–4, 92*t*, 98–9, 109

Bangladesh 169–70
Barnett Formula 17n.10, 21, 61–2, 74–5
Bavaria 84*t*
Bechhofer, Frank 51–2, 111, 138–9
Better Together 9–10, 15, 28–9
Billig, Michael 197, 199–201
Bill of Rights 87, 87n.3
Blair, Tony 8–9, 11–12, 29–30
Bradbury, Jonathan 139
Brazil 98n.8
Breuilly, John 197, 201–2
British Election Survey (BES) 136–7, 212
British National Party (BNP) 208n.2
British Social Attitudes Survey (BSAS) 38–42, 63, 136–7, 164
Brittany 83, 84*t*
Brogan, D.W. 105–8
Brown, Gordon 8–10, 20n.17, 24, 27, 27n.24, 32, 63, 74–5, 209
Buenos Aires 169–70

Cameron, David 8, 99–102, 184*t*, 190–1, 199
Canada 37–8, 93, 98–9, 109, 169–70, 174n.5
Carmarthen (by-election) 13
Carswell, Douglas 10–11
Castilla La Mancha 84*t*
Catalonia 84*t*, 207
Chamberlain, Neville 31
Chesterton, G.K. 15
China 98n.8
Churchill, Winston 8, 11–12, 31, 87n.3, 93–6, 99
Cities and Local Government Devolution Act (2016) 184*t*
Clarke, Harold 210
Clarke, Kenneth 188–9
Clegg, Nick 19–20, 25, 32n.29
Coetzee, Ryan 29n.28
Cohen, Anthony 51
Colley, Linda 204–5
Commonwealth 93n.4, 98–9, 115*f*
Conquest, Robert 100–1
Constitutional Convention(s) 175*t*, 183
Conservative Party 2–3, 5, 9–25, 28–30, 33, 35–6, 46, 58, 110, 120–1, 122*t*, 158*t*, 160, 171–3, 175*t*, 178–80, 185–92, 198, 209, 209n.3
  Conservative Democracy Task Force 173, 190–1
  Conservative Party's English manifesto (2015) 14–15
Cornish Assembly 175*t*
Cornwall 15–16, 113*f*, 115*f*
Cowley, Philip 17–18, 22–4
Crosby, Lynton 16–18, 24–5, 29n.28

Cummings, Dominic 31, 183n.6
Curaçao 169–70
Curtice, John 36

Dacre, Paul 32–3
Daily Express 121n.5
Daily Mail 18–19, 30–1, 121n.5
Daily Star 121n.5
Daily Telegraph 121n.5
Daley, Janet 18–19
Darling, Alistair 8–9
Dayell, Tam 59n.2
Davidson, Ruth 29–30
Declaration of Independence
    87n.3, 106
Democratic Unionist Party (DUP) 24
Devo-anxiety 5, 10n.2, 58–9, 64–6, 117–23,
    118f, 122t, 127, 155, 195–6
Devon 15–16
Dhaka 169–70
Dodds, Nigel 24
Dominions 93, 93n.4, 98, 206

Eagle, Angela 29n.27
Eatwell, Roger 207–8
Efficacy 49–51, 50t, 56, 104–5, 120–3,
    122t, 129–34, 143, 165–6
Eichhorn, Jan 139
Eliot, T.S. 15
Empire 2, 26–7, 36, 81n.1, 93–4, 98–102,
    113f, 115f, 200–1
English Liberal Democrat Party 173
English Parliament 65–6, 65t, 67t, 78–9,
    149t, 183, 193–4
English and Welsh votes for English and
    Welsh laws (EWVEWL) 175t, 187–8
English votes for English laws
    (EVEL) 8–12, 27, 61–6, 62t, 64t, 65t,
    67t, 74–6, 78–9, 100, 147–8, 160–1,
    168–9, 174–9, 175t, 185–94, 205–6
Essex Continuous Monitoring project
    210–11
Ethiopia 169–70
European human rights law 85t, 87–8,
    149t, 153, 155–7, 155n.3
European Union membership (Brexit)
    referendum (2016) 1–2, 5, 25–36,
    35n.2, 40–2, 57–8, 72–3, 80, 82, 83t,
    88–9, 100–2, 110, 160, 170, 198–9,
    207–12

Euroscepticism 10–11, 25–32, 80, 103,
    183n.6, 195–6
Euroscepticism battery 84–9, 85t, 117,
    118f, 125–7, 126t, 149t, 154–7, 156t
relationship with British identity (in
    England) 82–90, 85t, 103, 148–61,
    165–6
relationship with British identity (in
    Scotland and Wales) 135–6, 146–61,
    147t, 165–6
relationship with English identity 5,
    81–90, 85t, 99–103, 205
relationship with Scottish identity 135–6,
    146–61, 147t, 165–6
relationship with Welsh identity 135–6,
    146–61, 147t, 165–6

Farage, Nigel 15–16, 20–1, 25, 27, 30
Federalism 9–10, 65
First World War (*see also* Second World
    War; World Wars) 110
Food (as source of English/British
    pride) 112, 113f, 115f
Forsyth, Michael 24
Foster, Joanne 11n.4
France 92t
Future of England Survey (FoES) 4–5,
    11n.3, 38–9, 40–2, 48n. 4, 52, 58, 60–2,
    65, 68–73, 82, 89–90, 98–9, 119–20,
    124, 134, 190, 191–2, 196

Gàilhealtachd (*see also* Gaelic) 51
Gaelic 98n.6, 159
Galicia 84t
Gamble, Andrew 17n.11
Gellner, Ernest 198n.1
General Election(s) (UK) 189–90, 212
General Election 1964 12–13
General Election 1966 13
General Election 1974 (February)
    14n.7
General Election 1974 (October) 13
General Election 1987 181
General Election 1997 178, 185–6
General Election 2010 179, 189
General Election 2015 5, 12–25, 28–30,
    33–6, 58, 63, 77–8, 80, 173–4, 178–9,
    190–1, 209
General Election 2017 13
General Election 2019 2–3, 5

Glasgow 51, 139
Greater Manchester Combined
    Authority 184*t*
Greenfeld, Liah 205
Grender, Olly 20
Goodwin, Matthew 207–8, 208n.2, 210
Gove, Michael 17–18
Government Offices for the Regions
    (England) 175*t*
Guernsey 169–70

Hague, William 190–1
Hamilton (by-election) 13
Hannan, Daniel 27
Heath, Anthony 36
House of Commons 9–10, 12–14, 20, 31,
    78–9, 100, 112, 168–70, 185–92
House of Lords 58, 67*t*, 110, 112,
    169–70, 175*t*
Hroch, Miroslav 58, 197–8

Ignatieff, Michael 196
Ile de France 84*t*
Immigration 5, 29n.27, 31–2, 57–8, 88–94,
    90*t*, 92*t*, 98n.7, 198, 207–8
India 98, 98n.8
Ireland 91–4, 92*t*, 98, 171, 194
Irish nationalism 3–4, 33–4, 80–1, 81n.1
Isle of Man 169–70

Jeffery, Charlie 12–13
Jersey 169–70
Johnson, Boris 25–7, 29n.27, 30–1

Kaltwasser, Cristóbal Rovira 207–8, 208n.2
Kavanagh, Denis 17–18, 22–4
Kenny, Michael 204
Khan, Naushabah 21–2
Khan, Sadiq 29n.27
Kohn, Hans 196–7

Labour Party 2–3, 5, 11–25, 28–9, 32–3,
    59–60, 59n.2, 158*t*, 160, 163, 171–3,
    175*t*, 178–82, 183n.6, 185–8, 190–2,
    198, 203–4
Lampedusa, Guiseppe di 81, 101–2
Law, Richard 107–8
Laws, David 17n.11
Leadsom, Andrea 29n.27
Levinger, Matthew 197–9

Liberal Democrats (*including pre-1988
    Liberal Party*) 11–13, 11n.4, 15–16,
    19–22, 28–9, 110, 120–1, 122*t*, 158*t*,
    171–4, 179, 186n.8, 189–91
Lloyd George, David 172–3
Local Enterprise Partnerships (LEPs) 184*t*
London 2–3, 5, 13, 18–19, 23–4, 28–9, 39,
    97, 113*f*, 114n.3, 115*f*, 164, 175*t*, 180–1
    National identities in 46–9, 47*t*,
    50*t*, 130*t*
London Assembly 164, 175*t*, 183n.7
Loughlin, John 204–5
Lower Saxony 84*t*
Lytle, Paula Franklyn 197–9

Magna Carta 87, 87n.3
Mandelson, Peter 32–3
McCrone, David 51–2, 111, 138–9
McGrattan, Cillian 139
McKay Commission 11, 168–9, 175*t*, 189
McKay, William 189
Midlands 113*f*, 115*f*
Miliband, Ed 17–25
Minister for England 175*t*, 179–80
Mitchell, James 163
Monarchy (*see also* Queen, the) 51–3, 113*f*,
    114, 115*f*
Moreno Question 35n.2, 39–48, 41*t*, 42*t*,
    43*t*, 47*t*, 56, 65–79, 67*t*, 71*t*, 75*t*, 77*t*,
    82–100, 83*t*, 85*t*, 90*t*, 92*t*, 95*t*, 117,
    118*f*, 121, 136–9, 136*t*, 144, 148–59,
    149*t*, 156*t*
Morgan, Kenneth O. 171
Mudde, Cas 207–8, 208n.2
Müller, Jan-Werner 207–8, 208n.2
Murdoch, Rupert 32–3
Murphy, Jim 23n.21

Nairn, Tom 197–9, 214
National Assembly for Wales (*see also* Welsh
    Assembly; Welsh Parliament) 139, 164,
    180–1, 186n.8, 188n.10
National Health Service (NHS) 15, 52–4,
    53*f*, 55*t*, 89–90, 113*f*, 114, 115*f*
National Identity (survey measures
    of) 37–45
Nationalism 6, 24, 35–6, 78–9, 99,
    108, 136
    Alleged English antipathy towards 35,
    45, 106–7, 196

Nationalism (*cont.*)
　As lens for understanding the politics of
　　England 3–5, 36–7, 58, 80–1, 103,
　　116, 135–6, 196–203, 214
　Banal Nationalism 197, 199–200, 214
　How English nationalism differs from
　　Scottish, Welsh and Irish
　　nationalism 3–4, 33–4, 80–1, 135
　Majority Nationalism 206–7
　Relevance of academic literature on 6,
　　58, 140–1, 196–210
　The domestic challenges of
　　accommodating English
　　nationalism 167
　Triadic structure of nationalist
　　rhetoric 198–201
　See also Irish nationalism; Scottish
　　nationalism; Welsh nationalism
Newfoundland 93n.4
New Zealand 93, 98–9
Northern Ireland 3, 12–15, 24, 28, 36, 57n.1,
　　165, 169–73, 175*t*, 178, 186–7, 212
　Attitudes in England towards 59–62,
　　67*t*, 70, 71*t*, 72–4, 78, 95–6, 98,
　　100, 109
　Attitudes in England, Scotland and
　　Wales towards 147–8, 161–3, 162*t*
　Border poll 9
　Northern Ireland Assembly 71*t*, 126*t*
Northwest Territories (Canada) 174n.5
Nuttall, Paul 17n.11

O'Grady, Frances 29n.27
Oliver, Craig 29n.28
Ontario 169–70
Oprington (by-election) 13
Orkney 12n.6
Oromia 169–70
Orwell, George 105–8, 204
Osborne, George 17n.10

Pakistan 91–4, 92*t*, 139, 169–70
Parliament (as source of English/British
　　pride) 52–4, 53*f*, 55*f*, 109, 112, 115*f*
Paxman, Jeremy 59–60
Philippines 98
Plaid Cymru 13, 158*t*, 160, 172–3
Populism, relevance of academic
　　literature on 207–10
Powell, Enoch 13, 59n.2, 97, 98n.7

Prescott, John 184*t*
Punjab 169–70

Quebec 207
Queen, the (*see also* Monarchy) 52–4, 53*f*,
　　55*f*, 55*t*, 113*f*, 115*f*, 190

Reckless, Mark 10–11, 23
Referendum on Assembly for North-East
　　England (2004) 179, 181–2,
　　183n.6, 184*t*
Regional Assemblies/Government
　　(England) 59–60, 65–8, 65*t*, 67*t*, 76–7,
　　164, 175*t*, 179, 181–5, 184*t*
Regional Development Agencies
　　(RDAs) 175*t*, 184*t*
Regionalizing England 174–85, 175*t*,
　　184*t*, 192–4
Rochester and Strood (by-election) 21–3
Romania 91–4, 92*t*, 202
Rose, Richard 108–11
Ross, Tim 15–16, 24
Rudd, Amber 29n.27

Saatchi, M&C 16–17
Salmond, Alex 16–19
Salzburg 84*t*
Scotland 2–4, 25, 27n.24, 28, 29n.27, 33,
　　59, 84*t*, 87n.2, 135, 167, 169–74, 175*t*,
　　179–82, 185–7, 190–1, 210–13
　Attitudes in England towards 5, 35–6,
　　57, 98, 100, 103, 116–27, 117*t*, 126*t*,
　　129, 134, 198, 205–6, 209
　Attitudes towards the 'two
　　unions' in 135
　Independence referendum (2014) 8–12,
　　14, 57–8, 72–6, 73*t*, 75*t*, 76*t*, 77*t*
　Independence referendum (prospect of
　　second) 2, 194
　National identities in 6, 45, 51–2,
　　136–46, 136*t*, 142*t*, 145*f*, 146*t*, 148–61,
　　149*t*, 165–7, 195, 203, 205, 211
　Smith Commission 190–1
　see also English Votes for English
　　Laws (EVEL)
Scottish Conservatives 29–30, 158*t*,
　　160, 172–4
Scottish Election Study 164
Scottish Labour 15–16, 22–4, 158*t*, 160,
　　172–4, 182

Scottish Liberal Democrats 11, 158*t*, 172, 190–1

Scottish nationalism 3–4, 13, 33–4, 80–1, 81n.1, 135, 200, 207

Scottish National Party (SNP) 5, 13, 15–25, 29n.28, 33, 63, 72–3, 138–9, 158*t*, 160, 191, 215

Scottish Parliament 14, 68, 69*t*, 71*t*, 76*t*, 77*t*, 117*t*, 125–7, 126*t*, 132, 164, 172n.4, 206–7, 209–10

Scottish unionism 8–9, 11n.5, 24, 30, 182–3, 203

Second World War (*see also* First World War; World Wars) 31, 46, 94, 108–9, 198–9, 203–5

Shetland 12n.6, 51

Shipman, Tim 209n.3

Sinclair, Jeremy 16–17, 24, 29n.28

Singapore 98

Sint Maarten 169–70

Social Democratic and Labour Party (SDLP) 171–2

Somerset 15–16

South Africa 93n.4, 138

'Special relationship', The 94–9, 95*t*, 126*t*, 148, 149*t*, 155–7, 155n.3

Spellar, John 23–4

Sport 36–7, 48–9, 51–2, 53*f*, 105–6, 112, 113*f*, 115*f*, 200

St George's cross/flag 11, 20, 23, 51–2, 59–60, 60n.3, 113*f*, 115*f*

St George's Day bank holiday 62, 63*t*, 66, 67*t*, 124–5, 126*t*, 175*t*, 180

Stuart, Gisela 29n.27

Sturgeon, Nicola 17–19, 21, 22n.20, 29–30

Sun 17–19, 121n.5

Sunday Telegraph 18–19

Syria 91–4, 92*t*

The Leopard 81, 101–2

Thornberry, Emily 23–4

Thuringia 84*t*

Times, The 18–19

Towler, Gawain 21

Ulster Unionist Party (UUP) 12–13, 59n.2

Union Jack flag 51–4, 55*t*, 60n.3, 113*f*, 115*f*

'Union of Ignorance' 135–6, 161–5

United Kingdom Independence Party (UKIP) 10–11, 16, 17n.11, 20–5,

28–9, 31, 46, 110, 120–1, 122*t*, 158*t*, 160, 171–3, 175*t*, 178–80, 183, 209

Upper Austria 83, 84*t*

Verba, Sidney 132

Vienna 84*t*

Wales 2–3, 6, 9, 12–15, 28, 36, 45, 84*t*, 135, 169–74, 175*t*, 179–82, 185–91, 210–13

Attitudes in England towards 36, 57, 98, 100, 116–27, 117*t*, 126*t*, 129, 134, 198, 205–6, 209

Attitudes towards the 'two unions' in 135

National identities in 6, 45, 136–46, 136*t*, 142*t*, 145*f*, 146*t*, 148–61, 149*t*, 165–7, 195, 203, 205, 211

St David's Day process 190–1

see also English and Welsh votes for English and Welsh laws (EWVEWL); English Votes for English Laws (EVEL)

Watson, Iain 17–18, 17n.9

Wellings, Ben 205

Welsh Assembly (*see also* National Assembly for Wales; Welsh Parliament) 14, 117*t*, 126*t*

Welsh Conservatives 158*t*, 160, 172–4

Welsh Election Study 164

Welsh Labour 158*t*, 172–4

Welsh (language) 95n.5, 98n.6, 144–6, 159, 182

Welsh Liberal Democrats 12n.6, 158*t*, 172–4

Welsh Life and Times Survey 164

Welsh nationalism 3–4, 13, 33–4, 80–1, 81n.1, 135, 200, 207

Welsh Parliament (*see also* National Assembly for Wales; Welsh Assembly) 71*t*, 72

'West Lothian question' 8–9, 59, 59n.2, 168–9, 175*t*, 178–9, 185, 187–8, 190–1

Whiteley, Paul 210

Williams, Sophie 139

Wincott, Dan 12–13

World Wars (*see also* First World War; Second World War) 53–4, 53*f*, 55*f*, 55*t*, 108, 113*f*, 115*f*

Yorkshire Parliament 175*t*

Young, G.M. 107

Printed and bound by CPI Group (UK) Ltd, Croydon, CR0 4YY